LORDS OF THE SEA

LORDS *of the* SEA

A HISTORY OF THE BARBARY CORSAIRS

ALAN G. JAMIESON

REAKTION BOOKS

Published by
REAKTION BOOKS LTD
33 Great Sutton Street
London EC1V 0DX, UK
www.reaktionbooks.co.uk

First published 2012
Copyright © Alan G. Jamieson 2012

Printed and bound in Great Britain
by TJ International, Padstow, Cornwall

British Library Cataloguing in Publication Data
Jamieson, A. G. (Alan G.)
Lords of the sea : a history of the Barbary corsairs.
1. Pirates–Mediterranean Region–History. 2. Pirates–
Africa, North–History. 3. Mediterranean Region–
History–1517-1789. 4. Africa, North–History–
1517-1882.
I. Title
364.1'64'091638-dc23

ISBN 978 1 86189 907 1

Contents

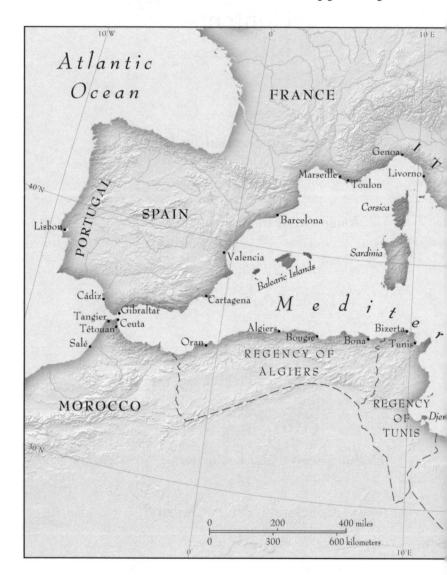

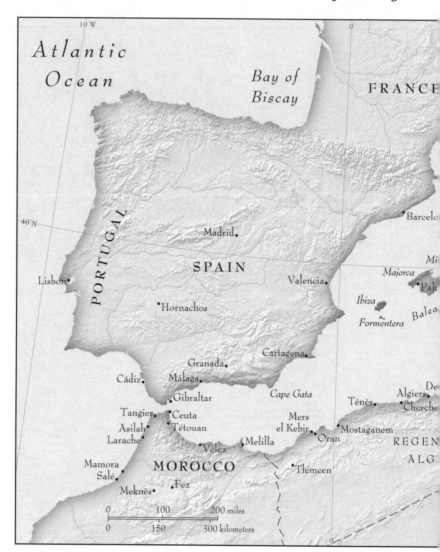

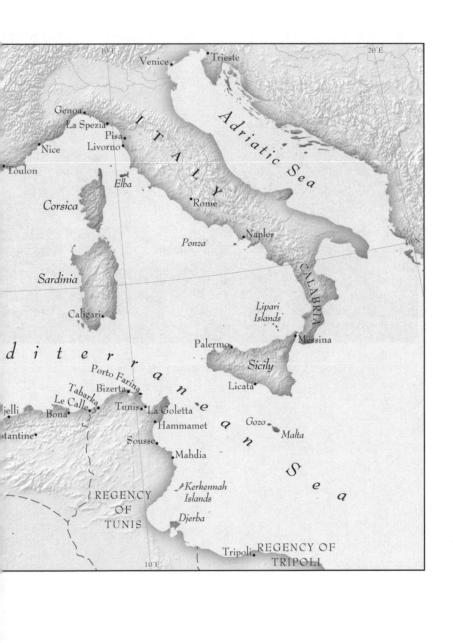

George Chambers, *The Bombardment of Algiers in 1816*, 1836.

INTRODUCTION:
The Barbary Legend

The captain was sure they were safe. His valuable ship and its equally valuable cargo had passed the zone where the pirate danger was greatest. Then suddenly everything changed. The Muslim pirates were climbing aboard the ship. It seemed impossible, but it was happening. The captain told his crew not to resist. Soon the ship was under the control of the pirates. They turned it about, heading for their home port on the African coast. Once they arrived there, the negotiations for a lucrative ransom could begin.

This sequence of events might have taken place in the Mediterranean Sea in the sixteenth century when the Muslim Barbary corsairs of North Africa seized a rich Christian merchant ship. In fact it took place in the Indian Ocean on 15 November 2008 when Muslim pirates from Somalia captured the tanker *Sirius Star*, which was, at over 300,000 tons, the biggest ship ever captured by pirates up to that date. In the sixteenth century the corsairs would have thought the crew almost as valuable as the ship and its cargo, since slave-taking was one of their principal activities. In the twenty-first century the main aim of the Somali pirates is to ransom the ship and its cargo. The ship's crew is almost irrelevant. The *Sirius Star* was released on 9 January 2009 after a ransom was paid. The ransom was said to be US $3 million, but was probably larger. Yet for a ship and its cargo valued together at almost US $250 million the sum paid in ransom probably did not seem great to the shipowners.[1]

The Barbary corsairs targeted Christian ships and the coastal regions of Christian countries bordering the Mediterranean Sea. They claimed the 'eternal war' between Christendom and the lands of Islam as justification for their predatory actions. The modern Somali pirates are purely criminals. Indeed their capture of the *Sirius Star* was deeply ironic. The ship was owned by a subsidiary of Saudi Arabia's national oil company. The king of Saudi Arabia is the protector of the most holy shrines of Islam in the cities of Mecca and Medina. The *Sirius Star* was carrying a cargo of crude oil from Saudi Arabia to the USA when it was captured. The Islamic militants in Somalia condemned this capture of a 'Muslim ship' and threatened to attack the home ports of the Somali pirates. No such attack took place at that time, and the Somali pirates continue to seize ships from Muslim countries.

Despite this, many of today's Muslims seem to see the Somali pirates as heirs of the earlier Barbary corsairs, as daring sea raiders who perpetuate the Barbary legend. Arabic media use the word 'corsair' to describe them, not the Arabic word for 'pirate', which is literally 'sea robber'.[2] Even Western commentators are falling into step, with talk of Somalia becoming the 'new Barbary', a base for Muslim pirates whose activities even the powerful navies of the USA and its allies may be unable to suppress. The exploits of the Barbary corsairs are remembered in Muslim countries, and especially in Turkey, where a number of ships of the Turkish navy are named after famous Barbary corsair commanders.

Westerners are less likely to remember the time when Barbary corsairs terrorized the Mediterranean and beyond. Few of those who enjoy the Mediterranean resort beaches of Spain, France and Italy stop to wonder about the ruined watchtowers along the coast or the Dragut festivals held in some villages. In Britain *The Bombardment of Algiers*, a painting by the nineteenth-century artist George Chambers, is one of the most widely reproduced images from the art collection of the National Maritime Museum at Greenwich, but few British people know why the Royal Navy was bombarding a city on the Barbary coast of North Africa in 1816.

Perhaps unusually, knowledge of the Barbary corsairs is probably more widespread in the USA than in Europe. The Barbary corsairs were the first major foreign enemy of the young American republic in the late eighteenth century, and they were the principal reason for the creation of a permanent United States Navy. The first Barbary war (1801–5), against Tripoli in Libya, and the second Barbary war (1815), against Algiers, loom large in any study of the USA's early foreign policy. The 200th anniversary of the first of these wars came just as 9/11 and its aftermath were increasing interest in all aspects of Christian–Muslim conflict and books about the war flew from the presses. Once called 'forgotten wars', America's Barbary conflicts have now had more written about them in English than any other aspect of the history of the Barbary corsairs.[3]

Americans may be more conscious of the history of the Barbary corsairs than Europeans, but their interest is narrowly focused on a very late period of that history. By the early years of the nineteenth century, despite a revival during the French Revolutionary and Napoleonic wars, the power of the Barbary corsairs was visibly in decline. Their heyday had been during the sixteenth and seventeenth centuries, when the Barbary 'pirates' were feared by all sea-going Christians. Although the Barbary corsairs are included in most general histories of piracy, it should be made clear that they were more privateers than pirates, similar to great French privateers like Jean Bart or Robert Surcouf, not pirates like Blackbeard and Captain Kidd.[4] Pirates are by definition criminals acting outside the law, like today's Somali pirates. The Barbary corsairs, like Christian European privateers, operated within a legal framework. They had to obtain permission from their rulers to send out their privately owned warships, and when they returned with prizes those captured ships, cargoes and crews were disposed of according to set legal rules. The Barbary corsairs were different from most European privateers in that they were engaged in a war which was 'eternal'. French privateers, for example, only attacked enemy shipping during clearly defined wars, which began with a declaration of hostilities and ended with a peace treaty. Since the struggle between Islam and Christianity was held to be never-ending, interrupted only by truces, the Barbary corsairs could sail out against the Christians whenever they wished.[5]

This ideological/religious element was also lacking in the motivation of ordinary pirates, most of whom were only out to get money and nothing else. Certainly the religious justification for the ravages of the Barbary corsairs began to seem weak over the years, and in their later days some of them even attacked the ships of Greek subjects of the Ottoman sultan. Nevertheless the religious justification, like the legal framework governing their activities, helped to set the corsairs apart from true pirates.[6] The Somali sea raiders of today act outside any legal framework and, although they are Muslims, they do not allege any religious justification for their actions. They are not the heirs of the Barbary corsairs.

Undoubtedly in the realities of war at sea the legal and religious cover for the depredations of the Barbary corsairs did wear thin at times, and they did appear more as pirates than privateers, yet they never truly fitted into the pirate mould. Piracy, meaning robbery at sea, had been a feature of life in and around the Mediterranean Sea for thousands of years. Similarly, the Christian–Muslim war at sea in the Mediterranean had been going on in varying forms and at varying levels of intensity since the seventh century. Up to the tenth century the Muslims had the upper hand, but from the eleventh century to the fifteenth the balance swung in favour of the Christians, largely thanks to the activities of the Italian maritime republics of Pisa, Genoa and Venice. Yet in the sixteenth century piracy/privateering in the Mediterranean and Christian–Muslim conflict at sea in the Mediterranean were to join together and achieve a new level of importance that was to endure for more than three centuries, only ending in the first decades of the nineteenth century.[7] Why did the Barbary corsairs arise when they did? Why did they achieve such power? And why did that power last for so long?

The Barbary corsairs had such a strong impact in the sixteenth century because they were the naval vanguard of the Ottoman Turks whose empire was rapidly becoming the most powerful Islamic state in the world. Although primarily land warriors, the Ottomans began expanding their naval activities in the second half of the fifteenth century. In the next century, Turkish corsairs began to move westwards in the Mediterranean, taking control of ports along the coast of North Africa, and becoming known as the Barbary corsairs. (The term Barbary probably derives from the original Berber inhabitants of North Africa.) Their attacks on Christian shipping and coasts made them widely feared, not just for their own activities but because they represented the advancing power of the Ottoman Empire and militant Islam.[8]

The frontier role of the Barbary corsairs was not entirely unique in Ottoman lands. The semi-independent Crimean Tatars on the north shore of the Black Sea performed a similar function on behalf of the Ottoman sultan. Their fast-moving cavalry launched raids aimed at collecting Christian slaves in neighbouring Russia, Ukraine and Poland, and also at extending the Ottoman sphere of influence in the steppe lands.[9] When the Ottoman sultan went on a land campaign against the Christians, for example in Hungary, the Crimean Tatars sent a contingent of cavalry to join his army. In similar fashion, when the Ottoman sultan assembled his main fleet for a campaign in the Mediterranean, the Barbary corsairs sent a squadron of ships to join that fleet, and they sometimes provided the fleet commander as well.

To oppose Muslim frontier warriors like the Crimean Tatars and the Barbary corsairs, the Christian side also produced unique military bodies. The Crimean Tatars were opposed by the Cossacks, Christian horsemen of the steppes, who were only very loosely under the authority of the rulers of Poland and Russia.[10] Unlike the Crimean Tatars, the Cossacks also made the transition from land to sea warfare, sending craft to raid Turkish territory around the Black Sea in the early seventeenth century. They even raided near the imperial capital Istanbul.

The specialist Christian opponents of the Barbary corsairs were the Knights of St John of Jerusalem (or Knights Hospitaller). This military religious order had experience of fighting on the Christian–Muslim frontier that went back to the time of the Crusader states in Palestine. After being driven out of their castles in the Holy Land, the knights made the switch from land to sea warfare. Based at the island of Rhodes, the galleys of the knights attacked Muslim ships and ports. In 1522 the Ottoman sultan Suleiman the Magnificent drove the knights out of Rhodes, and their new home was to be the island of Malta, which was more conveniently placed to resist the expanding power of the Barbary corsair states in North Africa.[11] The Knights of Malta, as they became known, were later supported by a new military religious order, the Knights of St Stephen, established by the ruler of Tuscany and based at Pisa and Livorno. Both knightly orders, like the Christian Mediterranean states, reinforced their own efforts against the Muslims by licensing Christian privateers to attack the infidel enemy as well.

The sixteenth century was a period when private military forces were as important as the slowly emerging state armies and navies. If the Barbary corsairs were a vital support to the Ottoman sultan's own fleet, a similar situation also existed in Christian lands. Much of Spain's galley fleet in the Mediterranean consisted of private galleys hired from Italian princes and maritime states, with the contingent from Genoa being especially important. The Doria family of Genoa not only hired their own galleys to the Spanish, but also provided them with naval commanders, above all Andrea Doria. In England maritime adventurers like John Hawkins and Francis Drake made the transition from pirates (as their Spanish victims called them) to privateers (with royal and aristocratic investors in their ventures) to commanders in the state navy when they brought their ships to assist royal warships in the fleet assembled by Elizabeth 1 to resist the Spanish Armada in 1588.[12]

Nevertheless, while Elizabethan 'sea dogs' like Hawkins and Drake had their own private warships, they were still under the authority of the English queen and her government. They did not set up their own semi-independent states as the Barbary corsairs did. Also men like Drake were native Englishmen, not foreign outsiders like the Turkish corsairs who imposed their rule on the native Muslims of North Africa. For three centuries North African Arabs and Berbers were ruled by a foreign Turkish military caste which recruited new members not from local Muslims but from the peoples of the Ottoman heartlands, chiefly Anatolia. Each year new recruits from there, and also from the Balkans and the Levant, were sent to the Barbary coast to reinforce the ranks of the Turkish corsairs and soldiers.[13]

The Mamluks had ruled Egypt in a similar fashion between the thirteenth century and their overthrow by the Ottoman sultan Selim 1 early in the sixteenth century. The Mamluks were Turco-Circassian slave soldiers originally brought to Egypt to serve its rulers, but they later rebelled and took control of the state.[14] They continued to replenish their ranks by bringing in slave soldiers from abroad (chiefly the Caucasus region), but they also developed family links within Egypt. The Barbary corsairs were much more exclusive. The offspring of marriages between the Turkish overlords and local women could not become part of the ruling elite. Instead new Turkish recruits were brought in from the Ottoman heartlands or captive Christians were converted to Islam and joined the corsairs. These Christian renegades were just as much outsiders as the Turkish elite. By the eighteenth century these harsh rules were breaking down in Tunis and Tripoli, but they largely endured in Algiers right up to the French conquest in 1830.

Although happy to serve the Ottoman sultan in his wars with the Christians, the Barbary corsairs were, like many frontier warriors, less keen about being closely controlled by the central Ottoman government in Istanbul. By the start of the seventeenth century revolts and disorder in the heartlands of the Ottoman empire further weakened the control that rulers in Istanbul had over their distant provinces in North Africa.[15] If control from the Muslim centre was weakening, so was the level of military resistance put up by the Christian powers to the activities of the Barbary corsairs. Spain was in decline, but France, England and the Netherlands did not yet have sufficiently strong navies to pose a serious threat to the corsairs. These circumstances meant that the Barbary corsairs enjoyed their heyday in the first half of the seventeenth century. In addition at this time they made the transition from oar-powered galleys to sailing ships, and this allowed their fleets to raid widely outside the Mediterranean for the first time, going as far as England, Ireland, Iceland and the Newfoundland fishery in North America.

Not only did the corsairs from the Ottoman regencies undertake these more distant voyages, but also ships from the other branch of the Barbary corsairs, those corsairs based in Morocco. They were not as well known as the Ottoman corsairs during the sixteenth century, but they were to enjoy a similar period of great success during the first half of the seventeenth century. The Moroccans were not subjects of the Ottoman sultan, but the central government in Morocco collapsed after 1603 in a similar manner to the decline of Ottoman central power. This allowed the Moroccan corsairs to set up their own authorities in their ports, above all the so-called 'pirate republic' of Salé.[16]

The taking of Christian captives had always been one of the principal aims of the Barbary corsairs, and this activity probably peaked in the early seventeenth century after reaching a high level in the sixteenth century. The magnitude of the Barbary corsairs' success in taking slaves is hard to evaluate precisely, but informed guesses have been made. It has been suggested that between 1530 and 1780 the Barbary corsairs took around 1.25 million captives from Christian Europe.[17] Some writers have suggested this figure is too high; others that it may be too low because the scholar who made the calculation relied mostly on figures relating to the corsairs operating from the Ottoman regencies of Algiers, Tunis and Tripoli and took little account of captives taken by the Moroccan corsairs. Even if one accepts a figure of one million Christian captives taken by the Barbary corsairs between 1500 and 1800, how does that compare with other slave-taking operations of the period?

The most obvious comparison is with the activities of the Crimean Tatars, the leading Muslim slave raiders on land. Between the fifteenth century and the conquest of their state by the Russians in the late eighteenth century, the Crimean Tatars may have taken as many as three million Christian captives, mostly from Russia, Ukraine and Poland, but also in raids as far west as Hungary and Austria while serving with the Ottoman sultan's army.[18] Cavalry raiders may have found it easier to round up Christian captives, the so-called 'harvest of the steppe', than maritime predators. So how does the Barbary corsair figure compare with the great maritime slave trade across the Atlantic from Africa to the New World?

Between the fifteenth century and the nineteenth over eleven million black slaves were taken across the Atlantic, with perhaps 80 per cent of them being carried across in the eighteenth and nineteenth centuries.[19] In the seventeenth century and especially in the sixteenth, the Atlantic trade in black slaves was probably at a lower level than the seizure of white Christian slaves from Europe by Muslim slave raiders, chiefly the Crimean Tatars and the Barbary corsairs. Indeed in the sixteenth century the Barbary corsairs alone may have taken more Christian captives than the number of black slaves that the Christian Europeans shipped across the Atlantic from Africa to the Americas.

This level of success in capturing Christian slaves was bound to provoke retaliation from Christian states. Spain and Portugal had been the principal opponents of the Barbary corsairs during the sixteenth century. Their power began to wane in the first half of the seventeenth century, but new sea powers were arising in the shape of the navies of France, England and the Netherlands. However, before 1660 these navies were not sufficiently strong to curb the activities of the Barbary corsairs. Only between 1660 and 1690 did the new sea powers launch significant naval attacks on the Barbary corsairs and force them to come to terms. By 1690 the three Ottoman regencies of Algiers, Tunis and Tripoli had all been forced to make peace treaties with France, England and the Netherlands which gave the merchant ships of those three countries immunity from corsair attack. Morocco was not finally compelled to give similar guarantees until the 1720s. Yet if the three main European sea powers were strong enough to force major concessions from the Barbary corsairs, why did they not seek to remove the Barbary corsair menace altogether?

One reason was cynical great power calculation. The Barbary corsairs would be allowed to continue attacks on the merchant fleets of the smaller European maritime states because this would prevent such fleets from prospering and becoming rivals to the merchant shipping of the great naval powers. In the eighteenth century the Barbary states were to reduce this great power advantage by making treaties with the smaller maritime states like Sweden and Denmark which offered immunity from corsair attack in return for annual tribute payments. However, even this concession could not be extended to all states all the time. The Barbary corsairs had to be notionally at war with some Christian state or they would have no income and no threat to hold over European merchant shipping.

Another reason the great European sea powers did not finally destroy the Barbary corsairs was that between 1689 and 1815 they were more likely to be at war with each other than hunting down Barbary sea raiders. In such a context the European sea powers were anxious to appease the Barbary corsairs to prevent attacks on their own shipping and to encourage the corsairs to launch attacks on the ships of their enemies. The Barbary states sensibly avoided going to war for either side, while playing the rival powers off against each other to win new concessions.

Collecting occasional 'presents' from the major sea powers and regular tribute payments from many of the smaller European maritime countries, the Barbary states had no need to keep up large-scale corsair attacks. By the middle of the eighteenth century their operations had sunk to a low level, just enough to remain a credible threat to the countries that were forced to meet their demands for tribute. Then came the French revolution of 1789 and the long European wars which followed it. With the international system thrown into chaos, the regular payment of tribute to the Barbary states began to dry up. Corsairing was now revived and it was even extended to attacks on new maritime targets, chiefly the merchant ships of the new United States of America.[20] Building a permanent navy for the first time, the Americans hit back hard and forced the Barbary corsairs to come to terms. Other maritime states were less ready to confront the corsairs. Amazingly one of these was Britain, the world's greatest naval power. Dependent on food supplies from the Barbary states to feed British garrisons in Gibraltar, Minorca, Sicily, Malta and the Ionian Islands; the men of the British Mediterranean fleet; and later British armies in Portugal and Spain, Britain was surprisingly indulgent towards the Barbary corsairs as long as they did not attack British-protected shipping.

With the end of the wars against France in 1815, the new Europe which emerged was much less tolerant of the activities of the Barbary corsairs. Britain was accused of hypocrisy because it made a great fuss about ending the black slave trade across the Atlantic from Africa to the Americas but seemed reluctant to crush the last vestiges of the white slave trade in the Barbary states. Eventually the British changed their position and their bombardment of Algiers in 1816 forced the Barbary corsairs to promise an end to the enslaving of white Christians. As in the past, such promises seemed unlikely to be kept for long, and during the 1820s many people began to agitate for an outright European conquest of the Barbary states of North Africa.

When the French attacked Algiers in 1830 it seemed at first that this might be just another punitive expedition to punish the Barbary corsairs after which the European forces would be withdrawn. In this case, however, the invasion was the beginning of a French conquest of Algeria which would take several decades to complete, establishing a French colony, later officially joined to metropolitan France, which would not be given up until 1962. The French invasion of Algeria began a process of European conquest in Africa that was to continue for the rest of the nineteenth century.[21] By the time the First World War broke out in 1914, all of North Africa from Morocco to Egypt was under European colonial rule. However, Barbary corsairing had disappeared long before then, the last Moroccan efforts having been discouraged by European naval action in the 1840s.

European conquest finally turned the Barbary corsairs from a terrifying reality into a picturesque legend.[22] Yet a European conquest of North Africa had been proposed as long ago as the 1490s and if it had begun at that date, the Barbary corsairs would never have arisen in the first place. How they arose and how they endured for more than three centuries is a story that needs to be examined in more detail.

The Ottoman attack on Spanish-held Tunis and La Goletta in 1574, from Georg Braun and Franz Hogenberg, *Civitates orbis terrarum*, vol. II (1575).

ONE

Vanguard of the Sultan
1492–1580

---⚓---

ALGIERS 1541

In the year 1500 Algiers was just a minor Muslim port on the coast of North Africa. Forty years later it was considered such a threat to Christendom that Emperor Charles V was ready to lead a massive military and naval expedition against it. Algiers was now the principal base of the Barbary corsairs, who were ravaging the coasts of Spain and Italy, much to the terror of their Christian inhabitants.

Charles, Habsburg ruler of half of Europe, Holy Roman Emperor, and secular leader of Christendom, had already driven Barbarossa, the Algiers-based leader of the Barbary corsairs, out of Tunis in 1535. This had been seen as a great Christian triumph which was all the more sweet because it redressed a much earlier crusader defeat at that port city. In 1270 Louis IX, king of France and one of the great medieval crusaders, had died of disease while trying to capture Tunis. Now Emperor Charles V had achieved what the French king, later canonized as Saint Louis, had failed to do. If Charles could lead a successful crusade against Tunis, surely Algiers could not resist his power?

Since the 1520s Charles V had been engaged in a titanic struggle with the ever-expanding Muslim empire of the Ottoman Turks, led by their sultan Suleiman, called the Magnificent by the Christians and the Lawgiver by his own subjects. The two main theatres of this struggle were the Danubian basin in central Europe and the Mediterranean Sea. By 1540 the Ottomans effectively dominated both Hungary on the first front and the eastern Mediterranean on the second. In central Europe the Ottoman threat to Austria and Germany was growing. In the western Mediterranean the Barbary corsairs were acting as the vanguard of the Ottoman sultan, steadily spreading their influence. Their chief base was Algiers and this was now the principal Ottoman stronghold in the western Mediterranean. That was one of the main reasons why Charles v was determined to conquer the port city.

As a reward for his successful corsair activity, the sultan had appointed Barbarossa to the post of 'kapudan pasha', commander-in-chief of the Ottoman navy. Barbarossa had defeated the Christian fleet of Charles v's principal naval commander, Andrea Doria, ruler of the republic of Genoa, at Preveza in 1538. It seemed the Ottomans might soon take control of the whole Mediterranean. However, in the summer of 1541 both sultan Suleiman and his naval chief Barbarossa were busy on the central European front. Barbarossa, the terror of the Christian Mediterranean, had the mundane task of ensuring supplies for the sultan's army in Hungary passed unhindered up the river Danube.

With both Suleiman and Barbarossa fully occupied in central Europe, Charles v considered it was an ideal time to launch his expedition against Algiers. After successfully achieving at least temporary agreement with the Protestant dissidents in Germany, the Catholic emperor left Regensburg in August 1541. Accompanied by thousands of German mercenary troops, commanded by the duke of Alba, a Spanish nobleman, Charles crossed the Alps into Italy and made his way to Genoa. There Andrea Doria, who was to command his fleet, tried to convince the emperor that it was too late in the season to send an expedition to Algiers. Autumnal storms would soon be racing across the Mediterranean. Doria, like the pope, tried to convince Charles that his troops would be more use fighting the Turks in Hungary than at Algiers.

Charles v was unconvinced. He had spent much of the year preparing his expedition against the main stronghold of the Barbary corsairs. Troops and ships were assembling; much money had already been spent on the preparations. The emperor decided to push on with his plans, trusting in God's support. He could also point out that if the expedition captured Algiers late in the year, the Ottomans would be unable to launch a counterattack until the spring of the following year at the earliest. By then Algiers would have been turned into a Christian fortress.

In late September Charles left the Genoese port of La Spezia with Doria and Alba, the German troops, 37 galleys (mostly Genoese) and other shipping. The rendezvous for the expeditionary forces was to be at Palma on the island of Majorca. There Charles was joined by Ferante Gonzaga, his viceroy in Sicily, who brought more galleys, along with Spanish and Italian troops. The last contingent, troops and galleys direct from Spain under Bernardino de Mendoza, did not join the emperor's fleet until it arrived off Algiers on 19 October.

In all Charles V had 65 galleys and about 400 troop transports and supply ships. The fleet was manned by 12,000 sailors and carried 24,000 soldiers, nearly all Spanish, Italian and German. In addition there were about 150 Knights of the Order of St John of Jerusalem, better known as the Knights of Malta after their new home, which had been given to them by Charles V in 1530. The force also included hundreds of 'adventurers', warrior noblemen who had joined the emperor's expedition at their own expense. They viewed it as nothing less than a crusade against the infidel. They came from all over Christian Europe, including France and England, but the largest group was made up of Spanish nobles, including Hernando Cortés, the conqueror of Mexico.

Rough seas caused an initial delay in landing the troops, but eventually the Christian forces began to come ashore on beaches a few miles to the east of Algiers. They encountered little resistance, and soon Charles was leading his troops westwards towards the city. The Spanish were on the left, covering the nearby hills; the emperor and his German troops were in the centre; and the Italians, along with the Knights of Malta, were on the right, marching along the seashore.

Barbarossa had left Hassan Aga, originally a Christian from Sardinia who had 'turned Turk' to become a renegade, as his deputy in charge of Algiers. With the bay of Algiers literally covered in ships and a vast Christian army approaching, Hassan could hardly be anything else but alarmed. He had barely 1,000 Turkish soldiers and perhaps 5,000 other forces, mostly corsairs and Andalusian Moriscos who had fled to North Africa from Spain. Charles sent in a demand that Hassan should surrender Algiers to him immediately. Some citizens were ready to give in, hoping to avoid the horrors of a bloody storming such as had been inflicted on Tunis in 1535. However, a marabout, a Muslim holy man, called Kara Josef claimed that he had received divine guidance in a dream. Allah would protect the people of Algiers if only they would resist the infidels. Whether influenced by the marabout or not, Hassan rejected the emperor's demand for surrender.

The Christian army now began to dig siege trenches near the walls of Algiers. All seemed to be going well until a severe storm suddenly swept in, bringing torrential rain and gale force winds. Without tents the emperor's soldiers were soon wet and cold. Only a few days' worth of food supplies had so far come ashore from the fleet, so the troops were soon hungry as well. Furthermore the downpour quickly rendered useless the gunpowder supplies for their firearms and the few artillery pieces that had so far been landed.

All night the rain and wind continued. Next morning Hassan seized his chance to launch a surprise attack on the bedraggled and demoralized Christian troops. His infantry charged out of Algiers and began to drive back the besiegers. It was an old-fashioned clash of sword against scimitar and halberd against spear because firearms had been rendered useless by the rain. In face of the Muslim onslaught, only the Knights of Malta stood firm. Inspired by their conduct, the other Christian troops rallied and soon the Muslim attackers were pushed back inside the walls of Algiers.

However, Hassan had not finished. He unleashed a cavalry force which all but routed the Italian troops until the Knights of Malta stepped in once again to form a strong rearguard. Charles now sent forward his German troops, but initially they had little impact. Surrounded by his bodyguard, the emperor decided to intervene personally. Suitably inspired by the appearance of their leader, the Christian troops drove the Muslim cavalry back into Algiers. Although finally victorious, these clashes had cost the Christians at least 300 dead, including a dozen Knights of Malta.

The weather improved for a time, but the fleet was still unable to land supplies and artillery in any quantity because of the heavy swell. Then on 25 October a fierce storm roared in from the north-east, causing immediate chaos among the Christian shipping. Within six hours some 150 ships had been sunk or driven ashore. These included fifteen galleys. Their shipwreck brought freedom to the Muslim slave rowers who got ashore, but death or slavery to the Christian sailors and soldiers who emerged from the raging surf. Andrea Doria took his surviving galleys out to sea to avoid being caught on a deadly lee shore in the bay of Algiers. Everywhere men struggled to survive in the stormy seas. An English 'adventurer', Thomas Chaloner, dived overboard from his sinking ship. He was so exhausted from swimming that he could not grasp a rope thrown to him from a Spanish vessel. He only saved himself by gripping the rope with his teeth until he could be pulled aboard to safety.

The storm eventually passed and Doria led the remains of the fleet back into the bay. Charles V now decided that his army must make a temporary retreat to a place where it could be safely resupplied by the fleet. The troops marched eastwards around the bay. Amazed at the turn of events, Hassan led out his forces from Algiers and began harassing the retreating Christians. In addition Berber tribesmen came down from the hills to join in the assault on the infidels. The Italian and German troops were still demoralized, but the Spaniards and the Knights of Malta formed a solid rearguard. Eventually the emperor's army reached the bay of Tementfoust near Cape Matifou (now Bordj El Bahri), where the Christian fleet had collected. Cortés, who had experience of wresting victory from the jaws of defeat during the conquest of Mexico, begged the emperor to make one last effort to conquer Algiers. However, Charles believed that the destruction caused by the repeated storms showed God's hostility to his enterprise, and he insisted on re-embarking his army.

Although the army had lost perhaps only 2,000 men in battle or due to sickness, the fleet had lost a massive one-third of its vessels. Where could room be found for the soldiers? Nearly 2,000 horses had come with the expedition to provide mounts for cavalrymen and for the noble commanders. Few had gone ashore. Charles now ordered that the horses should be forced overboard to make room for the soldiers. Despite protests from the nobles, many fine mounts were propelled over the side to a watery grave. On 2 November Charles waded out to a ship's boat. He was almost the last man of his expedition to leave the North African shore.

The weather had not finished with the emperor. A new storm sent further ships onshore near Algiers, while Charles and Doria were forced to find refuge in the Spanish-held port of Bougie further east along the coast. Yet more gales followed and the emperor did not finally reach Spain until the last week of November 1541.

The Muslims exulted that from Dellys, east of Algiers, to Cherchell, west of the city, the coast was littered with the bodies of Christian men and their horses. In all, the Christians lost around 12,000 men, with 8,000 soldiers and sailors dead and 4,000 rounded up to become slaves. There were soon so many Christian captives in Algiers that the price for them in the slave market dropped dramatically. It was said that a Christian slave could hardly even be bartered for an onion.

The Algiers expedition of 1541 was the worst defeat of Charles v's career. Christians were left to wonder why God had deserted their cause. Muslims were strengthened by this dramatic demonstration of the power of Allah. The emperor claimed that nobody could have predicted such terrible weather. Andrea Doria and the other naval commanders had made just such predictions, but Charles, trusting to divine support, had ignored them.

For the Barbary corsairs of Algiers these events of 1541 made up their greatest ever victory over the Christians. For almost another three centuries their city would successfully defy the armed might of Christendom. Charles v had failed to conquer the main Ottoman base in the western Mediterranean, and the Christian populations along those shores would soon have reason to lament his failure as the Barbary corsairs increased their attacks year after year.[1]

BEGINNINGS

Two events in the late fifteenth century set the context in which the Barbary corsairs would emerge as a unique phenomenon that would endure for more than three centuries.

First, in the eastern Mediterranean the Ottoman Turks arose as a new militant Islamic force which threatened not only the Christian states of south-east Europe, but also older Muslim polities such as the empire of the Mamluks in Egypt, Syria and Arabia. The Ottomans were primarily a land power, but after their conquest of Constantinople (now Istanbul), the last remnant of the Christian Byzantine empire, in 1453, their rulers saw an increasing need to develop naval forces as well. Their main initial target was the republic of Venice which had a number of colonies in the eastern Mediterranean.[2]

The second event was the end of the 700-year struggle by the Christians to regain control of the Iberian peninsula from the Muslims. Known as the 'Reconquista', this struggle had created a long-lasting crusading spirit among the Spanish kingdoms. In 1492 the so-called 'Catholic Monarchs', the married couple Queen Isabella of Castile and King Ferdinand of Aragon, completed the subjugation of Granada, the last Muslim state in Iberia. Although a large Muslim population remained in the peninsula, these people were now totally subject to their Christian rulers. However, this triumph was not enough to assuage the crusading zeal of Spaniards. Plans were put forward to carry the holy war to Muslim North Africa through an amphibious invasion. The kingdom of Castile was largely a land-based power, but the crown of Aragon, which included the port of Barcelona, already had a history of seafaring and had built up a maritime empire, including the islands of Sicily and Sardinia, in the western Mediterranean. There seemed no reason why Spanish power should not be extended across the strait of Gibraltar and into the Maghreb, the Arabic name for Muslim North Africa.[3]

Thus, by the late fifteenth century, a successful Muslim power in the eastern Mediterranean was moving westwards, threatening Christendom, while in the western Mediterranean a victorious Christian power was preparing to advance eastwards, hoping to subdue the Muslim states of North Africa. A clash between these opposing powers might seem inevitable, but in contemporary terms the distance between the two powers was still great. Only fleets sent by either side could bridge that gap and initiate conflict between them.

When the war between Granada and the Spanish kingdoms broke out in the early 1480s, the Muslim state naturally looked to other Muslim countries for support. The states of North Africa were too weak and divided to be of much assistance, so Granadan emissaries went on to the great Muslim powers of the eastern Mediterranean, the Mamluks and the Ottomans. The Mamluks lacked adequate naval forces to carry an army to the Iberian peninsula. In Cairo, the Mamluk capital, the Granadans received words of support, but no action was taken to make them a reality. Indeed the Mamluks were in secret trying to win Ferdinand of Aragon's assistance against their Muslim rivals, the Ottomans. The Ottoman sultan had a growing, if limited, navy, but his armies were busy on his own frontiers. The only aid the sultan could offer was to give approval for Turkish corsairs to head to the western Mediterranean, base themselves at North African ports, and carry out raids on Christian coasts and shipping.

The most famous of these corsairs was Kemal Reis, who also took along with him his nephew Piri Reis, a skilled sailor but most famous for the sea charts he prepared. ('Reis' was the title given to a Turkish corsair captain.) Kemal had taken part in the Ottoman capture of the Venetian-held island of Negroponte (now Euboea) in Greece in 1470. He settled there and came to command a force of corsairs based on the island. In 1487 Sultan Bayezid II ordered Kemal to take a naval force to assist the Granadans in their fight against the Christians. He used North African ports such as Bougie (now Bejaia) and Bona (or Bône; now Annaba) as bases. Over five years he was active against the Spanish and their allies, raiding not only the Spanish coast but also the Balearic Islands, Corsica and Italy. However, by 1492 Kemal was reduced to ferrying Muslim refugees from Granada to ports in North Africa. Once Granada had fallen, Kemal returned to Ottoman territory. He won several naval victories over the Venetians in the Ottoman–Venetian war of 1499–1502, and because Spain sent military aid to the Venetians, he returned to the western Mediterranean in 1501 to attack Spanish targets.[4]

During the Granada war Castile had few warships with which to oppose the Turkish interlopers, but it did hire some galleys from the republic of Genoa and a force of Catalan galleys was provided by the crown of Aragon. However, the war was largely one of sieges on land, where Castile's superior artillery was decisive. Turkish corsairs could in the end do little to save Granada, but their movement to North Africa to wage war against the Christians was to set a valuable precedent for other Turkish corsairs in the first decades of the sixteenth century.

The use of North African ports as corsair bases was one reason the Catholic Monarchs began to think of extending their war against the infidels to the Maghreb. Another reason was that historically the Muslim states of North Africa had often intervened in Iberia to reverse Christian successes and strengthen Muslim resistance. In the eleventh century the Christians had taken Toledo, the ancient Visigothic capital, from the Muslims and forced many Muslim states in the peninsula to pay them tribute. Then the Almoravids, a fundamentalist Islamic sect, had come over from North Africa, defeated the Christians and retaken many of their gains. Similarly, in the twelfth century, Christian successes were neutralized from mid-century by the Almohads who came across to Iberia from North Africa.

The situation seemed more favourable to the Christians by the middle of the thirteenth century. All the Muslim states of Iberia had been conquered, except for Granada. Yet once again a North African power, in this case the Marinids, would repeatedly send armies into Spain with the intention of driving back the Christians and restoring Muslim power. Only in 1340 was the last Marinid invasion defeated, but Granada did not fall until 1492. Christian victory now seemed final, but Spaniards still worried that some new Muslim force would sweep out of the Maghreb once more to revive Muslim fortunes in Iberia. Only a Spanish conquest of the Maghreb could make sure that this would never happen.

The Spaniards were aware that they would not be the first Iberians to aim at making permanent conquests in North Africa. The Portuguese had captured Ceuta on the Moroccan shore of the strait of Gibraltar as long ago as 1415. Tangier was added in 1471, and the Portuguese also forced the rulers of ports further down the Atlantic coast of Morocco to acknowledge their sovereignty. This expansion owed something to the crusading spirit, but there were also economic motives for taking control of these ports. They were to support the steady movement of Portuguese traders and explorers down the Atlantic coast of Africa. In 1488 the Portuguese would sail around the Cape of Good Hope, and in 1498 they reached India. Soon they were establishing a Christian maritime empire around the Indian Ocean which challenged both Muslim and Hindu local rulers.[5]

In 1493 the Catholic Monarchs sent secret agents to North Africa to report on the state of the country. Since the collapse of Marinid power in the mid-fourteenth century, the Maghreb had split into a number of weak principalities. The Spanish agents reported that there was no single strong Muslim power that could resist a Spanish invasion. In 1494 the pope fixed the dividing line between Portuguese and Spanish areas of expansion in North Africa and the Catholic Monarchs decided that their first attacks would be directed against the ports of Melilla and Oran. However, in the same year the king of France invaded Italy to press his claim to the kingdom of Naples. Ferdinand of Aragon also had a claim to that kingdom, so all thoughts of attacking the Maghreb were put aside as Ferdinand concentrated Spanish forces against the French in Italy.[6] Nevertheless North Africa did not totally slip from Ferdinand's mind. Aragon had a long standing political and economic interest in the Maghreb, especially eastern areas like Tunis which were near to the Aragonese possessions of Sicily and Sardinia. The Castilians had little past connection with North Africa, but the Andalusian nobles who had played a major role in the conquest of Granada were glad to continue their war against the Muslims in a new area. In 1497 the duke of Medina Sidonia asked for royal permission to send an expedition to capture Melilla. The permission was given, the port taken and Moroccan counterattacks driven off. Spain had its first outpost in the Maghreb.

After the conquest of Granada in 1492 the Catholic Monarchs had made various concessions to their new Muslim subjects, granting them a degree of religious freedom. These concessions were steadily undermined by zealous Catholics, above all Cardinal Francisco Jiménez de Cisneros, archbishop of Toledo and primate of Castile. The new restrictions led to a Muslim revolt in Granada in 1499 which was not finally suppressed until 1501. The Christian victors now ordered all Muslims in the kingdom of Castile to convert to Christianity or leave the country. (A similar order would not be applied to Aragon until 1526.) Most of the Muslims accepted nominal conversion to Christianity, becoming known as Moriscos, while the others fled to North Africa. Another effect of the revolt was to reinforce calls for a Spanish conquest of the Maghreb since the rebels in Granada had received some support from North African ports. Cardinal Cisneros and Queen Isabella were particularly keen to carry the holy war to North Africa, but Ferdinand still seemed obsessed with events in Italy and the queen died in 1504.[7]

In August 1505 Cisneros took matters into his own hands, obtaining royal approval to organize an expedition to take the port of Mers el Kebir near Oran. Troops from both Spain and Italy formed the landing force, but little fighting was required. At the appearance of the Spanish force in September, the governor immediately surrendered the town. In July 1508 the small outpost of Vélez de la Gomera was taken by the Spanish, but Cardinal Cisneros wanted a bigger success. He put up money from his diocese to fund an expedition against Oran and Ferdinand gave his approval, allowing Cisneros to accompany the attacking army, said to number 20,000 men, although the actual military commander was Pedro Navarro, count of Oliveto, an experienced soldier and military engineer.

In mid-May 1509 the army was transported to the Spanish outpost of Mers el Kebir and then it marched on neighbouring Oran, which had about 12,000 inhabitants. Cisneros exhorted the troops to fight for the Christian faith and crush the infidels. However, the conquest of Oran was more a massacre than a battle. Two of the town's officials turned traitor and opened the gates to the Spanish army. By nightfall on 17 May Oran had been secured: 30 Spaniards had died, but at least 4,000 Muslims had been slaughtered. Most of the remainder of the Muslim population was sold into slavery. Some 300 Christian slaves were freed. After this success Cisneros wanted to advance into the interior and capture the major city of Tlemcen as a first step towards the complete conquest of the region. Navarro refused, claiming his orders related only to Oran. The cardinal was disgusted at such an attitude and returned to Spain, never again going on crusade in North Africa.[8]

Although no soldier, Cisneros may have been wiser than Navarro in the long run. Just seizing Spanish outposts, known as 'presidios', on the coast of North Africa did not bring security to Spain; it merely added military and financial burdens. Most of the outposts could not get supplies from the Muslim territories around them and had to be supplied from Spain or Spanish possessions like Sicily. Usually unpaid and half-starved, the troops in the garrisons died of disease or deserted to the enemy. If Cisneros had been listened to and North Africa had been conquered by Spain in the early years of the sixteenth century, the Barbary corsairs would never have come into existence. The European conquest of North Africa would not take place until the nineteenth century.

Freed of his religious adviser, Navarro was sent back to North Africa by Ferdinand in January 1510. With a force of 4,000 men he captured the port of Bougie. He also compelled other ports in the region to recognize Spanish sovereignty over them. One of these ports was Algiers. To make sure the agreement was observed, Navarro, the military engineer, established a fortress on an island facing the city and left a small Spanish garrison in it. Later in the year Navarro struck much further to the east along the North African shore. On 25 July he took the port of Tripoli in Libya, killing or enslaving most of the Muslim inhabitants. The city was put under the control of Ferdinand's kingdom of Sicily as being the nearest Spanish possession. In August Navarro and his naval commander García de Toledo attempted to capture the island of Djerba which lay to the west of Tripoli. Here Spanish luck ran out. The local inhabitants and Turkish corsairs based there repulsed the attackers. Several thousand men of the Spanish force were said to have perished, most dying when four ships sank in a storm. Undiscouraged, the Spanish laid plans to capture Tunis in 1511, but once again Ferdinand was distracted by affairs in Italy and the plans were cancelled. There were no further Spanish conquests in North Africa up to the time of Ferdinand's death in 1516.[9]

Among the defenders who repulsed Navarro's attack on Djerba in 1510 was a Turkish corsair called Aruj. He was accompanied by his brother Khizr. Together they would be known as the Barbarossa ('red beard') brothers and they became the principal founders of the Barbary corsairs. Their participation in the battle with the Spanish at Djerba meant that the Ottoman advance in the Mediterranean from the east had finally met up with the Spanish advance from the west, a clash that was soon to have major consequences for both sides.

BARBAROSSAS

Aruj and his brother Khizr were born during the 1470s on the island of Lesbos (sometimes known as Mitylene after the name of its main town) off the west coast of Anatolia. They had a Muslim Turkish father, Yakup Aga, and a Christian Greek mother, Katerina. Yakup was originally a sipahi, an Ottoman cavalryman, and he had participated in the conquest of Lesbos in 1462 when it was taken from the Genoese. Yakup was given a land grant on the island and married a local Greek girl. He later set up a pottery and his sons probably first went to sea in vessels carrying their father's wares.[10]

Although the Ottoman Turks had taken most of the islands in the Aegean Sea, a few remained under Christian control. Most troublesome for the Muslims was the island of Rhodes, which was the headquarters of the Knights of St John of Jerusalem. A military religious order set up in the Holy Land in the time of the Crusades, the Knights of St John (also known as the Knights Hospitaller for their medical aid to Christian pilgrims) were driven out of Palestine when the Muslims destroyed the last Crusader states in 1291.

At first resident in Cyprus, the Knights of St John seized the island of Rhodes from the Byzantines early in the fourteenth century. It became the base for their new vocation, to take the holy war to sea. For several centuries the galleys of the knights sallied out from Rhodes to attack Muslim coasts and shipping, and the order was always ready to assist larger expeditions by Christian nations in the eastern Mediterranean. Sultan Mehmed II, the conqueror of Constantinople, realized the Knights of Rhodes were a threat that had to be removed. Shortly before his death in 1480, the sultan sent an Ottoman army and fleet to take the island, but they failed to do so. The knights remained a threat to both the Ottoman Turks and the Mamluks of Egypt and Syria.[11]

Sometime during the 1490s a galley of the Knights of Rhodes intercepted a vessel commanded by Aruj. After a short fight he was taken prisoner. He was a galley slave of the knights for three years, but then he was ransomed or escaped, returning to his family. His sufferings imbued Aruj with a powerful hatred of Christians in general and the Knights of Rhodes in particular. He became a corsair captain, first launching attacks on the Christians from Anatolian ports, then later from Egypt.

Shortly after 1500 Aruj, accompanied by Khizr, moved on to Tunisia. The Hafsid sultan of Tunis permitted Aruj to base his corsairing activities in La Goletta, the port of Tunis, in return for a share of his profits. Aruj soon made a reputation for himself, among his exploits being the capture of two papal galleys off Italy in 1504 and the capture near the Lipari Islands of a Spanish ship taking troops and treasure to Naples in 1505. However, Aruj and Khizr were not the only Turkish corsairs active in North Africa. Another was Kurtoglu Muslihiddin, whom the Hafsid ruler of Tunis allowed to operate from the port of Bizerta from 1508. Kurtoglu Reis launched many raids on the coasts of Italy and Spain, even co-operating with Aruj and Khizr on occasion.

Possibly because of threats of retaliation from Christian states, the ruler of Tunis encouraged Aruj and Khizr to move their corsairing base to the more distant island of Djerba in 1510. As already noted, the brothers played a role in helping local people to repulse Pedro Navarro's attack on Djerba in the same year. By 1512 Aruj and Khizr were said to have a corsair fleet of twelve galliots (small galleys), eight of their own and four belonging to other Turkish corsair captains who worked with them. In that year a message reached Aruj from the former ruler of the port of Bougie, which had been captured by the Spanish in 1510. He asked for Aruj's assistance in an attempt to retake the port. Aruj and Khizr took their corsair fleet north to carry out this operation. However, the siege was a failure. In one clash Aruj was severely wounded in the left arm and it had to be amputated.

As the corsair fleet withdrew to the temporary refuge of La Goletta, it captured a Genoese ship on its way to Tabarka, the Genoese trading outpost and coral fishery on the coast of North Africa. Angered when they learned of this loss, the Genoese were not slow to retaliate. Before the end of 1512, a force of Genoese galleys, under the command of Andrea Doria, raided La Goletta and destroyed most of Aruj and Khizr's ships.

This was the first encounter between the brothers and Andrea Doria. The latter was to become perhaps the greatest Christian admiral in the Mediterranean during the sixteenth century. Living to a great age (he died in 1560 a few days before his 94th birthday) and remaining an active commander into his eighties, Doria probably participated in more maritime conflict than any of his Christian or Muslim naval contemporaries. Genoese galleys, including those of the Doria family, were available for hire to other Christian states when not active on behalf of the

republic of Genoa. Up to 1528 Andrea Doria generally supported France
in its struggles with Emperor Charles V in Italy. In that year, however,
Doria changed sides and he remained a loyal servant of the Spanish
Habsburgs for the rest of his career.[12]

In 1512 Andrea Doria probably felt he had delivered a deadly blow
to Aruj and Khizr, but during 1513 they carefully rebuilt their corsair
fleet at Djerba. In 1514 the brothers once again attacked Bougie, but the
Spanish garrison received reinforcements and again the siege failed.
Reluctant to return to Djerba and probably unwelcome in Tunis, Aruj
and Khizr took their forces to winter in the port of Djidjelli (now Jijel),
not far from Bougie. Probably Aruj was thinking of making yet another
assault on Bougie, but in the meantime the corsairs still carried out raids
in the western Mediterranean from their new base.

In 1516 the corsair Kurtoglu Reis was said to have co-operated with
Khizr in a raid on the Italian coast. On returning to his base at Bizerta,
Kurtoglu found it under attack by Christian forces. He helped the
Tunisians to drive away the enemy, and immediately counterattacked
with a raid on the Italian coast near Rome. According to legend it was
on this occasion that Kurtoglu tried to capture Pope Leo X, who was out
hunting, but the pontiff escaped from the infidel raiders. Later in the
year Kurtoglu received a summons from Sultan Selim I to command
the Ottoman naval forces supporting the sultan's attack on the Mamluks
in Syria and Egypt. Kurtoglu was transformed from Barbary corsair into
Ottoman naval commander, the first of many who would make that
transition, and he played an important role in the Ottoman conquest of
Egypt in 1517.

The year 1516 saw the death of King Ferdinand of Aragon, and his
vassal the Muslim ruler of Algiers felt that his loyalty ended with the
Christian king's death. The ruler now requested the help of Aruj and
Khizr in capturing the Spanish-held fortress which stood just offshore
from the city of Algiers. Aruj was happy to assist, but on his way to
Algiers he took a short detour to the port of Cherchell. Another Turkish corsair had taken control of Cherchell, but Aruj wanted no rivals on
this coast. He killed the corsair and made the port subject to his rule.
Arriving at Algiers, it was soon clear to Aruj that he would not be able
to take the Spanish fortress. Instead he overthrew and killed the ruler of
Algiers and added the city to his fast-growing chain of territorial
possessions. The inhabitants of the city now plotted a revolt against their

new Turkish overlords, but the plot was discovered and Aruj executed all those involved in it.[13]

Both the Spanish and the native Muslims of North Africa were unhappy about the growing power of the Turkish corsairs in the region. Cardinal Cisneros, the conqueror of Oran, died in 1517. One of his last acts was to send a Spanish force under Diego de Vera to remove Aruj and Khizr from Algiers, but the expedition was defeated with considerable loss. Next it was the turn of the local Muslims to act. The ruler of the port of Tenes led his troops, aided by tribesmen from the mountains, against Algiers. Aruj now assembled a force of Turkish corsairs and Muslim refugees from Spain, both groups outsiders in the Maghreb, and attacked the approaching army. He was victorious and added Tenes to his possessions.

While many Moors (the Spanish term for the native Muslims of Iberia and the Maghreb) feared the growing power of the Turks, others still wanted to exploit their military prowess. A deputation from the important inland city of Tlemcen asked Aruj to come and remove their pro-Spanish ruler. As ever he was happy to oblige, and he seized Tlemcen with little trouble in September 1517. Aruj undoubtedly reached his peak as a ruler in the winter of 1517–18. Controlling most of the coastal region of what is today Algeria, he felt he could write to the sultan of Tunis and the ruler of Fez in Morocco as an equal, inviting them to join him in destroying the last Spanish outposts in the area. Similarly Aruj wrote to the Ottoman sultan describing his achievements and seeking Selim's approval and support.

Once again the Spanish tried to take back Aruj's gains. In 1518 the governor of Oran, the marquis of Comares, led a Spanish army, assisted by local Muslim tribesmen, in an expedition to Tlemcen. Although he had been promised Moroccan support by the ruler of Fez, Aruj soon realized he could not successfully resist the Spanish forces. He left Tlemcen and retreated towards Algiers, where his brother Khizr awaited him. However, the Spanish pursuit was faster than expected. Aruj was overtaken and killed in a short skirmish. Comares might have followed up this success by attacking Algiers. Instead he installed a pro-Spanish ruler in Tlemcen and returned to Oran.[14]

Khizr inherited not just the territorial possessions he and his brother had seized in the last few years, but also Aruj's nickname: Barbarossa ('red beard'). Its origins have been disputed. At its simplest it may just be that both brothers had red beards, and Aruj received the name first because he was the eldest and the leader. Others have claimed the name came from a corruption of Baba Aruj, 'Father Aruj', a Muslim nickname for the older brother. Whatever its origins, the name Barbarossa was now to be firmly applied to Khizr by his Christian enemies. The Ottoman sultan later gave Khizr the honorific title Khair ad-Din ('best of the religion' [of Islam]), but it is as Barbarossa that he survives in the folk legends of Christian Mediterranean countries right up to the present day.

The Spanish now began to prepare a direct attack on Algiers, so Barbarossa felt it was time for him to submit formally to the Ottoman sultan Selim and ask for his assistance. Selim had recently completed the conquest of the Mamluk empire. This included Egypt, and a further extension of Ottoman control to Algiers would increase the sultan's hold on the southern shore of the Mediterranean. Previously the most westerly Ottoman outposts in that sea had been in Greece. Now Algiers would be an Ottoman base deep within the western Mediterranean and a direct threat to Spain. Selim was happy to accept Barbarossa's submission and to make Algiers a new Ottoman frontier province.

The sultan gave Barbarossa the Ottoman rank of beylerbey and sent him 2,000 janissaries along with a quantity of artillery. Janissaries were the elite infantry of the Ottoman army. They were raised by a levy of young boys from Christian families in the Balkans and Anatolia. These boys became Muslims and were given a rigorous training, so that their only loyalties were to the sultan and their fellow janissaries. They provided a vital professional backbone to Barbarossa's force of Turkish corsairs and Spanish Moors, and their arrival was to have long-term effects on the future political development of Algiers.[15]

Charles I, the youthful new king of Spain, and soon to become Holy Roman Emperor Charles V, ordered Hugo de Moncada, the viceroy of Sicily, to assemble an army and fleet with which to conquer Algiers. The Spanish forces reached Algiers in August 1519, but Barbarossa's reinforced army was ready to oppose them. Muslim resistance, plus storms at sea, soon ruined the Spanish expedition and the survivors departed leaving many dead and captives behind them. Once again the Spanish had failed to take Algiers, but their garrison still survived in the fortress just offshore from the city.

Yet where the Spanish had failed, the local Muslims were to succeed. In 1520 a major revolt of the mountain tribes, encouraged by the ruler of

Tunis, made the situation so difficult for Barbarossa that he left Algiers and retreated to Djidjelli. Not until 1525 was he able to regain possession of Algiers. Nevertheless every year his corsairs set out to raid the coasts of Spain and Italy as well as Sicily, Sardinia, Corsica and the Balearic Islands, doing much damage and taking many Christian captives.

After Selim's conquest of Egypt, the trade route from Istanbul to Alexandria took on new importance. The Knights of Rhodes were ideally placed to prey on ships using this route. When Selim's son Suleiman came to the Ottoman throne he was determined to conquer Rhodes. In 1522 he led a large army and fleet to the island. The naval contingent was commanded by Kurtoglu Reis, former comrade in arms of Barbarossa. Although Barbarossa had been temporarily driven out of Algiers, he began the long tradition of Barbary corsairs reinforcing the Ottoman fleet in time of war when he sent some galleys to join Kurtoglu's ships at Rhodes. Under their grand master, Philippe Villiers de l'Isle-Adam, the knights beat off attacks by the besieging Ottomans for five months, but by the end of 1522 they entered into negotiations with the sultan. In a moment of generosity he was later to regret, Suleiman agreed to let the knights leave Rhodes unmolested instead of taking them prisoner. After their departure in early 1523, Kurtoglu Reis became the first Ottoman governor of Rhodes.[16]

The Knights of St John went first to the island of Crete, a Venetian colony, and then via Sicily to Civitavecchia in the territory ruled by the pope in central Italy. Emperor Charles v offered the order new possessions: the island of Malta (a dependency of Sicily) and the port of Tripoli on the north coast of Africa. The knights, many of whom were French, were initially reluctant to accept anything from an emperor who was frequently at war with the king of France. Most knights hoped they could recapture their old home of Rhodes. However, as the years passed this seemed more and more unlikely. The knights finally accepted the emperor's offer. In 1530 they took over Malta and Tripoli. Although they continued to send raiding galleys into the eastern Mediterranean, the new Knights of Malta would find much of their time taken up in conflict with their new neighbours, the Barbary corsairs.[17]

Before the knights arrived in their new homes, Barbarossa was back in control of Algiers. Although during his exile he had secured new possessions such as the ports of Bona and Mostaganem and the inland city of Constantine, Barbarossa regarded Algiers as the principal city of his dominions. Its only drawback was the continued presence of the offshore Spanish fortress which meant corsair ships could not use the harbour of Algiers and had to be based at other ports. Finally, in May 1529, Barbarossa decided to remove this Spanish thorn from his side. Barbarossa summoned the Spanish commander Martín de Vargas to surrender, but he refused. After a fierce bombardment the Algerines stormed the Spanish fort. The survivors of the Spanish garrison were enslaved and their first task was to construct a stone breakwater linking the fortress island to the city of Algiers on the mainland, thus creating a more sheltered harbour for corsair vessels.[18]

If Aruj had been bold and daring, leading to an ultimately fatal recklessness, his younger brother, the new Barbarossa, tempered his own military and political abilities with caution and patience. He laid the foundations of a state which would endure for more than three centuries. He was also careful in his choice of subordinates, most of whom were both able corsair captains and loyal to him. They were nearly all Turks or renegade Christians and Jews (Sinan Reis was known as the 'Jew of Smyrna'). The greatest of Barbarossa's captains was Turgut Reis, of whom more later, but in 1529 his captains Aydin Reis and Salih Reis won a particularly notable victory over the Spanish.

Barbarossa had sent the two captains, with fourteen ships, to raid the Balearic Islands. They carried out a number of attacks there, then extended their operations to the gulf of Valencia on the coast of Spain. As was common practice, Aydin Reis sent messengers ashore to contact the Moriscos, the Moors of Spain who had supposedly converted to Christianity. They were particularly numerous in the Valencia area and often gave useful intelligence to the corsairs to guide their raids. On this occasion Aydin learned that a number of Morisco families on the estates of the count of Oliva wished to leave Spain and find refuge in North Africa. The reis took them aboard his ships and withdrew to Formentera, one of the smaller of the Balearic Islands, which was a rendezvous for the corsair force. A Spanish force of eight galleys under Rodrigo de Portundo was sent after the raiders and the count of Oliva offered a financial reward for the return of his Moriscos. Aydin and Salih were initially taken by surprise when Portundo's vessels arrived at Formentera, but they fought back to such good effect that the Spanish commander was killed and seven of his galleys were captured. The Muslim slaves at the oars were freed, the prizes were taken back to Algiers in triumph, and this success was the first major victory of the Barbary corsairs over Spanish naval forces in a battle at sea.[19]

Stung by this defeat, the Spanish were determined to hit back. In 1530 Andrea Doria, now in Charles v's service, was sent to the Barbary coast with a fleet that attacked the port of Cherchell. The town was taken and Christian slaves liberated. Then Doria learned that Barbarossa was approaching with a naval force from Algiers. He immediately ordered his men to leave Cherchell and return to their ships. Happily plundering the town, many of the men ignored their admiral's orders. Eventually Doria tired of waiting and his ships sailed away, leaving his men on shore to be captured and enslaved by the Muslims. If Doria had found his operations against the Barbary corsairs unsatisfactory, he had more success against the main Ottoman enemy. In 1532 he captured the ports of Coron and Patras in Greece and defeated Ottoman efforts to retake them in the following year.

Worried by the poor performance of his naval forces, Sultan Suleiman the Magnificent decided to call Barbarossa to Istanbul to take command of the Ottoman navy. He would hold the office of 'kapudan pasha' and be in charge of both the administration of the fleet and its operations against the Christians. Barbarossa was the first of several leaders of the Barbary corsairs who would be called to take on this office during the sixteenth and seventeenth centuries. In August 1533 Barbarossa left Algiers to take up his new post. He left Hassan Aga, a Christian from Sardinia who had converted to Islam and become a renegade corsair captain, to be his deputy in the city.

After a winter spent reorganizing the Ottoman fleet, Barbarossa led it out from Istanbul in the spring of 1534. Initially he launched a series of raids on the coast of Italy, but these were only to mislead the Christians about his true intentions. His main target for this year's campaign was the city of Tunis, whose pro-Spanish ruler, Moulay Hassan, was unpopular with his subjects. In mid-August Barbarossa swooped down on Tunis, meeting little resistance when he captured it and La Goletta, his home in his early days as a corsair in North Africa. Moulay Hassan fled and called on the Spanish to help him regain his throne.[20]

The first Ottoman base in the Maghreb had been Algiers, which primarily threatened Spain. With the fall of Tunis, there was now a second Ottoman base in the area, primarily threatening Italy. It was a challenge Emperor Charles v could not ignore. However, instead of just sending Andrea Doria or some other subordinate commander to recapture Tunis, the emperor decided to do the job himself. More than that, he decided to turn his military expedition into a veritable crusade.

In early June 1535 Charles assembled his forces at Cagliari in Sardinia. There were 74 galleys (from Spain, Sicily, Naples, Genoa, the papal states and the Knights of Malta); more than 300 sailing ships (not only troop transports and supply ships, but also warships from the emperor's possessions in the Netherlands and from his brother-in-law the king of Portugal); and some 26,000 Spanish, Italian, and German soldiers. Andrea Doria commanded the fleet and the marquis of Vasto the army; the emperor was in overall command. It was the most powerful Christian fleet and army that had ever been assembled in the western Mediterranean. It had cost Charles v one million ducats to prepare this expedition, a vast sum the emperor could only afford because of a financial windfall that had reached him from the New World.

In 1533 Francisco Pizarro had overthrown and killed Atahualpa, the Inca ruler of Peru, and seized his treasures. The emperor's share of the treasure, some two million ducats, had only recently arrived in Spain. Now half of it could be used to fund the holy war against the Muslims in the Mediterranean. Charles was conscious of the greatness of his endeavour, both in financial and military terms. He expected to win an historic victory, and to record his triumph he took along the Flemish artist Jan Vermeyen and the Spanish poet Garcilaso de la Vega.[21]

On 14 June 1535 the mighty fleet appeared in the gulf of Tunis and began to land the Christian troops. Barbarossa made no attempt to oppose the landings. Tunis lies on a lake which connects to the sea via a narrow channel on which stands the town of La Goletta. The fortress at La Goletta was the first target of the Christian invaders and it was soon besieged. At first the siege proceeded only slowly, and a lack of fresh water and an outbreak of dysentery began to sap the strength of the Christian army. As Barbarossa had little chance of defeating the emperor's army in the field, his only hope was for disease to cripple it. Charles ordered an assault on La Goletta on 14 July. The Knights of Malta led the way and soon the fortress had been taken.

The deposed ruler Moulay Hassan now arrived from the inland city of Kairouan with his own forces and he begged the emperor to press on to Tunis. Despite the continuing shortage of fresh water, the Christian army moved closer to Tunis and a siege of the city seemed about to begin.

Within its walls, Barbarossa and his commanders discussed what to do with the thousands of Christian slaves held there. The slaves would use up valuable food and water if there was a siege. There were suggestions that most of the captives should be put to death. News of this possibility reached the Christian slaves and they broke into revolt, possibly aided by Christian renegades among the Muslims who had now decided to revert to their former allegiance. The armoury was seized and a city gate was opened to receive the approaching Christian army. While Barbarossa and several thousand of his men fled from Tunis to the port of Bona, the emperor's soldiers poured into Tunis on 21 July.

Charles v gave his troops the traditional right to sack a city that had not surrendered at first summons. Estimates of the Muslim dead in the subsequent massacre go as high as 30,000, but while that figure is probably too high, the victims certainly numbered more than 10,000. It was perhaps the most brutal slaughter of the inhabitants of a Muslim city by Christians during the sixteenth century. At least it caused Charles v less embarrassment than an earlier atrocity committed by his soldiers when they sacked Rome, the religious capital of Christendom, in 1527.

Once the massacre was over the emperor generously returned the ruined city of Tunis to its former ruler Moulay Hassan, who once again became a Spanish vassal. To ensure the returned ruler's future security, a Spanish garrison was left at La Goletta in a much strengthened fortress. Charles had a series of rich tapestries made on which were shown scenes from his victorious expedition to Tunis. Unsurprisingly the massacre of the city's Muslim inhabitants did not feature in any of those scenes.

Despite this Muslim defeat, Barbarossa proved himself as resilient as ever. Collecting ships from Bona and Algiers, he launched a raid on the Balearic Islands, which had little protection because Spanish forces had been removed to go on the Tunis expedition. The port of Mahon on the island of Minorca was taken and all the inhabitants, variously estimated at between 2,000 and 6,000 persons, were taken away to become slaves in Barbary. The loss of Tunis had done nothing to reduce the ability of the Barbary corsairs to launch successful raids on Christian territories.[22]

When they captured La Goletta the soldiers of Charles v found French artillery on the shattered ramparts. These guns had not been captured by Muslim corsairs; they had been supplied by France to its secret Turkish ally. That alliance was openly proclaimed in 1536, making

France the first European Christian power to forge a link with the greatest Muslim power in the Mediterranean. There was much talk of a joint Franco-Ottoman assault on Charles v's possessions in Italy. In 1537 the Ottoman sultan decided to take Corfu as a base from which to launch an invasion of Italy. The island was owned by the Venetians. Since 1502 the republic of Venice had been careful to avoid war with the Ottomans lest it lose its valuable trade with the Turkish empire. However, there could be no question of tamely surrendering Corfu to the sultan. Barbarossa brought the fleet to support Suleiman's army in its assault on Corfu, but the Venetians defeated the Ottoman attack.

What now seemed to be a direct Ottoman threat to Italy caused the pope to seek the formation of a wide Christian alliance to oppose the infidel enemy. A holy league that included the papal states, Spain, Genoa and Venice was brought into being. In May 1538 Charles v seemed to think this new alliance would permit him to launch a massive Christian assault on the Turks which would recapture Constantinople (Istanbul), but the Christian forces were slow to assemble. Barbarossa, with a fleet of 90 galleys and 50 smaller galliots, struck first, aiming to capture Corfu during the new campaigning season. Some 80 Venetian and papal galleys went to oppose him in June, but neither side was ready to take decisive action. When Andrea Doria belatedly appeared with 50 Spanish and Genoese galleys, accompanied by sailing ships, the Christians finally outnumbered Barbarossa. The Turkish admiral merely retreated into the gulf of Preveza on the west coast of Greece, putting Ottoman artillery batteries on both sides of its narrow entrance channel. Unwilling to force an entry into the bay, Andrea Doria, now overall commander of the holy league fleet, could only cruise off its mouth, using up his supplies.

Finally, with his supplies running out, Doria decided to withdraw his fleet on the night of 27–8 September 1538. As he did so his fleet began to straggle and by dawn the wind had died. This was no problem for Doria's galleys, but his fleet also included sailing ships, both warships and transports. These might now be at the mercy of Barbarossa's galleys if they appeared. This they duly did, coming out from the gulf of Preveza on the morning of 28 September. Barbarossa's fleet, including a contingent from the Barbary coast under commanders such as Turgut Reis, Salih Reis and Sinan Reis, attacked the dispersed ships in the rear of Doria's fleet and the Christian commander was slow to send assistance to them. One Venetian galleon had to fight off the Turkish galleys surrounding it for hours, and its eventual escape owed nothing to any help from Doria. In all the Ottoman fleet took about a dozen Christian sailing ships and galleys, only a small part of Doria's fleet, but the Genoese admiral had definitely suffered a defeat. Enemies claimed his lack of zeal was due to the age-old Genoese hatred of the Venetians, who made up a large part of his fleet or, it was said, Doria did not wish to commit the Genoese galleys he actually owned to the battle lest they be damaged or lost.[23]

The significance of the battle of Preveza has often been exaggerated. Tactically it was a minor Ottoman success, which was largely negated by a storm shortly afterwards that sank more of Barbarossa's ships than he had taken from the Christians. Strategically it has been claimed that the battle won for the Ottomans a naval domination of the Mediterranean that lasted until their great defeat at the battle of Lepanto in 1571. However, concepts like 'command of the sea' had little meaning in the context of sixteenth-century galley warfare in the Mediterranean Sea. As on land, naval warfare was a seasonal activity. One side might lose heavily in one summer campaign (with storms more likely to sink galleys than enemy action), but the opponent's advantage rarely lasted beyond that year. In the next campaigning season the positions could easily be reversed. A victory one year did not guarantee continued naval domination the next, let alone 'command of the sea' for decades.

Battles between galley fleets were relatively uncommon. More important was the battle for ports, and in this context the struggle for control of Tunis in 1534–5 was more significant than the battle of Preveza in 1538. Galleys were essentially short-range vessels, with little capacity to carry extensive supplies of food and water for their crews. To advance the Ottoman naval frontier with Christendom in the Mediterranean, new naval bases needed to be taken so that Turkish galleys could extend their operations into new areas. Barbarossa's capture of Tunis was far more threatening to the Christian powers than losing a few of their ships at the battle of Preveza. That was the reason Charles v had to hit back immediately, retaking Tunis the following year.

Nevertheless naval battles are always more striking events, especially given their rarity in the Mediterranean struggle, so Barbarossa's success at Preveza cemented his reputation as the great Ottoman naval hero and he returned to Istanbul in triumph. More important were the divisions that Doria's conduct in the battle had opened up on the Christian side. Venice was increasingly unhappy with the way the war was being conducted, and in 1540 the republic made a separate peace with the Ottoman sultan, paying him a substantial financial indemnity. As we have already seen, in 1541 Charles v tried to repeat his great success at Tunis in 1535 with a similar expedition aimed at conquering Algiers. It ended in disaster, more due to bad weather than Muslim resistance, but the effects were lasting. Charles would make no further efforts to destroy the Barbary corsairs.

The Franco-Ottoman alliance had so far brought little benefit to either side, while the French king had incurred hatred throughout Christian Europe for being in league with the infidels. In 1543 Barbarossa took the Ottoman fleet into the western Mediterranean with the intention of co-ordinating his operations with the French. After raiding along the Italian coast, he arrived at Marseille to find the French commanders had few plans for the campaigning season. Eventually a Franco-Ottoman attack on the city of Nice was agreed. Nice eventually fell, but its brutal sacking was largely carried out by the French rather than the Ottoman forces. Before going into winter quarters, Barbarossa sent Salih Reis with a squadron to raid along the coast of Spain, and he ravaged towns such as Rosas and Palamos on the Catalonian coast before rejoining the main fleet.

Instead of returning to Istanbul, the Ottoman fleet was to winter in the port of Toulon in France. All the Christian population of the town had been removed and churches were temporarily converted into mosques. This was amazing enough to contemporary Christians, but what particularly enraged them was that the French king allowed thousands of Christian slaves to languish in Turkish galleys in one of his own ports without making any effort to help or ransom them. In 1544 Barbarossa found the French unwilling to campaign alongside his forces so he decided to take the Ottoman fleet home. Before doing so, he had some unfinished business to conclude. His most valued corsair captain, Turgut Reis, had been captured by the Genoese in 1540. Barbarossa now took the entire Ottoman fleet off Genoa and threatened to blockade the port unless Andrea Doria agreed to negotiations about freeing the captive. Doria complied and Turgut was released on payment of a large ransom. Given Turgut's successes against the Christians in the coming years, Andrea Doria had made a bad bargain, but Barbarossa was at the height of his fame and even his greatest Christian opponent was forced to recognize his power. After further raids along the Italian coast and allowing the Barbary corsair contingent to leave for their home ports, Barbarossa took the remainder of the Ottoman fleet back to Istanbul.[24]

In 1545 Barbarossa retired to his palace in Istanbul and dictated his memoirs, the only Barbary corsair leader ever to do so. He died in July 1546 and was buried in his mausoleum in the Besiktas district of the imperial capital. As a Turkish chronicler put it: 'The king of the sea is dead.' In his lifetime Barbarossa had established the Ottoman navy as a formidable naval force throughout the Mediterranean, and he had also established a corsair state at Algiers that would last for centuries and make the Barbary corsairs a legend in both Christian and Muslim worlds.

TURGUT REIS

Turgut Reis (called Dragut by his Christian enemies) was born in a small village outside Bodrum on the west coast of Anatolia sometime in the 1480s. (His birthplace is now named after him as the town of Turgutreis.) The son of a Turkish peasant, he initially became a soldier and served in the Ottoman conquest of Egypt in 1517. Originally linked to the corsair Sinan Reis, Turgut came under the command of Barbarossa around 1520. Proving himself a successful corsair, Turgut served as a commander in Barbarossa's fleet in his victory at the battle of Preveza in 1538.[25]

In 1540, however, Turgut's luck ran out. His force of twelve corsair galleys had been run ashore on a beach in Sardinia so that repairs to them could be undertaken while the crews rested and collected water. Genoese galleys, under the command of Giannettino Doria, the nephew of Andrea Doria, then appeared. Taken by surprise, Turgut and his men were quickly forced to surrender. Initially Turgut became a slave rower in a Genoese galley. There is a story that one day Turgut the galley slave had a conversation with a visiting Knight of Malta, Jean Parisot de la Valette, about the fortunes of war and how quickly the victor might become the vanquished. Some years earlier it had been the knight who had been a slave rower in a Turkish corsair galley until freed. Whether the story is true or not, the two men were to meet almost a quarter of a century later. At the siege of Malta in 1565 de la Valette would be grand master of the defending Knights of Malta, while Turgut led the Barbary corsair contingent among the besiegers and died in the struggle.[26]

Barbarossa was anxious to free Turgut from captivity, but his initial overtures were rejected by the Genoese and they later moved Turgut out of his galley and into a prison at Genoa. As mentioned, in 1544 Barbarossa and the whole Ottoman fleet paid a visit to Genoa and threatened to blockade the port or mount an attack on it if Turgut was not released. Andrea Doria agreed to release Turgut in return for a ransom of 3,500 gold ducats, which was duly paid. Once again free, Turgut did not forget his years as a Genoese captive. The Genoese coastline in Liguria and the Genoese-controlled island of Corsica were to be favourite targets of his future corsair raids.

After the death of Barbarossa in 1546, a truce in the Mediterranean was agreed between Emperor Charles v and the Ottoman sultan Suleiman. However, as on the plains of Hungary, a truce between Christian and Muslim rulers did not mean an end to small-scale raiding by their frontier forces. Turgut Reis, now governor of the island of Djerba, carried out a number of raids on Christian coasts and islands, but in 1550 he took action which Charles v considered to be a serious breach of the truce. After a dispute with a neighbouring Muslim ruler in Tunisia, Turgut seized the port of Mahdia from his opponent and showed every intention of developing it into an Ottoman corsair base. After his protest to the sultan received no response, Charles v sent Andrea Doria with a galley squadron and a force of Spanish troops to take back Turgut's prize. The Knights of Malta were happy to contribute forces to this expedition as well. Turgut was away raiding along the Italian coastline, but his Turkish garrison in Mahdia resisted the Christian attack for some months. Eventually, however, Mahdia was stormed and most of its inhabitants killed or enslaved. A Spanish garrison was installed, but it proved difficult to supply, so in 1554 it was withdrawn after the fortifications of Mahdia had been blown up.

Andrea Doria was not satisfied with his Mahdia success alone. He was determined to crush Turgut Reis personally. He led a force to the island of Djerba and took Turgut by surprise, trapping the corsair fleet in the channel separating the island from the North African mainland. The Spanish controlled one end of the channel while the other end was blocked by reefs. Turgut escaped from this trap by cutting through the reefs and dragging his galleys to open water. Thwarted by Turgut's escape, Andrea Doria could only ravage Djerba and then depart. Turgut now went to Istanbul and consulted with the sultan about future naval operations, since the Habsburg–Ottoman war in the Mediterranean had obviously begun once more.[27]

In 1551 an Ottoman fleet was sent into the central Mediterranean. Turgut accompanied it, but the commander was Sinan Pasha, the kapudan pasha or commander-in-chief of the Ottoman navy. This was the post once held by Barbarossa, but Sinan Pasha was no sailor. He was an imperial official who largely owed his position to the fact that he was the brother of the grand vizier, Rustem Pasha, and was married to one of the daughters of Sultan Suleiman the Magnificent. The sultan had told Sinan Pasha to take Turgut's advice on naval matters, but the relationship between the two men was soon strained.

After some initial raids on the Italian coast, the Ottoman fleet went to the island of Malta, intent on driving out the knights. Turkish forces overran most of the island as the knights retreated within their fortifications, but it soon became clear that the Ottoman invaders lacked both numbers and the necessary supplies to sustain a long siege. Leaving Malta, the Ottomans sacked the nearby island of Gozo and carried away all its inhabitants, said to be 6,000 in number, to become slaves. Joined by forces under Salih Reis from Algiers, the Ottoman commanders now set their sights on capturing the other, weaker possession of the Knights of Malta: the port of Tripoli in Libya.

The governor of Tripoli was the Frenchman Gaspard de Vallier and he had 30 other knights (all French) and 600 soldiers (mostly Italian) under his command. The fortifications had been neglected and they were steadily broken down by Ottoman cannon fire. As conditions worsened, the soldiers of the garrison threatened to mutiny. In the meantime, the new French ambassador to the Ottoman sultan, Gabriel d'Aramon, had reached Malta on his way to Istanbul. The grand master of the Knights of Malta asked him to go to Tripoli and mediate between the embattled garrison and France's Ottoman allies. D'Aramon did so and arranged generous terms of surrender for de Vallier and the other French knights. They were permitted to go to Malta, but the soldiers of the garrison were all enslaved by the victorious Turks. The grand master was outraged at de Vallier's conduct, but pressure from the king of France and from the French knights who dominated the order ensured that de Vallier spent only a short time in prison as punishment for his selfish actions. The Ottomans were cynically amused by the fact that although the French were supposedly their allies, at the siege of Tripoli they were also their principal enemies in the guise of Knights of Malta. Turgut Reis had hoped to be named the first Ottoman governor of Tripoli, but Sinan

Pasha appointed Murad Aga, the commander of the nearby Ottoman outpost of Tajoura, instead.[28]

In the summer of 1552 the Ottoman fleet, commanded by Sinan Pasha with the assistance of Turgut Reis, once again appeared in the central Mediterranean. It was supposed to join with the French galley fleet near Naples, but the French failed to appear. Sinan wanted to return to Istanbul, but Turgut convinced him to launch a series of raids along the Italian coastline. King Henry II of France had promised the pope that his Ottoman ally would not attack the papal states, but Turgut did not feel bound by this promise, launching raids in papal as well as Neapolitan territory. Although outnumbered by the Ottoman fleet, Andrea Doria's force of galleys was compelled to take some sort of action to disrupt Turkish raiding. In the end he clashed with the Ottoman forces off the island of Ponza, was beaten, and was lucky to escape with the loss of only seven galleys. The French galley fleet under Paulin de la Garde now belatedly joined the Ottomans, but it was too late in the year for further operations.

Franco-Ottoman naval co-operation was to be more successful in 1553. Partly this was due to the fact that when the Ottoman fleet came west it now had Turgut Reis in sole command, the ailing Sinan Pasha being left behind (he died at the end of the year). After sacking the island of Pantelleria and the port of Licata in Sicily, Turgut attempted to persuade the sultan of Tunis, known to be on bad terms with the Spanish garrison at La Goletta, to come over to the Ottoman side, but without success. Turgut then took his fleet north along the west coast of Italy, attacking Elba, before joining up with the French galleys under Paulin de la Garde. The Franco-Ottoman fleet then escorted a French army and a force of Corsican exiles, under Sampiero Corso, to Corsica. The island was invaded and by the end of September its Genoese overlords had lost almost every important town to the invaders. Despite French requests to stay on and complete the conquest, Turgut Reis withdrew his fleet because of the lateness of the season, and its ships, laden with captives and booty, set off for home.[29]

The invasion of Corsica was important because of the threat it posed to Spanish sea communications with Italy. The southern route to Italy, from Cartagena in Spain to Naples, passing south of Sardinia and north of Sicily, was already insecure because of the proximity of the bases of the Barbary corsairs in North Africa. The northern route, from Barcelona in

Spain to Genoa in Italy, passing near the north point of Corsica, had previously been quite safe, but if Corsica fell into French, or even Ottoman, hands, it would endanger that route as well. Spain could not afford to lose safe communications with its possessions in Naples and Milan, the latter being reached via Genoa. Before 1553 was over Andrea Doria was landing more Genoese forces on Corsica, but the struggle on the island was to last for several more years. The French claimed the Ottomans did not give them enough support; the Genoese voiced similar complaints about the Spanish.

Salih Reis, ruler in Algiers, decided to remove the last Spanish outposts from his territory, and in 1555 he began a siege of the port of Bougie. The small Spanish garrison, under Alonso de Peralta, was soon forced into negotiations for surrender. Peralta wanted a guarantee that he and 40 companions of his choice would be given safe passage back to Spain. Salih Reis agreed to this and took possession of the town. Peralta and his friends went home while all the other Christians in Bougie became slaves. De Vallier survived his disgrace at Tripoli in 1551, but Peralta was not so fortunate. Arrested as soon as he reached Spain, Peralta was publicly executed at Valladolid in May 1556 for his disgraceful conduct. After his success at Bougie, Salih Reis moved against the last remaining Spanish strongholds on his coast, Mers el Kebir and Oran, in 1556, but had no success in taking them.[30]

In 1556 Turgut Reis was finally made ruler of Tripoli in Libya and set about developing it as a corsair base. He might have entertained hopes of being made kapudan pasha like Barbarossa before him, but the post of head of the Ottoman navy continued to be given to imperial officials rather than sailors. Between 1533 and 1587 six men held the post, four imperial officials and only two sailors, Barbarossa and Uluj Ali, both Barbary corsairs. Piyale Pasha had held the post since Sinan Pasha's death in 1553, but unlike the latter he was prepared to listen to advice from sailors and was to enjoy a good relationship with Turgut Reis.

In 1558 Piyale Pasha brought the Ottoman fleet into the central Mediterranean and Turgut Reis joined him. Once again the plan was to co-ordinate operations with the French, but after sailing north along the Italian coast and making a number of raids, the Ottomans arrived off the French coast to find their allies unprepared. The Ottoman fleet then went to raid Spain's Balearic Islands. The town of Ciutadella on Minorca was seized and thousands of its inhabitants were taken away as slaves.

The sudden appearance of the main Ottoman fleet within sailing distance of the coast of mainland Spain led to panic along that shore. It was particularly pronounced in Valencia, where it was feared there might be a revolt among the Morisco population to aid Turkish invaders. Fortunately for the Spanish, the French recalled the Ottoman fleet and offered to join it for operations against Corsica. Piyale Pasha refused and sailed for home. Disease had broken out among his slave rowers, killing many and leading to some galleys being towed by others, which was one reason to withdraw, but there were also rumours that the Genoese had bribed Piyale Pasha not to attack their island of Corsica.[31]

The Algerine conquest of Bougie in 1555 had alarmed not just the Spanish but also the Moroccans, who had beaten off an Algerine invasion in 1553–4. Both parties wished to see the power of Algiers reduced. The Spanish governor of Oran, the count of Alcaudete, negotiated with the Moroccan ruler for a joint attack on Algerine territory and by 1557 preparations were underway. In early 1558 the ruler of Algiers, Hassan Pasha, the son of Barbarossa, staged a pre-emptive attack on the Moroccans but was defeated. Hearing that Alcaudete was assembling a Spanish army at Oran, Hassan retreated to his own territory and prepared to meet it. As a first step, Alcaudete sought to capture the port of Mostaganem, east of Oran, but soon Hassan was closing in on his army with Algerine forces and mountain tribesmen. An attempt to retreat from Mostaganem to Oran soon degenerated into confusion. The Spanish army of 12,000 men was surrounded and destroyed. Half the men, including Alcaudete, were killed, and the rest, including his son, were taken prisoner. Oran was open for the taking, but Hassan chose to return to Algiers to enjoy his triumph. His large number of prisoners proved troublesome. Not only did they drive down prices in the slave market, but Alcaudete's son tried to organize a slave revolt. He was thwarted and later freed in return for a large ransom. In the following year, Hassan offered captured Spanish soldiers their freedom if they would convert to Islam and join his army to suppress a revolt by mountain tribes. Hundreds accepted his offer. After the disaster at Mostaganem, the Spanish did not again conduct major military operations within North Africa until the mid-nineteenth century.[32]

The new king of Spain, Philip II, was still in the Netherlands in early 1559 when he received a request to approve an expedition to recapture Tripoli from Turgut Reis. The request came from the Spanish viceroy in Sicily, the duke of Medinaceli and Jean Parisot de la Valette, who had become grand master of the Knights of Malta in 1557. Philip no doubt saw this as a chance to take revenge on the Barbary states for the defeat at Mostaganem the previous year, and he gave his approval. By late summer the Knights of Malta were ready to go on campaign, but the Spanish and their Italian allies moved more slowly.

In the past such an expedition would have been led by Andrea Doria of Genoa, but having reached the age of 93 he had finally decided to retire, dying in 1560. His successor was his great nephew Gian Andrea Doria, who was only twenty years old and without command experience. The Spanish raised no objection to this change in leadership, but it was to have a major impact on the coming campaign, when not only would the younger Doria's competence be called into question, but also his courage. There seems to have been some hope of seizing Tripoli late in 1559 so that the Ottomans could not counterattack until the following year, but delays meant that the last Christian ships did not assemble at Malta until January 1560.

The expedition consisted of 55 galleys, including vessels from Spain, Sicily, Genoa, the papal states and Malta; 65 sailing ships, mostly transports; and 5,000 Spanish, Italian and German soldiers. Medinaceli was to command the troops and Gian Andrea Doria the fleet, but who had the overall command was unclear. After calling at the island of Djerba to collect fresh water, despite attacks by the local Muslims, the Christian force went on to land on the North African coast some distance to the west of Tripoli. After several weeks of indecision, the Christian commanders decided to capture Djerba rather than assault Tripoli.[33]

They returned to the island in early March, quickly overran it, and began to build a fort on the north coast to hold a permanent Spanish garrison. Unfortunately news that the expedition had set out from Malta had reached Istanbul and Piyale Pasha had been ordered to take the Ottoman fleet to sea to oppose it. At short notice he could only assemble 86 galleys, but it was felt this might be sufficient if Piyale could find out quickly where the Christians had gone. When the Ottoman fleet reached the central Mediterranean, Piyale was fortunate to meet the corsair Uluj Ali who told him that the Christian force was at Djerba. The pasha immediately led his galleys towards the island.

By the start of May the fort on Djerba had been completed, but the main Christian forces were slow to leave the island. On the evening of

10 May a vessel arrived to warn the Christian commanders that the Ottoman fleet was approaching. After desperate discussions during the night, it was decided that all the Christian troops should be re-embarked and the island abandoned. This operation was underway on the morning of 11 May when Piyale's Ottoman galleys appeared and swept down on the disordered Christian shipping. In the ensuing battle 30 Christian galleys were captured or sunk, and a similar number of sailing ships suffered the same fate. Amid the chaos, Doria and Medinaceli fled in a couple of fast vessels. The remaining soldiers took refuge in the fort under the command of the Spanish colonel Álvaro de Sande.

Piyale Pasha landed troops to begin a siege of the fort, and several days later Turgut Reis arrived from Tripoli with sixteen galleys and siege artillery. The soldiers in the fort put up a prolonged resistance, but finally, due to lack of water, they had to surrender in late July. The siege and the earlier sea battle may have killed at least 9,000 Christians, and some 5,000, including de Sande, became prisoners. Piyale took most of the captives back to Istanbul, where they were triumphantly paraded through the streets. Unlike most of his companions, Álvaro de Sande was ransomed quickly and fought the Turks again at the siege of Malta in 1565.

The disaster at Djerba in 1560, following so quickly after the defeat at Mostaganem in 1558, marked a new low for Spanish fortunes in the Mediterranean struggle between Christians and Muslims. The Ottomans now seemed to dominate that sea from end to end and every Christian attempt to oppose them seemed doomed to failure. Further blows were to come, but this darkest hour in fact marked the turning point in both Spanish and Christian fortunes.

When Charles v passed the post of Holy Roman Emperor to his brother Ferdinand, this divided the Habsburg inheritance in Europe. Germany and the struggle against the Turks in Hungary now became the exclusive concerns of Ferdinand. Charles v passed his other possessions, chiefly Spain, his Italian lands and his empire outside Europe, to his son Philip, along with the Netherlands. Philip II took up residence in Spain and could now concentrate his efforts on Spanish concerns. Charles v had often been distracted by events all over his vast empire, especially in Germany. Even before the disasters at Mostaganem and Djerba, the war against the Turks in the Mediterranean was always going to dominate Philip's policies in a way it had never dominated those of his father Charles.

In addition, although it would not be confirmed for some years, the position of France in international affairs would weaken dramatically after the Franco–Spanish peace treaty of 1559. This was not just another pause in the wars between the two powers that had been going on since the 1490s, chiefly in Italy. Religious civil wars would soon tear France apart and render it powerless in international affairs until the end of the century. Spain thus lost its main Christian enemy and its dominance in Italy was confirmed. The Ottoman sultan lost his only Christian ally and no longer could his fleets find refuge in French ports.

In terms of the Mediterranean naval balance, the collapse of French power was even more dramatic. The French galley fleet in the Mediterranean was stood down after the 1559 peace. France would not possess another significant naval force in that sea until the 1620s. Philip II could direct all his naval resources against the Barbary corsairs and their Ottoman masters. Philip's fleets would also be more Spanish in content. The death of Andrea Doria and the poor performance of his great nephew at Djerba made the Spanish more reluctant to depend on Genoese naval expertise and hired galleys. Great efforts were made to expand the production of galleys at Barcelona in Catalonia and at the principal ports of Spain's Italian possessions, Palermo in Sicily and Naples on the mainland. However, the tide of misfortune for the Spanish had still not peaked.

The Spanish-ruled kingdom of Sicily had lost its entire force of eight galleys in the Djerba disaster in 1560, but it quickly rebuilt the fleet, with seven galleys ready to put to sea in the following year. However, experienced sailors and rowers could not be replaced so easily. In July 1561 the Sicilian galleys, commanded by a Catalan Knight of Malta, Guimeran, were ambushed by a superior corsair fleet led by Turgut Reis near the Lipari Islands. The Christian force was overwhelmed, all the galleys taken, and Turgut went on to raid extensively around Naples. Despite these losses more galleys were produced in Sicily, and in September 1562 Juan de Mendoza could collect 28 galleys of Spain and Sicily to escort a supply convoy to Oran on the North African coast. Returning to Malaga in Spain, Mendoza's force was struck by a sudden storm and 25 of the galleys, along with several thousand men, were lost in Herradura Bay. It seemed that no sooner did the Spanish add new galleys to their fleet than they were lost to the corsairs or bad weather.[34]

Nevertheless between 1561 and 1564 the Spanish were given a valuable breathing space in which to build up their naval forces because the Ottomans did not send fleets into the central or western Mediterranean in these years. In this period it was the Barbary corsairs who carried on the fight against the Christians, confirming their reputation as the vanguard of the sultan.

Encouraged by the Spanish losses at Herradura Bay, Hassan Pasha, the victor of Mostaganem, decided he could muster sufficient forces to capture Oran without assistance from the Ottoman sultan. The attack was launched in April 1563, and the attackers decided to concentrate on capturing the port of Mers el Kebir, taking the view that if it fell the defence of Oran could not continue. Oran was held by Alonso de Córdoba, Count of Alcaudete since his father's death in battle in 1558, and Mers el Kebir by his brother Martín, who had been briefly a captive in Algiers after the 1558 battle. Hassan's forces captured several outlying forts in fierce struggles which cost him many men. Then there were repeated attacks on the walls of the town itself. It seemed Mers el Kebir might be about to fall when a relief fleet, under Francisco de Mendoza, arrived from Spain with 34 galleys and 4,000 troops. Hassan ordered his army to retreat, while several of his ships cruising offshore were taken by the Spanish warships.[35]

Relieving Mers el Kebir and Oran was an encouraging success for the Spanish, and the following year was to bring further achievements. So many new galleys were now being produced that early in 1564 Sancho de Leyva, commander of the galleys of Naples, was given permission to take a naval squadron along the Barbary coast to capture sufficient Muslim male slaves to provide rowing crews for the new vessels. Spain's newly appointed Captain General of the Sea, García de Toledo, then began to prepare an expedition aimed at capturing one of the corsair bases on the North African coast.

By the end of August 1564 Toledo had collected a large force on the south coast of Spain: almost 100 galleys, including the galleys of Spain under Álvaro de Bazán and Genoese galleys under Gian Andrea Doria; a similar number of sailing ships, mostly transports; and 15,000 Spanish, Italian and German soldiers. For such a formidable force, assembled with great publicity, the target was to be rather puny: the fortress of Vélez de la Gomera off the coast of Morocco. Once held by the Spanish, then retaken by the Muslims, it was one of the smaller bases for the Barbary corsairs. Most of its inhabitants and the corsairs simply fled at the approach of such a mighty Christian force. Spain took possession of this offshore rock in September 1564 and still holds it almost 450 years later. The capture of Vélez de la Gomera was a small but encouraging success for the Spanish, and the fact that they could assemble such a large fleet to carry out the operation showed that Spanish naval expansion since 1560 had achieved considerable success.[36]

Another event of 1564 was less publicized but was to have greater consequences. One of the most successful Knights of Malta raiding Ottoman Turkish coasts, islands, and shipping in the eastern Mediterranean was Mathurin Romegas. In the summer of 1564 he made a series of successful captures of large Ottoman merchant ships off Greece. Among the captives he secured were important Ottoman officials and members of the sultan's court. For years people like Turgut Reis had been begging Suleiman to put an end to the ravages of the Knights of Malta once and for all. Now he decided to take action, to redress the folly of his youth when he had allowed the knights to leave Rhodes on such easy terms. During the winter of 1564–5 a large Ottoman fleet was collected at Istanbul and an army assembled for it to carry westwards.[37]

Philip II was well aware of the Ottoman preparations and his initial thoughts were that they presaged an Ottoman strike in revenge for his capture of Vélez in 1564. In the battle of bases, the loss of one Muslim base could only be made good by the Ottomans taking a Spanish-held port. The most likely target was La Goletta, the most easterly and vulnerable of Spain's outposts along the North African coast, and a garrison whose loss would almost certainly bring Tunis under Ottoman control. While they waited to see where Suleiman would send his fleet and army, the Spanish continued operations against the Barbary corsairs. The Moroccan port of Tetouan had long been an important base for corsairs and it was very close to the Spanish coast. In March 1565 a naval squadron under Álvaro de Bazán succeeded in blocking the river leading to Tetouan by sinking several old ships to block its mouth. Yet while this operation was going on, other corsairs were capturing Spanish ships off Malaga, not very far away. However, the minor war of the corsairs was soon to be overshadowed by the return of a major Ottoman fleet and army to the central Mediterranean after an absence of nearly five years.[38]

Piyale Pasha commanded a fleet of around 150 vessels, mostly galleys and galliots. They carried some 30,000 soldiers, under the orders of Mustafa Pasha. The overall commander was unclear. Piyale claimed he was the equal of Mustafa, but the latter said he was superior, at least with regard to land operations. To add to the confusion, the sultan had told both Piyale and Mustafa to consult Turgut Reis before reaching decisions. The Ottoman forces came ashore on the south coast of Malta on 18 May 1565 and Jean Parisot de la Valette ordered his forces to retire within their fortifications, chiefly those at Senglea and Birgu on the south side of the Grand Harbour and Fort St Elmo on the north side. The defending Christian forces numbered only around 8,000 men, including 500 Knights of Malta and around 600 Spanish and Italian soldiers. The rest were mostly Maltese militia.[39]

As the Ottoman forces began to set up their siege lines around the Grand Harbour, other Muslim forces came to join them. On 27 May Uluj Ali, now governor of Alexandria in Egypt, arrived with four galleys and 600 men; Turgut Reis arrived from Tripoli on 2 June with fifteen galleys and galliots, carrying 2,500 men; and another contingent of Barbary corsairs, 2,500 men in 27 galleys and galliots from Algiers, arrived on 12 July. Thus the Ottoman land forces rose to about 36,000 men, and they had brought a substantial number of heavy siege guns with them. Despite being told to consult Turgut, Piyale and Mustafa had begun an attack on the isolated Fort St Elmo even before the aged corsair reached the island. By taking the fort, they would allow the Ottoman fleet to move up to the Grand Harbour from its present anchorage in a bay on the south coast of Malta. This would permit the fleet to give more direct support to the army.

Whatever Turgut's views about the wisdom of attacking Fort St Elmo first, he took an active part in emplacing the siege guns and directing the fire which, it was hoped, would swiftly force the small fort to surrender. Unfortunately the garrison of St Elmo offered a fierce and prolonged resistance. Ottoman attempts to storm the fort were repulsed and Ottoman casualties rose rapidly. On 17 June Turgut Reis became one of them. A cannon ball struck the ground near him and peppered his body with sharp chips of rock. Some said the ball had been fired from the Christian Fort St Angelo on the far side of the Grand Harbour; others believed it was a Turkish cannon ball which had fallen short, an early example of a 'friendly fire' casualty. One account says that Turgut died soon after he was hit; another account claims that he lingered for days and died on 23 June, the day Fort St Elmo finally fell to the Ottoman besiegers.

After the fall of St Elmo, the Ottomans launched fierce attacks on the positions the Knights of Malta held in Senglea and Birgu, but all their assaults failed with heavy casualties. As the battle in Malta raged on during the summer of 1565, a Christian relief force was slowly being collected in Sicily. As a reward for his conquest of Vélez in 1564, García de Toledo had been made viceroy of Sicily and he had the task of gathering the force. It finally headed for Malta in September. At the same time Piyale and Mustafa despaired of ever taking Malta and began to re-embark their forces in the Ottoman fleet. Thus as the first of the 11,000 troops of the relief force landed on Malta, with Álvaro de Sande, defender of the Djerba fort in 1560, among their commanders, the Ottomans were already in the process of leaving the island. An Ottoman covering force tried to hold off the new arrivals, but it was beaten back. Nevertheless the Ottomans made their escape without suffering much inconvenience from García de Toledo's relief force.

Christians throughout Europe saw the successful defence of Malta against the Ottoman Turks as a great victory, but such a defensive achievement could not seriously undermine the power of the Ottoman sultan. Even as they cleared the ruins around the Grand Harbour, the Knights of Malta were fearful of a new Ottoman attack in 1566. Turgut Reis, however, would never campaign against his old enemies on Malta again. The corsair Uluj Ali took the old man's body back to Tripoli and it was buried in the mosque which Turgut had built in that city. Barbarossa and Turgut Reis were gone, but now Uluj Ali would take their place as the leader of the Barbary corsairs.

ULUJ ALI

Desperate to find some explanation for the sudden resurgence of Muslim sea power in the Mediterranean after centuries of Christian dominance, Christian commentators in the sixteenth century (and later) pointed to the supposed Christian roots of the greatest Barbary corsair commanders. It was a strange kind of comfort. The Barbarossas certainly had a Greek Christian mother, but it now seems certain their father was a Muslim Turk. Attempts were made to give Greek Christian parents to Turgut Reis, but all the indications are that he came from a Muslim Turkish peasant family.

Even if one was to concede Christian parentage to the Barbarossas and Turgut Reis, it would hardly matter. All these corsairs were brought up as Muslims and subjects of the Ottoman sultan. Repeated Christian attempts to bribe them into changing sides (whether as independent Muslim rulers or 'returning' to Christianity) all failed. Their prowess in naval warfare was not due to any traits derived from a Christian heritage. If Christian origins were so important, why did the sailors of Christendom perform so badly in their maritime war with the Muslim corsairs?

Christian apologists were on stronger ground with the origins of the last great Barbary corsair leader of the sixteenth century, Uluj Ali (usually known to the Christians as Ochiali). Born Giovanni Dionigi Galeni in the village of Le Castella in Calabria, Italy, around 1520, his father was a fisherman, but both his parents hoped their son might find a career in the lower ranks of the Catholic church. However, in 1536 young Giovanni was captured by one of Barbarossa's corsair captains. For a number of years he served as a galley slave, but then he converted to Islam and was given the name Uluj Ali ('convert' Ali). Despite his impeccably Christian origins, Uluj Ali never wavered in his new loyalties, despite later Christian attempts to suborn him. The Spanish tried to bribe him not to support the Morisco rising of 1568–70, and after he took Tunis they offered to recognize him as king of Tunis if only he would become a vassal of Philip II. Uluj Ali ignored both offers.[40]

Uluj Ali was a Christian renegade, just one of hundreds of thousands of Christian men and women who, willingly or unwillingly, between 1500 and the start of the nineteenth century converted to Islam and found new lives as Muslims. One estimate says that around 300,000 Christians became renegades between 1550 and 1700.[41] Although most had originally been captured by Muslim raiders on land or sea, some of the Christians had chosen freely to pass over into the Islamic world. It was largely a one-way traffic. Relatively few Muslims taken captive by the Christians ever converted to Christianity, and Muslims who willingly went over to the Christian side were almost unknown. Some Christian renegades later reverted to their original loyalty, but most never returned to Christendom. The huge numbers of Christians who became Muslims was a considerable embarrassment to Christian commentators, especially the religious ones. They could only allege that most renegades were either forced to convert by brutal Muslim ill treatment or, if the Christians converted willingly, that the converts did so from the very worst motives, often to sample the supposed sexual freedoms (for men) in the Islamic world. Naturally all Christian renegades were said to come to a bad end, despite the well-known cases of men like Uluj Ali who came to hold important positions in the Ottoman government or armed forces.

In a reworking of the Christian origins explanation for the new Muslim prowess in naval warfare, Christian commentators (and some later historians) pointed out that because so many Barbary corsair captains were Christian renegades, they must have brought their superior maritime skills over from the Christian side. This seems unlikely since most of these renegades originally fell into Muslim hands when they were children or teenagers (like Uluj Ali). The training they received in maritime war was all undertaken after they became Muslims.

The fact was that in the sixteenth century the Barbary corsairs offered an especially attractive route for advancement for even the most humble men, whether Muslim-born or Christian converts. In the rigid hierarchical societies of Christian Europe the chance of a fisherman's son rising to become commander of an empire's navy (as Uluj Ali did) was nil. The Christian naval commanders who confronted the corsairs were all aristocrats or princes. In the Ottoman empire there was no hereditary aristocracy and all the population were in theory the slaves of the sultan. Christians denounced this as oriental despotism, but it also meant that the sultan could choose the best men for his government, army and fleet without concern for racial or class origins. Able young men, often Christian converts, could be raised from humble backgrounds to the highest offices of state as long as they remained loyal servants of both Islam and the Ottoman sultan.

Such aspirants were trained in the imperial schools at Istanbul. The Barbary corsairs were not formally part of this system, hence the occasional clashes between their experienced sailors and Ottoman officials when the corsairs were given command positions in the main Ottoman fleet. Nevertheless the Barbary corsairs, operating in the freer world of the Ottoman–Christian naval frontier, were always ready to reward and promote young sailors who showed skill and daring in their maritime pursuits. Once such men had made a name for themselves, the Ottoman sultan might well choose them as commanders in his main fleet.

After the death of Barbarossa in 1546 Uluj Ali served under Turgut Reis, but soon won a reputation as a successful corsair in his own right. In 1560 he passed on vital intelligence to Piyale Pasha which led to the

Ottoman victory at Djerba. In 1565 the sultan made him governor of Alexandria, and Uluj Ali brought his forces to the siege of Malta later in the year. After Turgut Reis was killed during the siege, Uluj Ali took the body of his old mentor back to Tripoli for burial. Piyale Pasha then made Uluj Ali the new ruler of Tripoli. Early in 1568 the post of ruler of Algiers fell vacant and Piyale Pasha recommended that the sultan, Selim II, should give the position to Uluj Ali. This was done and Uluj Ali became effective leader of all the Ottoman Barbary corsairs.

Despite the boost their successful defence of Malta in 1565 had given to Christian morale, the growing Spanish navy took little action to follow up the success. Similarly the Ottomans did not mount the expected new attack on Malta in 1566, nor did they launch new naval offensives in the Mediterranean in the following years. Suleiman the Magnificent died in 1566 and his successor, Selim II, had other concerns as he sought to establish his position. From 1566 onwards Spain began to be distracted by the revolt in its possessions in the Netherlands, but an even more dangerous threat was to be posed suddenly by the enemies within Spain itself, the Moriscos.

Although all the remaining Muslims in Spain had been ordered to leave or become Christians in the first half of the sixteenth century, those who had nominally converted – the Moriscos – were not trusted by the native Christian inhabitants. Most of the Moriscos continued Islamic practices in secret and they retained close links with the Muslims of North Africa. Barbarossa had encouraged many Moriscos to come over to Algiers to live in his new state, while those who remained in Spain were happy to assist Barbary corsairs in their raids on the Spanish coast. For example, when corsairs attacked the Andalusian coastal town of Tabernas in 1566, local Moriscos joined them in sacking the town and then went with the corsairs to North Africa.

In early 1567 Philip II decreed that all remaining Islamic practices among the Moriscos were to be suppressed and the edict came into force a year later. In 1568 Moriscos began to plot a revolt against their Christian rulers and they sent letters to Uluj Ali in Algiers and Sultan Selim II in Istanbul asking for their support. The revolt was to begin in what had formerly been the kingdom of Granada, with Christmas Eve 1568 chosen as the starting date. An attempt to seize the city of Granada failed, but the Moriscos had more success in the nearby Alpujarras mountains, killing Christians and destroying churches.[42]

By the spring of 1569 the Moriscos held much of rural Andalusia, but few of its towns. The rebels had hoped their actions would spark Morisco risings in other areas, above all in the kingdom of Valencia where there was a large Morisco population, but there was little reaction. The initial Spanish military response to the Morisco rising was weak and confused. All their best troops were in Italy or the Netherlands, and it took time to assemble counter-insurgent forces in Andalusia. As a royal mark of the importance of the struggle, Philip made his half-brother, Don Juan of Austria, the bastard son of Emperor Charles v, commander of the army in Andalusia. The young man had already served in the Spanish galleys chasing Barbary corsairs, and he now had a new chance to further his military career.

Despite Spanish efforts to maintain a naval blockade along the coast of Andalusia, the Barbary corsairs sent men, arms and supplies from North Africa to support the Morisco rebels. The Moriscos had no money to pay for supplies, but their Christian captives were a useful substitute currency. It was said that one Christian captive would be exchanged for one musket. Turkish soldiers and Berber volunteers were among those anxious to cross over and join the holy war in Spain, but after initial enthusiasm Uluj Ali began to take a more realistic view of the Morisco revolt. It was a serious blow to the Spanish, but it seemed unlikely to succeed in the long term. Uluj Ali felt his best troops would be more useful elsewhere. By autumn 1569 he was only willing to let Muslim volunteers from less respectable sources go over to aid the Moriscos. Muslims in prison or wanted by the law were promised forgiveness if they went to fight in Spain. Several hundred did so. Of the estimated 25–40,000 Muslims who took part in the Morisco revolt, probably 4,000 had come over from North Africa to join the rebel side.

Uluj Ali saw that the Spanish were distracted both by the Morisco revolt at home and the revolt of the Netherlands in northern Europe. It seemed a good time for him to exploit Spain's difficulties. In October 1569 Uluj Ali led an army of around 5,000 troops east from Algiers and invaded Tunisia. The pro-Spanish ruler of Tunis, Moulay Hamida, sent forces to oppose the invaders, but they were scattered in an encounter at Beja. In January 1570 Uluj Ali took possession of Tunis and other ports in northern Tunisia. Moulay Hamida fled for safety to the Spanish fortress of La Goletta. Uluj Ali was reluctant to attack La Goletta, but continued Spanish possession of it meant that he could not use the port of Tunis. Instead he used Bizerta as a base from which to launch new corsair attacks on Spanish-held Sicily, Sardinia and Naples. When Barbarossa had seized Tunis in 1534, Charles v had launched a massive crusade to retake it in the following year. How would his son Philip react to this second Barbary corsair capture of Tunis?[43]

As Uluj Ali had calculated, the Spanish were slow to react to the new Ottoman success. Gian Andrea Doria assembled a force of galleys at Sicily, but then refused to attack Uluj Ali's ships in the harbour of Bizerta because he said the port was too strongly defended. The reality of the threat from Uluj Ali's new base in Tunisia was shown in mid-July 1570. Four galleys of the Knights of Malta, which represented most of their fleet, had gone to Sicily to join Doria's squadron. However, their commander, the French knight François de St Clément, then decided to return to Malta, despite warnings that Uluj Ali's force of twenty galliots was in the neighbourhood. The feared encounter duly occurred, and the Maltese galleys fled back towards the Sicilian coast. With the chance of freedom so near, it was said that the Muslim galley slaves rowed as slowly as they dared. The corsair galliots took two galleys, a third escaped, and St Clément ran his flagship ashore on the Sicilian coast. Its Muslim galley slaves rose in revolt and the corsairs swarmed ashore to help them. The Christian survivors fled to the safety of a coastal watchtower from where they could observe the corsairs towing away the Maltese flagship. In this disaster 60 knights and hundreds of Maltese soldiers and sailors were said to have been killed or captured, but St Clément escaped. Faced with a possible revolt by the enraged inhabitants of Malta, the grand master of the knights was forced to put his defeated commander on trial. St Clément was found guilty of misconduct and executed. With three out of four galleys lost, the knights faced a difficult situation. Philip II stepped in to help them. Three newly built Spanish galleys were sent to Malta, but the knights still had problems in manning the replacement vessels.[44]

One reason Gian Andrea Doria failed to take urgent action after Uluj Ali's success at Tunis was that during the winter of 1569–70 the Ottoman sultan was known to be assembling a large fleet and army at Istanbul. Its destination was initially unknown and there were Spanish fears that the force would be sent against La Goletta, aiming to complete Uluj Ali's work by capturing the Spanish-held fortress. Doria hoped he might be able to intercept the Ottoman force before it reached Tunisia. Then news arrived in late July 1570 that the great Ottoman armada had instead attacked the Venetian-controlled island of Cyprus in the eastern Mediterranean. By early September its capital, Nicosia, and most of the island had fallen to the Turks, and only the port of Famagusta (now Gazi-magusa) still held out. Under pressure from the pope, Pius v, Philip II reluctantly agreed to send Gian Andrea Doria and his fleet to assist papal and Venetian naval forces in trying to break the Turkish blockade and take relief supplies to Famagusta. The combined relief attempt was a failure, but the Venetians alone did get some supplies through to the beleaguered port later in the winter of 1570–71.[45]

If the struggle over Cyprus was a new problem, at least the Spanish had largely suppressed the Morisco revolt by the autumn of 1570. Most resistance had been crushed and the remaining Andalusian Moriscos were scattered in small groups in other parts of Spain, except for those who had escaped to Muslim North Africa. With the revolt over, the Spanish now had additional ships and troops to deploy. The pope wanted them sent to the eastern Mediterranean to fight the Ottomans, but Philip II hoped to use them in North Africa, particularly aiming at the recapture of Tunis. Eventually the Spanish king succumbed to papal pressure, and in May 1571 he agreed to join a holy league against the Ottoman Turks with the papacy and Venice. Nevertheless Philip still had an article included in their agreement which would permit attacks on the Barbary corsairs in North Africa. The combined fleet of the holy league was at Philip's insistence to be commanded by his half-brother Don Juan of Austria, fresh from his successes against the Moriscos in Spain.[46]

The Christian intention was to go to the relief of Gazimagusa but, leaving a small naval blockading force at Cyprus, the main Ottoman fleet, under Muezzinzade Ali Pasha, came westward even before the siege had been concluded. Soon after leaving Cyprus, the fleet was joined by a force of Barbary corsair ships under Uluj Ali. The next Ottoman target was the Venetian-held island of Crete, but their attacks on the island in June never went much beyond raiding. Next month the Ottoman fleet moved on to the Adriatic Sea. Attacks were made on Christian targets along its shores, with Uluj Ali and another corsair, Kara Hodja, even raiding as far north as the waters close to Venice. In August the Ottomans concentrated their attack on the Venetian possession of Corfu, but although they ravaged much of the island, the main fortress held out.

Meanwhile a large Christian fleet had been assembling at Messina in Sicily. There were just over 200 galleys, including vessels from Spain,

Sicily, Naples and Genoa, but with the largest contingent, 106 galleys, coming from Venice. The dozen galleys contributed by the pope had in fact been hired from the Grand Duke of Tuscany. They included several galleys of the new Knights of St Stephen, a military religious order which the grand duke had set up in 1562 to imitate the Knights of Malta and fight against the infidel.[47] The Knights of Malta, still recovering from Uluj Ali's victory over their fleet in 1570, could only contribute three galleys to the great Christian fleet. There were 13,000 sailors and 43,000 rowers manning the fleet. Not all the rowers were captives (either Muslim slaves or Christian convicts), since at this time the Venetians still largely used free rowers who could fight as soldiers once the galleys were locked together with those of the enemy. The fleet carried 28,000 soldiers (9,000 Spanish, 5,000 German and the rest Italian). Taken together, it was one of the largest Christian military forces ever assembled to fight the Muslims.

With the Ottomans ravaging the shores of the Adriatic, the Christian fleet gave up any hopes of sailing to Cyprus to relieve Gazimagusa (Famagusta). In September 1571 Don Juan moved his fleet towards Corfu and the Ottomans pulled back to the gulf of Patras in Greece. The season was getting late and the opposing fleets might normally have been expected to withdraw to refit over the winter. However, both commanders were, unusually, under pressure to seek battle with the enemy. Such pressure increased on the Christian side when news of the fall of Famagusta reached them. After surrendering on the promise of mercy, the Christian garrison had been massacred, with its commander flayed alive. Intent on revenge, Don Juan led his fleet southwards and, as he entered the gulf of Patras on the morning of 7 October, Ali Pasha brought out his fleet of over 250 galleys and galliots (including 43 vessels from the Barbary corsair bases of Algiers and Tripoli), carrying 25,000 troops, to meet him near the port of Lepanto (now Nafpaktos).[48]

Both fleets were drawn up in similar formations, with ships in line abreast. The Christian left, under the Venetian Agostino Barbarigo, faced the Ottoman right, under Mehmet Scirocco, governor of Alexandria, near the Greek coast. Don Juan's centre, with Álvaro de Bazán's reserve behind it, faced the Ottoman centre under Ali Pasha, which also had a small reserve division behind it. Uluj Ali commanded the Ottoman left division, facing the Christian right under Gian Andrea Doria. Each Christian division had two Venetian galleasses (large oar-driven ships carrying more guns than an ordinary galley) in front of it. The Ottoman aim was to break the Christian line and then use their superiority in number of vessels to overwhelm isolated Christian ships. The Christian ships carried more guns than those of the Ottomans and they intended to preserve their disciplined formation while destroying the enemy ships with firepower. The galleasses would begin this process, damaging and disordering the Ottomans before the two battle lines even met. In an attempt to avoid one Christian contingent failing to support another (especially due to the hatred between Venice and Genoa), Don Juan had arranged that a variety of vessels should be put in each Christian division, although this did not stop the Christian left being largely Venetian.

Uluj Ali's division included most of the Barbary corsair ships from Algiers and Tripoli. It also had Muslim corsair ships from Valona (now Vlore) on the coast of Albania, a port sometimes used by Barbary corsairs as a forward base when they ventured into the Adriatic. Nevertheless the division also included galleys from Istanbul, Anatolia and Greece. Uluj Ali's opponent Gian Andrea Doria had an even more mixed force. In addition to his own Genoese galleys, Doria had papal, Neapolitan and Spanish galleys, as well as the three galleys of the Knights of Malta and a dozen Venetian galleys whose commanders had little faith in Doria's abilities. Some historians believe Doria brought his division into battle in some disorder and that his two Venetian galleasses were left behind and did not take up their agreed position in front of his line. Other historians believe this view is incorrect and that Doria brought his division into battle in the same ordered formation as the two other Christian divisions. This latter view seems preferable as it makes for a clearer understanding of the subsequent battle between Doria and Uluj Ali.[49]

As with the other Ottoman divisions, fire from the Venetian galleasses disrupted and damaged Uluj Ali's ships before they could reach the Christian line. Unlike the other Ottoman divisions, Uluj Ali had the sea room to move his ships away from the guns of the two galleasses. As the Ottoman ships veered off southwards, Doria thought Uluj Ali was trying to get around his flank. To prevent this, Doria began to move his ships southwards as well, leading to some disorder in his formation. As Doria drew away from the Christian centre, some of the Venetian ships in his division refused to follow, possibly believing Doria was trying to avoid battle, and this led to further confusion on the Christian side. Seeing a gap opening up between Doria and the Christian centre, Uluj

Ali promptly led his ships into it. His forces quickly overwhelmed half a dozen Christian ships which had become separated from the rest of Doria's division. One of these was the flagship of the Knights of Malta, which had most of its Christian crew killed and the great banner of the knights captured.

Uluj Ali now threatened the right flank of Don Juan's centre division, and if he had done this earlier there might have been serious consequences for the Christian side. However, in the centre, as in the clash of divisions along the Greek coast, the Christian side had already defeated their Muslim opponents. Galleys from Don Juan's centre and Bazán's reserve could move to oppose Uluj Ali, while Doria brought his ships round to attack Uluj Ali's rear. Seeing the battle was lost, Uluj Ali now sought to escape and got away with at least 30 Muslim ships, the only large Muslim force to escape from the disaster of the battle of Lepanto. He was forced to leave or destroy the Christian ships he had taken, but Uluj Ali made sure to take away the captured banner of the Knights of Malta.

Lepanto was the last and greatest battle between galley fleets. The Christian victors lost twelve galleys and 10,000 men. The defeated Ottoman Turks had just over 200 galleys sunk or captured, losing 30,000 men, including their fleet commander. Some 12,000 Christian galley slaves were freed from the Ottoman ships. For much of the sixteenth century there had seemed a real danger that the Muslims would become dominant at sea throughout the Mediterranean, a situation that had not existed for centuries. Now it seemed that Christian sea power had reasserted its superiority. Lepanto had shown that the Ottomans were not invincible at sea. Yet it was too late in the year for the Christians to exploit their great victory. Only if the Ottomans failed to restore their fleet by the next campaigning season would the battle of Lepanto have any long-term significance.

Collecting other Ottoman ships that had been absent from the battle, Uluj Ali arrived in Istanbul with around 60 ships in November 1571. Normally an Ottoman commander who had been involved in such a severe defeat would have been executed as a punishment. However, Selim II wanted to play down the magnitude of the blow. Since Uluj Ali had brought back the banner of the Knights of Malta as a trophy, it was decided to treat him as a hero rather than a failure. He was renamed Kilic Ali ('sword' Ali, his usual name in Turkish writings) to mark his heroic conduct in the battle and was made kapudan pasha, commander-in-chief of the Ottoman navy.[50]

Over the winter of 1571–2 Uluj Ali rebuilt the Ottoman fleet, receiving assistance in his task from the grand vizier, Mehmet Sokullu, who had once been kapudan pasha himself. Dozens of galleys were built and efforts were made to learn some of the lessons taught by the defeat at Lepanto. More guns were put on the galleys, the troops aboard them were to have more firearms and fewer bows, and an attempt was made to build Ottoman versions of the galleass, but without great success. Much has been made of the loss of experienced sailors by the Ottomans in their great defeat and it is certainly true that manning the new fleet was not without its problems. Nevertheless the Barbary corsairs were always regarded as the best sailors in the Ottoman fleet and their contingent had survived the battle with relatively few losses. They provided an experienced core around which the new fleet could be assembled. Although the cost of building this new fleet was heavy, possibly as much as a quarter of the empire's annual revenues, Uluj Ali would have a formidable force of over 200 galleys to lead out against the Christians in the campaigning season of 1572.[51]

Early in 1572 the Christian side decided to exploit their victory at Lepanto by carrying out a campaign against the Turks in the Levant during the coming campaigning season. However, Spanish agreement to this plan was only reluctant. Their preferred option was attacking the Barbary corsair bases in North Africa. After the death of Pope Pius v in May, Philip ii tried to get out of his commitment to operations in the eastern Mediterranean. The naval force that Don Juan had collected at Sicily was held back. The excuse was a fear that France might enter the war on the side of the Ottomans, but a more likely reason was the hope of launching an attack on Algiers or Tunis. The new pope, Gregory xiii, was as keen to strike the Turks in the east as his predecessor, so Philip eventually had to agree to send Don Juan to support the papal and Venetian galleys already cruising off Greece. They had put to sea because Uluj Ali had led the revived Ottoman fleet of over 200 galleys into Greek waters. The united Christian fleet tried to bring Uluj Ali to battle, but he retreated to the port of Modon, which the Christians blockaded. A stalemate resulted, and at the start of October the Christian fleet had to withdraw.[52]

After this failure to follow up the Lepanto victory, the Venetians tired of the war and longed to regain their lucrative Levant trade. They made peace with the Ottoman sultan in March 1573, giving up their claim to Cyprus and paying a heavy indemnity in return for a restoration of their trading rights. The pope was furious at this betrayal, but Philip II was glad his forces could now be concentrated against North Africa. The main Ottoman fleet, under Piyale Pasha and Uluj Ali, did not come into the central Mediterranean until late July and cruised without apparently having any clear objective. Don Juan had once again assembled Spanish forces in Sicily. If the Ottomans withdrew without making any major assault, he had decided to attack Tunis. By the end of September it was clear the Ottoman naval forces were heading back to Istanbul. On 7 October, the anniversary of Lepanto, Don Juan departed for Tunis. He had a fleet of 107 galleys, many sailing ships, and a force of more than 20,000 Spanish, Italian and German troops. The next day Don Juan reached Spanish-held La Goletta and began to land his soldiers. Faced with such a large Christian army, the Muslims simply fled from Tunis and the Spanish conquerors marched into an empty city, which they ransacked. Other Tunisian ports such as Porto Farina (now Ghar al Melh) and Bizerta also submitted to Don Juan without a fight.[53]

Unknown to Don Juan, Philip II had sent orders that all the Tunisian ports should have their defences destroyed and all Spanish forces should then be withdrawn from the country. Don Juan took the opposite course of action. Although he could not spare garrisons for places like Bizerta, he ordered the construction of a new fortress at Tunis and left 8,000 Spanish and Italian troops to garrison it. The garrison of 1,000 men at La Goletta would remain. Sicily and Naples had had enough trouble sending supplies to the latter garrison. Now they would have to support an even larger force in Tunisia. Philip would have preferred these large numbers of troops to go to fight in the Netherlands, but he accepted Don Juan's arrangements.

The problems in the Netherlands and elsewhere distracted the Spanish in 1574 and the Ottomans launched a strong counterattack in the central Mediterranean. In mid-July an Ottoman fleet including 230 galleys and carrying 40,000 sailors, soldiers and oarsmen arrived in the gulf of Tunis. Uluj Ali commanded the fleet and Koca Sinan Pasha the army. The Ottoman troops swarmed ashore and first laid siege to La Goletta. Its garrison surrendered after a resistance that lasted barely one month. Then the Ottomans assaulted the half-completed new fortress at

Tunis. After a half-hearted resistance it fell in mid-September. Thousands of Spanish and Italian soldiers became prisoners. They had been expected to resist as fiercely and as long as the Knights of Malta in 1565, and Don Juan had been assembling a force at Sicily to come to their relief. By the time it was ready to sail, the Christian captives were already on their way to Istanbul to be paraded in triumph. The only comfort for the Christian side was that the Ottoman conquerors had lost many men on their expedition, mostly from disease.[54]

Among the soldiers in the Ottoman army which took Tunis was Abd al-Malik, the Ottoman-supported pretender to the throne of Morocco. In 1575 the new Ottoman sultan, Murad III, ordered Ottoman forces in Algiers to place Abd al-Malik on the Moroccan throne. This was successfully achieved in 1576. So now it appeared that the Ottomans ruled all of North Africa, whether directly or indirectly. This achievement made the defeat at Lepanto seem relatively unimportant. However, Muhammad, the deposed Moroccan ruler, fled to Portugal, where King Sebastian promised to help him regain his throne and began to assemble an invasion force. The new Moroccan ruler Abd al-Malik proved insufficiently obsequious to his Ottoman sponsors, trying to play off the Spanish against them.

Having been granted crusading privileges by the pope, King Sebastian invaded Morocco in 1578. His army not only contained Portuguese troops but also Spanish volunteers, German and Italian mercenaries and even a few English and Irish would-be crusaders. Abd al-Malik naturally declared a holy war, a jihad, against the infidel invaders, and he met them in battle at Alcazarquivir (now Ksar el Kebir) in early August. It became known as 'the battle of the three kings' because Sebastian, Abd al-Malik and his deposed predecessor Muhammad all perished in this resounding Moroccan victory. Abd al-Malik's brother Ahmad reaped the fruits of victory, including thousands of Christian prisoners, and took the title al-Mansur, the Victorious. Sebastian's disastrous attack on Morocco was the last major Christian European invasion of North Africa until the French landed in Algeria in 1830. Victory at Alcazarquivir was a powerful boost to Moroccan prestige and Ahmad al-Mansur ignored his dead brother's obligations towards the Ottoman sultan. He was happy to recognize the sultan as caliph, the religious leader of the world's Muslims, but he would not acknowledge any political subjugation to the Turkish ruler.[55]

Thus the Ottoman control of Morocco proved short-lived, but the three regencies of Algiers, Tunis and Tripoli had been firmly established as Ottoman provinces and would remain the main bases for the Barbary corsairs for the next 250 years. But if the 1578 battle had important implications for the Muslim side, it was even more significant for the Christians. The death of King Sebastian left only an elderly cleric as the sole heir to the crown of Portugal and his reign was short since he died in 1580. Now Philip II of Spain put forward his claim to inherit the Portuguese kingdom. His genealogical claim was strong, and the backing of a powerful fleet and army made it irresistible. In 1580 Philip took over Portugal and its empire. This might seem to give him new resources with which to wage war on the Ottomans. In fact it was to confirm a shift of Spanish strategic concerns from the Mediterranean to the Atlantic that had been growing since 1566. The revolt of the Netherlands increased in strength and English support for the rebels became more open and aggressive. The Spanish now wanted a truce with the Ottomans in the Mediterranean so they could concentrate on their growing problems in the Atlantic area.

Fortunately for Philip II, the year 1578 also saw the start of a war between the Ottoman empire and Persia (now Iran) which would not end until 1590. The Ottoman rulers were no longer interested in war in the Mediterranean despite the pleas of Uluj Ali and others for further campaigns against Spain. Negotiations between Spain and the Ottomans led to a truce being agreed in 1580–81 and neither side was ready to return to conflict in the Mediterranean in the coming years. In fact the Spanish navy would never again fight the navy of the Ottoman empire, but it would still clash with the Barbary corsairs at various times over several centuries.[56]

Uluj Ali remained kapudan pasha, but despite his pleas the naval war with the Christians in the Mediterranean was not renewed. He saw more action suppressing revolts within the empire in the eastern Mediterranean and led an expedition in the Black Sea in 1584 to ensure the pro-Ottoman candidate became ruler of the Crimean Tatars. Despite the similar functions they both served on the Ottoman frontiers, this was perhaps the only time that the leader of the Barbary corsairs had close contact with the leader of the Crimean Tatars.

When Uluj Ali died in Istanbul in 1587 he was still nominally the ruler of Algiers, although deputies had carried out his functions for years.

The sultan's advisers thought this was a good opportunity to reorganize Ottoman government in North Africa. Previously Algiers had been the dominant authority in the region. Now there were to be three equal regencies, each under a pasha, appointed by the sultan, who would rule for only three years at a time. The aim of this governmental change was to increase control of the regencies by Istanbul. Yet in fact from the 1580s the Barbary corsairs were increasingly to escape from the sultan's control. Once the vanguard of Ottoman expansion in the Mediterranean, they would now become lords of the sea in their own right.

The redemptionist friars arrive at Algiers to ransom Christian captives during the 1630s, from Pierre Dan, *Histoire de Barbarie et de ses corsaires* (1637).

TWO
Lords of the Sea
1580–1660

ICELAND 1627

For a century the principal ship used by the Barbary corsairs in their predatory pursuits had been the oar-propelled galley in various forms. However, soon after 1600, the corsairs were introduced to the use of the far more versatile square-rigged sailing ship by Dutch renegades. Such ships not only ended the corsairs' need for large numbers of Christian slave rowers, but also extended the range of their operations.

The Dutchman Simon Danser was said to have been the first person to show the corsairs of Algiers how to construct and how to navigate square-rigged sailing ships. This new type of vessel allowed the Algerines to send their ships far into the Atlantic Ocean, often using Salé in Morocco as a forward base. By 1630 the corsairs had attacked the Atlantic coasts of Portugal, Spain, France, England and Ireland, as well as raiding Atlantic islands such as the Azores and even the distant Newfoundland fishery off North America. However, the most famous thrust by the Barbary corsairs into distant waters was their expedition to Iceland in the summer of 1627.

The commander of this expedition was the corsair Murad Reis, formerly known as Jan Janszoon and born in Haarlem in the Netherlands. He started his maritime career as a Dutch privateer preying on Spanish shipping, but made little money from such activity so he turned to piracy. In 1618 he was captured by corsairs from Algiers and soon 'turned Turk', becoming Murad Reis the Muslim corsair. Initially he served under another Dutch renegade, Suleiman Reis (formerly Ivan De Veenboer), but after the latter was killed in a battle with Christian vessels in 1620, Murad Reis left Algiers. He next based himself at the fast-growing corsair port of Salé on the Atlantic coast of Morocco, although he did not totally sever his links with Algiers. By the mid-1620s Murad was

75

one of the leading corsairs at Salé and he was raiding widely along the Atlantic coasts of western Europe.

In the summer of 1627 a Danish captive called Paul was said to have suggested to Murad Reis that he should raid Iceland. It was a possession of the kingdom of Denmark, well known for its rich fisheries, but the Danes had made little effort to provide it with adequate defences. Paul knew the northern seas well and offered to act as a pilot. In return he asked for his freedom, which Murad was prepared to give him if the expedition went well.

Four corsair ships reached the coast of Iceland in June 1627. One went to the harbour of Grindavik on the south-west coast, where fifteen Icelanders and a few Danes were quickly captured. Two Danish merchant ships were also seized. Captives and booty were put on board one prize and it was sent on its way to Algiers. The other prize accompanied the corsair ship to Bessastaðir, near Reykjavík, which was the residence of the Danish governor, Holger Rosenkrantz. The latter ordered that cannon be placed in a fort overlooking the bay, and an Icelander, Jon Olafsson, who had served in the Danish navy, was sent to the fort to act as gunner. The fort and the corsair ship exchanged shots, but without damage to either side. Then the corsair's prize ship ran aground and it could only be refloated after the captives and booty had been transferred to the corsair. While this was going on, the Danish governor ordered the fort not to fire on the corsairs. This conduct annoyed the Icelanders. Once the prize had been refloated, the corsairs made no attempt to land. They left the bay and headed for home.

Meanwhile two other corsair ships were raiding the east coast of Iceland. On 5 July they landed men at the Herutsfjord and for a week they hunted down local people. In all the corsairs captured 110 people and killed at least nine others. Returning to sea, the two corsair ships met the fourth corsair ship of the original fleet of corsairs. The three corsair ships now headed for the Vestmann Islands off the south coast of Iceland. On the way they met an English fishing vessel which was forced to hand over some men to act as pilots in those islands.

Of the island group, only the island of Heimaey was inhabited, and the local people had warning that the corsair ships were approaching. They tried to prepare some defences, but when the three corsair ships reached the harbour of Kaupstad no serious resistance was offered. A Danish merchant ship, the *Krabbe*, was seized in the port, and most of the local inhabitants were hunted down over the next few days, despite their attempts to hide. In all 242 men, women and children were taken captive, while between 30 and 40 others were killed, along with most of the livestock on the island. After burning the church, merchant warehouses and many houses, the Barbary corsairs departed with their booty, their captives and the prize ship.

Most of the captives were on board the prize *Krabbe*, which became separated from the three corsair ships in bad weather. One of those on board was the priest Olafur Egilsson, who had been captured along with his wife and two sons, and later wrote an account of his experiences. Like most of the prisoners Olafur was surprised to find that the corsairs were human beings like himself. Popular stories had portrayed them as nothing less than devilish monsters. The ex-Christian renegades were judged to be the most cruel of the corsairs, with the Turks and Moors taking a less brutal attitude toward their captives. The prisoners were given food, and also beer, mead and brandy to drink. The Muslims, including the renegades, drank only water.

As the prisoners much outnumbered the corsairs guarding them on the *Krabbe*, some of them made plans to rise up and seize the ship. Unfortunately one of the Danish captives mentioned these plans to Paul, the Dane who had originally proposed the expedition to Murad Reis. Paul naturally warned the corsairs, and the prisoners were put in irons until the *Krabbe* rejoined the other corsair ships.

The ships finally reached Algiers on 17 August 1627. In all the expedition had yielded around 400 Icelandic and Danish captives, who were all sold as slaves in Algiers. In 1628 the priest Olafur Egilsson was released so that he could go to Copenhagen to encourage King Christian IV to arrange ransoms for the captives, but it was a slow process. Many of the captives died of disease soon after arriving in North Africa, a few escaped and others 'turned Turk', renouncing Christianity and becoming Muslims.

By 1635 only about 70 of the captives from Iceland were known to be still alive. Some 34 were said to have been ransomed in 1636, but only 27 of them passed through Copenhagen on their way back to Iceland in 1637. At least two of those who had converted to Islam and remained in Algiers had notable careers. Jon Asbjarnarson obtained a high post in the court of the ruler of Algiers. Jon Jonsson Vestmann became a corsair captain, but it was believed that he later returned to Christian Europe and died in Copenhagen.

The small group of ransomed Icelanders who passed through Copenhagen in 1637 were thought to need re-education in the Christian religion after their years in an Islamic country. A young Icelandic religious student, Hallgrímur Pétursson, was given the job of instructing them. He became particularly close to Guðriður Símonardóttir, a married woman from the Vestmann Islands. Petursson returned to Iceland with the group, and shortly afterwards Guðriður gave birth to his child. Fortunately her husband had recently died, so she was able to marry her much younger lover. The scandal meant that Pétursson had to work as a labourer for a number of years before being allowed to take up religious duties once more, becoming not only a priest but also one of Iceland's greatest poets.

Among the other returnees of 1637 was Asta Þorsteinsdóttir, the wife of Ólafur Egilsson, the priest who had already been free for almost ten years. Their two sons did not return from Algiers. Like most of those captured in Iceland during the 'Turkish abductions' of 1627, they were lost forever.

Murad Reis carried out a similar raid on the village of Baltimore on the south coast of Ireland in June 1631. Some 109 men, women, and children were taken captive and sold as slaves in Algiers. Only a handful of them ever returned home from North Africa. The menace of the Barbary corsairs had once been something associated exclusively with the waters and the shores of the Mediterranean Sea. In the first half of the seventeenth century the corsairs used their new mastery of the square-rigged sailing ship to burst out into the wide expanse of the Atlantic Ocean. There seemed to be nothing the Christian maritime powers could do to stop these Muslim raiders. The Barbary corsairs had truly become lords of the sea.[1]

CORSAIR HEYDAY

In the years between the Ottoman capture of Tunis in 1574 and the Ottoman invasion of Crete in 1645, the Mediterranean did not witness any major naval war between state navies. Yet this period was a time of intense maritime conflict in that sea, a conflict carried on at a lower level by both Muslim and Christian corsairs. During this age of private warfare the Barbary corsairs were to reach the zenith of their power and influence. Against them were arrayed the forces of the Knights of Malta and the Knights of St Stephen, along with the Christian privateers licensed by those orders and Spanish territories, but it soon became clear that the Muslim corsairs were growing steadily stronger.[2]

Even as the war fleets of the king of Spain and the Ottoman sultan stood down in the Mediterranean, the Barbary corsairs showed their continuing power. In the summer of 1582 Hassan Veneziano, a Venetian Christian renegade and ruler of Algiers, left that port with a squadron of 22 galleys and galliots, carrying at least 1,500 janissaries and other soldiers. First Hassan struck at Sardinia, with his men ranging as far as 40 miles inland, and the island provided him with 700 Christian captives. Moving north, the Algerines struck Monticello in Corsica, taking 400 captives. Then it was on to the Italian mainland, sweeping up 130 more Christians from Sori near Genoa. Moving westwards, the coast of Spain was the next target. The village of Pineda near Barcelona yielded 50 Christian captives, but when Hassan moved south to the coast near Alicante he had another task to carry out. Some 2,000 Moriscos wished to leave Spain to start a new life in North Africa and were willing to pay for their journey. Somehow Hassan found room for them in his already overloaded vessels, and the squadron returned to Algiers after a highly successful cruise.[3]

Nor was Barbary corsair power to be restricted just to the Mediterranean. The Algerines had made their first ventures through the strait of Gibraltar and into the Atlantic Ocean in the 1580s. Murad Reis the elder may have passed through as early as 1582, and in 1585 he carried out a daring attack on Lanzarote in the Canary Islands, having come from Algiers and then used the port of Salé in Morocco as a forward base for his operation. These were tentative first steps. The Algerines did not go far into the Atlantic, raiding mostly the Canaries and the Algarve coast of Portugal. In part this reluctance to venture further was because the Algerines were still using galleys and galliots, Mediterranean craft which could not cope with the Atlantic swells for long.

As the Algerines tentatively ventured outside the Mediterranean, new maritime players from northern Europe were increasingly coming into that sea, above all the English and the Dutch. As both were at war with Spain, they might have expected a welcome from the Barbary corsairs, but their initial reception was mixed. There were certainly English merchants in Algiers before 1580, when one of them, John Tipton, became the unofficial English consul in the city. In the same year an

English envoy, William Harborne, had visited Istanbul and concluded a commercial treaty with Ottoman sultan Murad III. Harborne later returned to Istanbul as the English ambassador, but it is notable that his first journeys to and from the Ottoman capital were made by land across Europe, perhaps underlining the insecurity of sea routes in the Mediterranean at this time.[4]

Tipton, like so many English and then British consuls after him, had an insecure and generally unhappy time in Algiers. In 1583 he wrote to Harborne complaining that the sultan's grant of special privileges to the English was being ignored by the ruler of Algiers. Tipton was worried that English trade in the Mediterranean might be strangled because the ships carrying it would be attacked from all sides. The Muslim Barbary corsairs attacked the English because they were infidels; the Catholic powers, such as Spain, the Knights of Malta, and the Knights of St Stephen, attacked the English because they were heretics. In the following year Harborne sent his assistant, Edward Barton, and an Ottoman envoy from Istanbul to North Africa. They went to Algiers, Tunis and Tripoli to make clear to the local rulers that the sultan had granted his protection to English traders and ships. Although occasional English ships were still taken by corsairs, in general the Ottoman regencies were favourable towards the English for the rest of the century. For example, the English privateer Edward Glemham used Algiers as a base for supplies and repairs when he was cruising against the Spanish in the first half of the 1590s.[5]

Although the Spanish still maintained some galley squadrons in the Mediterranean, after 1580 most of their naval efforts were now concentrated in the Atlantic Ocean, the main zone of conflict with their English and Dutch enemies. When the English, with a little Dutch help, defeated the famous Spanish Armada in 1588, this was noted favourably in the Islamic world. The Protestant maritime powers now seemed worthy potential allies in the struggle against Spain; at least, that was the view of the Barbary states of North Africa. The Ottoman sultan remained reluctant to renew his war with Spain, despite the entreaties of the English ambassador in Istanbul. When the English attacked the Spanish port of Cádiz in 1596, the Moroccans supported them with supplies and in return the English released any Muslim slaves they found in captured Spanish vessels. Indeed in 1596 Spain seemed to be beset by enemies, both within and without. It was at war with England, the

Netherlands and France; Morocco was considering an attack on the Spanish; and the Moriscos were in secret negotiations with the French across the Pyrenees about the possibility of starting another revolt within Spain. Between 1600 and 1603 Elizabeth I of England and Ahmad al-Mansur of Morocco had serious negotiations about concluding a military alliance against Spain, aiming to launch attacks not just in Iberia but also against Spanish colonies in the Caribbean. However, no such alliance was ever agreed, largely because both rulers died in 1603.[6]

Despite English encouragement, Ottoman sultans showed little desire to renew war with Spain in the Mediterranean. As long as this was the case, the Spanish gave a low priority to naval operations in that sea. When the Barbary corsairs were seen as the vanguard of Ottoman expansion, opposing them was vitally important. Once they were only occasional raiders, stopping their attacks seemed less of a priority, even if the tempo of such attacks seemed to be increasing. Despite the growing complaints of the inhabitants of Spain's Mediterranean coasts and islands, the government in Madrid felt its military and naval priorities were elsewhere.

Given this Spanish policy, there was widespread alarm in the Mediterranean in the summer of 1601 when the king of Spain ordered naval preparations on a scale not seen for years. The Ottomans immediately thought they were the intended target of the fleet being collected by the aged Gian Andrea Doria and rushed to collect their weakened galley forces into some sort of fleet. However, Doria assembled his ships at Trapani in Sicily which did not seem a likely starting place for a thrust into the eastern Mediterranean. In fact Spain's rulers had finally responded to the complaints of its long-suffering coastal population. Doria was going to attack Algiers, the first major Spanish attack on the corsair base since Emperor Charles v's failed assault 60 years earlier. After all the large-scale preparations, the result was an anti-climax. Shortly before reaching Algiers, the Spanish fleet was struck by a storm and scattered. By the time it was reassembled, Doria had already decided to call off the attack. Spain would not again try to conquer Algiers until the attack of General O'Reilly in 1775.[7]

At the end of the sixteenth century Spain seemed to be surrounded by enemies, both Muslim and Christian, but by the end of the first decade of the seventeenth century the country would be at peace with all its Christian foes. Spain and France made peace in 1598, and peace was agreed with England in 1604. After the death of Elizabeth in 1603, the crowns of England and Scotland had been united under King James (James I of England and James VI of Scotland), who was not only pro-Spanish but also hostile to the Muslim powers, especially the Barbary corsairs. Spain was not yet ready to concede independence to the Dutch rebels it had been fighting since the 1560s, but it was ready to agree a temporary truce. In 1609 a twelve-year truce was agreed between Spain and the Netherlands. Suddenly Spain had no Christian enemies. This peaceful interlude seemed a good opportunity for the Spanish government to take action against its most persistent Muslim foes: the Moriscos within Spain and the Barbary corsairs in the waters around it.

After the revolt of 1568–70 there had been calls for the expulsion of all Moriscos from Spain, but initially more restrictive controls on them were preferred. In 1575 it was decreed that no Moriscos in Valencia could approach the coast without a permit; in Granada any Morisco found carrying a weapon could be put to death; and in 1588 extra vigilance was ordered on the French frontier to stop Moriscos in Aragon from contacting the Huguenots, French Protestants hostile to Spain. Despite such measures Moriscos were still caught assisting the raids of the Barbary corsairs. For example, in 1583 fifteen Moriscos were executed for allegedly assisting a corsair attack on Chilches near Malaga. This continued threat from the 'enemy within' could not be ignored. In 1582 the Spanish council of state had agreed in principle that the Moriscos should be expelled at a convenient moment. However, this moment would not come for almost 30 years.[8]

The Moriscos still had powerful protectors among the Spanish aristocracy, especially the nobles in the Valencia region who claimed they could not work their estates without Morisco labour. However, Juan de Ribera, the archbishop of Valencia, was a strong opponent of the Morisco presence and worked for their expulsion. King Philip III and his wife also felt that the continued presence of secret Muslims in Spain both endangered the country's security and offended God. After the peace treaties with France and England, negotiations began in 1607 for a truce with the Dutch rebels. Once it was concluded, troops and ships would be available to assist in the final removal of the Moriscos.

In April 1609, just before the Dutch truce was finally agreed, Spain's council of state approved the expulsion of the Moriscos, beginning with the large population in the Valencia region. King Philip gave his final approval to the measure in June 1609 and the expulsion began in Valencia in September. The local aristocrats had been promised compensation for their lost labour force. The Moriscos offered little resistance and soon large numbers of them were being shipped to the Spanish outpost of Oran in North Africa. From there they were driven across the border into the territory of the regency of Algiers. In all some 124,000 Moriscos were expelled from Valencia. Driven out of Spain for being 'bad Christians', they received a mixed reception in North Africa. Many were seen as 'bad Muslims' because they spoke Spanish rather than Arabic, wore Spanish clothes and had a poor understanding of Islamic religious practices.[9]

At the end of 1609 the Spanish government decided the next targets would be the Moriscos of Andalusia, Granada and part of Murcia, along with a particularly militant Morisco group at Hornachos in Extremadura. The duke of Medina Sidonia, captain-general of Andalusia and commander of the doomed Armada of 1588, had much experience of dealing with corsair raids on his territory and doubted that this expulsion would reduce such attacks. However, he obeyed his orders from the king and began to round up the Moriscos of Andalusia. These areas were cleared of Moriscos in early 1610, with the Moriscos of Hornachos using the threat of resistance so that they could leave on their own terms, taking their arms and their wealth with them. The summer of 1610 saw the removal of the Moriscos in Old and New Castile, most going to France from where they moved on to North Africa. Next came the Moriscos of Aragon and Catalonia, who were told they had to leave their children behind if they went direct to North Africa. Understandably most of these people went to France with their children and then travelled to North Africa and other Muslim lands.

The last remaining Morisco groups were in Murcia. Well integrated into Christian society and loyal to the Spanish crown, these people had many Christian friends who begged the government to treat them as an exception. Indeed the Moriscos of Murcia had largely remained loyal during the revolt of 1568–70 and had provided scouts to help the government forces crush the Morisco rebels. However, King Philip III decided there could be no exceptions. During December 1613 and January 1614 the last Moriscos of Murcia were expelled. Some Moriscos tried to hide, but once they had been rounded up King Philip could declare in August 1614 that his kingdom was now free of all Moriscos.

In less than five years some 300,000 Moriscos had been expelled from Spain. Although this was only about 4 per cent of the country's total population, the exodus had a serious economic impact in some areas. In Valencia the Moriscos had made up around 30 per cent of the population of the region, and many of the villages they left were never repopulated. The expulsion marked the end of a Muslim civilization that had existed in the Iberian peninsula for a little over 900 years. This was the final victory of the Renconquista, but would it do much to end the attacks of the Barbary corsairs?

The emigration of Moriscos from Spain to North Africa was nothing new. The expulsions of 1609–14 were notable chiefly for the large numbers coming across and the fact that they marked the end of a Muslim presence in Iberia. The earlier influx spread across the sixteenth century had been encouraged by some North African rulers, especially the Barbarossas at Algiers. The Turkish ruling elite was happy to be joined by other Muslim outsiders, who would not only support the maritime war against the Christians, but would help keep the local Muslims, both Arab and Berber, in their place. There were some examples of these earlier Morisco immigrants turning to corsairing and other military activities. A Morisco called Said Ben Faraj al-Dughali left Granada and went to Morocco in the 1560s. He carried on corsairing from his base at Tetouan, and in 1571 launched a raid on the Canary Islands. Al-Dughali also recruited Morisco soldiers for the army of the ruler of Morocco and these men played an important part in the defeat of the Portuguese at the battle of Alcazarquivir in 1578. However, most of the Moriscos arriving in North Africa were agricultural labourers or artisans, such as silk workers, and preferred to follow those activities rather than wage war on the Spanish.[10]

These trends were largely mirrored in the great influx of Moriscos after 1609. It has been claimed that this new wave of Morisco immigrants was one of the reasons for the expansion of Barbary corsairing in the first half of the seventeenth century, but this view seems exaggerated. As in earlier times, most of the Moriscos had not followed occupations with any military or maritime relevance. The rulers of Tunis did not welcome the 80,000 Moriscos who went to that regency because of their martial expertise. It was their agricultural and artisan skills which were valued because of the contribution they would make to the Tunisian economy.

There certainly were a few Morisco corsair captains, two of whom were captured with their ships by the Spanish in 1618. Julian Perez was a Morisco expelled from Moron de la Frontera who had been raiding the coasts of Andalusia and Valencia, while Ali Zayde, expelled from Zaragoza, was captured off the coast of Valencia. Another Morisco who became a corsair captain at Algiers was Blanquillo Morisco. His crew were all fellow Moriscos, Spanish-speaking and wearing Spanish clothes, who could fool Spanish naval patrols and raid widely on the Spanish coast. Nevertheless, the majority of captains on Barbary corsair vessels were either Turks or Christian renegades, and Moriscos were more likely to hold more lowly positions in corsair crews. As early as May 1610 the Spanish viceroy in Majorca was warning that twelve corsair ships had left Algiers carrying many Moriscos, but most of them were either soldiers or guides. Moriscos remained an important element in the armies of Morocco, but in the civil wars that broke out after 1603 they were more likely to be fighting fellow Muslims than Christian infidels. Some Moriscos undoubtedly served in the corsairs of Algiers, but more useful were the financial investments Morisco merchants made in such ventures.[11]

Nevertheless one must not go too far in downplaying the impact of the Morisco expulsions on corsairing from the Barbary states. The new Morisco influx reinforced an existing Morisco population in North Africa, especially in Morocco and Algiers, which was implacably hostile to Christians in general and the Spanish variety in particular. The local North African rulers could be sure that any weakening in their commitment to the maritime jihad would lead to unrest among their Morisco subjects. Generally this Morisco hatred of the Christians did not lead to active participation in the maritime war against them, but there was one major exception to this rule: the Moriscos who came from Hornachos. In only a few decades they turned the Moroccan port of Salé into a corsair base that could rival even Algiers. Their achievement will be considered in a later section, but they did not do this alone.

Thus the Moriscos expelled from Spain 1609–14 were not a major cause of the expansion of Barbary corsairing in the early 1600s, except in the case of Salé. The other new factor which had a greater role in boosting corsair activities after 1600 was the influx of Dutch and English pirates into Barbary shortly after the start of the new century. These men brought new technology and maritime skills which would boost the power of the Barbary corsairs, not only in the Mediterranean but also in their new hunting grounds in the Atlantic Ocean.

Even before Spain made peace with England and the Netherlands, many privateers from those two countries were finding it hard to make money in their licensed maritime war against Spain and its main ally, Portugal. As the supply of prizes which could be lawfully seized began to dry up, the temptation to seize any available merchant ship increased. Even before the outbreak of peace ended all privateering, many English and Dutch privateers had already become pirates, preying on the ships of all nations. For a while such pirates found bases in distant harbours such as those of south-west Ireland but, as they were steadily driven out of those refuges, the Barbary ports became more attractive as bases. Many of the pirates had already visited these ports when they were privateers carrying on war against the Spanish. Although the pirates were nominally Christian infidels, the Barbary corsairs were prepared to welcome them because of the many maritime skills they could impart. In any case many of the pirates soon converted to Islam and became renegades.[12]

The chief technological skills the newcomers had to offer were how to construct and sail square-rigged sailing ships. Unlike galleys such ships were strongly built and could carry more guns, along with booty and captives. Not needing galley slaves, the sailing ships carried only a small number of Christian captives to pull on ropes and similar tasks. More Christian captives would now be available for other tasks which might yield more income for their owners than labouring at an oar. The Barbary corsairs could now meet heavily armed European merchant sailing ships in the Mediterranean on more equal terms than when they possessed only galleys. Even more importantly, the strongly built sailing ships would allow the Barbary corsairs to range more widely into the Atlantic maritime world.

The prospect of new hunting grounds was welcome to many of the corsairs. A century of incessant raiding along Spanish and Italian coasts and islands in the Mediterranean had led to such heavy losses among the coastal populations that the remaining residents had fled. Many stretches of coastline and offshore islands were now deserted. The corsairs needed new targets for their 'Christian stealing' operations. They found them on the Atlantic coasts of Spain, Portugal, France, England and Ireland, and on distant islands like Madeira, the Azores and Iceland. Not only did the Dutch and English pirates provide the sailing ships that made Atlantic corsair operations possible, but they also provided the navigational skills and maritime knowledge so that the corsairs could find and exploit the best areas to cruise for prizes or launch land raids. The Newfoundland fishery would prove attractive, especially in the spring, when the corsairs could intercept English and French vessels going out to the fishery loaded with men who would soon fill the slave markets of Algiers and Salé. Venturing out further into the Atlantic also meant the corsairs could threaten the great Spanish and Portuguese fleets returning home carrying the wealth of the Indies. They had no hope of taking the great galleons loaded with bullion, but there were smaller ships which could still yield a rich return. These ships, which promised a quicker passage, often carried government officials and rich merchants anxious to get home. If such people became captives of the corsairs they were bound to yield large ransoms.

Simon Danser, said to have been born at Dordrecht in the Nether-lands, was the central figure in the transmission to the Barbary corsairs of how to build, set out and navigate square-rigged sailing ships. Around 1600 Danser was living in Marseille on the Mediterranean coast of France with his wife and family. For reasons unknown he then moved to Algiers, leaving his family in Marseille. Danser began building square-rigged sailing ships for the Algerine corsairs and advised them how such ships should be employed. This soon led to Danser becoming a corsair himself. He converted to Islam, becoming Simon Reis, and soon had a wife and family in his new home. Over a period of three years Danser was said to have taken at least 40 prizes in both the Mediterranean and the Atlantic. He worked closely with other European renegades and pirates in Algiers and Tunis, especially the Englishmen Peter Easton and John Ward. Spanish, French and English warships were said to have been sent in pursuit of Danser, but he escaped them all.[13]

Danser became a rich man, but it soon became clear he did not want to retire and enjoy his wealth in Algiers. In 1609 Danser captured a Span-ish vessel off Valencia and found a number of Jesuit priests on board. He agreed to release them if they would carry a message to King Henry IV of France. Danser wanted to be forgiven his crimes, to return to his original family in Marseille and to be allowed to keep his riches. The French king agreed to these terms, and in November 1609 Danser arrived at Marseille with four well armed ships. Unfortunately some of the cannon on board those ships belonged to the government of Algiers and not to Danser, a fact which would later poison relations between France and Algiers. To mark his return to Christendom, Danser handed over many Muslim members of his crews to become slaves in the French galleys.

Based in Marseille, Danser now became involved in attacks on Muslim shipping. In 1611 the French authorities asked him to go on a mission to Algiers to secure the release of French ships and sailors held there. Unwisely Danser agreed to undertake this task. Arriving at Algiers in a French ship, he initially found the Algerine government well disposed towards him. However, once Danser came ashore he was quickly seized and executed for being an apostate from Islam and for his attacks on Muslim ships.

One of Danser's officers during his time as an Algerine corsair had been Ivan De Veenboer, a fellow Dutchman, who had been born at Hoorn in the Netherlands. De Veenboer had originally been a Dutch privateer in the war against the Spanish, but on taking few prizes he had turned pirate and eventually reached North Africa. By 1617 he was said to have his own fleet of Algerine corsairs and had 'turned Turk', becoming known as Suleiman Reis. However, in secret he was negotiating with the Dutch consul in Algiers for a pardon which would allow him to return home. These negotiations eventually collapsed and De Veenboer returned to corsairing.

By 1620 De Veenboer was rich enough to retire, but he still remained committed to taking out his ships to hunt for rich Christian prizes. The Christian nations sent ships to hunt him down. De Veenboer managed to beat off an attack by Dutch warships in July 1620, but in October of that year he encountered a multinational squadron off Cartagena in Spain. The squadron was composed of one Dutch, two French and two English warships, and they were soon closely engaged with De Veenboer's corsair squadron. During the fierce battle De Veenboer's legs were smashed by a cannonball and he died soon afterwards.[14]

Among the Christian renegades who served in De Veenboer's ships was Jan Janszoon, born at Haarlem in the Netherlands. He had served in Dutch privateers during the war with Spain, but then turned to piracy. Janszoon was at Lanzarote in the Canary Islands in 1618 when a major raid by the Barbary corsairs struck the island. He was captured by the corsairs and taken back to Algiers as a slave. Janszoon quickly converted to Islam and took the name Murad (later being known as Murad Reis the younger to distinguish him from the earlier famous corsair of the same name). He joined one of De Veenboer's ships, but after his leader was killed in battle in 1620 Murad moved to Salé in Morocco, although he still maintained links with Algiers. As already noted, Murad Reis led corsair raids in the Atlantic which included the attack on Iceland in 1627. As he is most intimately associated with Salé, his story will be continued in a later section.[15]

The most famous Englishman on the Barbary coast in this period was John Ward. He was said to have originally been a fisherman at Faversham in Kent, but later served in English privateers and warships. As the war with Spain came to an end, he joined a gang of pirates in the English Channel in 1603. In the following year Ward became leader of the gang and set off in his pirate ship for the Mediterranean. After receiving a hostile reception at Algiers, Ward moved on to capture prizes at the entrance to the Adriatic Sea. In 1605 Ward was based at Salé in Morocco, but in 1606 he adopted Tunis as his home port.

Ward was said to have had a major role in introducing the Tunisians to the advantages of the square-rigged sailing ship, and later in 1606 he captured a large Venetian ship returning from Alexandria in Egypt, a prize so rich that it was said to have made his fortune. In 1607 Ward took two more rich Venetian prizes, prompting the Venetian government to complain to King James about the activities of English pirates in the Mediterranean. There were Muslims among Ward's sailors, but most of his crewmen were English, Dutch and Spanish. Ward even ransomed English captives in Barbary so that they could join his ships. In 1608 Ward took another Venetian ship off Greece, then some prizes in the western Mediterranean which he sent into Algiers. By the end of 1608 Ward, now worth 150,000 crowns, was said to be negotiating with the Grand Duke of Tuscany so that he could retire to Italy and enjoy his wealth, but the negotiations later collapsed.

In 1609, while Ward's pirate fleet was active in the Mediterranean, his subordinate Richard Bishop took another pirate squadron into the Atlantic and cruised for prizes off Ireland. Later in the year a Franco-Spanish squadron attacked La Goletta, the port of Tunis, and burned 30 ships, including some owned by Ward. Undismayed, Ward kept up his corsairing activities. His Christian enemies sent an assassin to kill him, but the attempt on his life failed. The English government then offered him a pardon if he would give up corsairing and come home, but the negotiations were unsuccessful.

In 1610 Ward was said to have a fleet of fifteen vessels, manned by 1,500 men, based at Tunis. Later in that year he converted to Islam, taking the name Yusuf Reis, although he was also known to Muslims as Captain Wardiyya. Ward's successes made him as famous as Simon Danser among Christians. He was the subject of Robert Daborne's 1612 play *A Christian Turn'd Turke*, but in this fictional account Ward as a Christian renegade had to meet a savage death. In reality Ward was wealthy and untroubled by Christian hostility, real or literary.

In 1615 the Scottish traveller William Lithgow dined with John Ward, alias Yusuf Reis, at his 'faire Palace' in Tunis and found the semi-retired corsair engaged in the improbable pursuit of rearing chicks by incubating eggs in camel dung. Having left a wife in England, Ward married Jessimina, a Christian renegade from Sicily, during his time in Tunis. Perhaps going on another corsairing cruise as late as 1622, Ward seems to have died in the plague outbreak at Tunis in 1623.[16]

Henry Mainwaring was another English pirate who came to Barbary in these years, but his origins were very different to those of John Ward. Born into a gentry family and educated at Oxford University, Mainwaring first served the English crown by pursuing pirates in the Bristol Channel. However, after a dispute with the Spanish in 1612, Mainwaring decided to turn pirate, aiming to attack the ships of all nations except England. With bases in Ireland and at Mamora (now Mehdya) in Morocco, the gentleman pirate soon built up a small but effective fleet. Mainwaring had some successes, but when he took his ships to raid the Newfoundland fishery in 1614 a Spanish expedition attacked and captured Mamora in his absence. On his return Mainwaring moved his operations into the Mediterranean. First he visited Tunis, but then he found a new home at Villefranche, then in the duchy of Savoy. Mainwaring defeated a Spanish force sent after him in 1615, but in the following year he left the Mediterranean and went to Ireland. There he negotiated a pardon from King James and, once this was granted, began writing a book about piracy, in part based on his own experiences. Despite the mercy shown to him, Mainwaring recommended in his book *Discourse of Pirates* (1618) that pirates should never be pardoned. In 1618 King James gave Mainwaring a knighthood and sent him to chase pirates in the English Channel.[17]

One of Mainwaring's lieutenants had been Robert Walsingham, and after Mainwaring had sailed for Ireland Walsingham set up his own pirate fleet which he based at Algiers. In February 1617, leading a squadron of five ships, Walsingham attacked a lone English ship, the *Dolphin* of London, off Sardinia. In a running battle, the supposed victim managed to beat off all the attackers, and Walsingham returned to Algiers humiliated. Perhaps discouraged by failures such as this, Walsingham went to Ireland in 1618 and followed his former commander's path by negotiating a pardon from the English government. Walsingham's knowledge of the Barbary corsairs did not go to waste. In 1620 he joined Admiral Mansell's fleet which was being sent to attack Algiers. Both Mainwaring and Walsingham had been at Villefranche, and the duke of Savoy's hospitality was extended to another English pirate, Peter Easton. After carrying on his piratical activities in Ireland, off Newfoundland and from Salé in Morocco, Easton was looking to retire. The duke was happy to welcome him and his fortune of 100,000 crowns in 1613. Becoming a Catholic, Easton reinvented himself as an Italian nobleman, just as John Ward had turned himself into a Turkish pasha.[18]

The Dutch and English pirates who came to North Africa in the early 1600s were clearly men of ever-shifting loyalties, but they did play a far more important role in boosting the power and range of the Barbary corsairs than the Moriscos expelled from Spain. Their impact was most obvious in the changing composition of the Barbary corsair fleets. For example, in 1581 the Algerine fleet consisted of 36 galleys and galliots. By 1634 the fleet had not only doubled in size, but was now largely composed of well-armed sailing ships, most carrying between 25 and 40 cannon. At this time the fleet of Tunis still included five galleys, but they were greatly outnumbered by the 40 sailing vessels in this corsair fleet.[19]

The shift to sailing ships allowed the Barbary corsairs to expand their operations into the Atlantic Ocean. Long used to bitter complaints from the victims of corsair raids on Spain's Mediterranean coast, the government in Madrid now received similar complaints from the Atlantic coast of the country. Before 1617 governors of Galicia in northwest Spain made no mention of raids by 'Turkish' corsairs. Then in December 1617 Muslim corsairs attacked and burned the village of Cangas in the Ria de Vigo, killing or taking away most of its inhabitants. After that date such raids became a regular occurrence. For example, in 1621 the village of Portonovo was sacked and many of its inhabitants were taken away by the estimated 1,000 North African corsairs who had arrived in fifteen vessels.[20]

In 1616 Sir Francis Cottingham, the English ambassador in Madrid, noted that 'the strength and boldness of the Barbary pirates is now grown to that height, both in the [Atlantic] ocean and the Mediterranean sea', that the Spanish court was in despair about how to contain this onslaught.[21] Nevertheless, since Spain was at peace with its European rivals, the Spanish did have forces available to take action against the Barbary corsairs, sometimes even in co-operation with those same rival nations.

Luis Fajardo de Cordoba was particularly associated with the anti-corsair efforts. In 1609 he co-operated with a French force under Beaulieu-Persac to launch a joint attack on La Goletta, the port of Tunis, which led to the destruction of 30 Muslim vessels. As France still had no real navy, the French squadron was made up of privateers from Marseille. In 1610 Muhammad al-Shaykh, one of the leaders in the Moroccan civil wars, agreed to hand over the port of Larache in return for Spanish support. Fajardo took possession of the new acquisition, which was well placed to threaten the corsair/pirate bases of Mamora and Salé. In 1611 the Spanish succeeded in sinking blockships in the river at Mamora, but these were soon removed by the inhabitants. Only in 1614 did Fajardo have the chance to take a large expedition to Mamora, quickly capturing the port.[22]

Spain and the Dutch rebels had been fighting bitterly for decades, but after the truce of 1609 they did on occasion co-operate to act against the Barbary corsairs. This co-operation reached its peak in 1618 when a Dutch squadron under Admiral Lambert and a Spanish fleet under Miguel de Vidazabal intercepted in the strait of Gibraltar a large Algerine force returning from a successful raid on the Canary Islands. Half the Algerine ships were captured or sunk, with some Christian captives freed, but a larger number drowned.[23] Heartened by events such as this, King James 1 of England proposed to set up more permanent co-operation between England, Spain and the Netherlands to destroy the menace of the Barbary corsairs. However, by the time James put forward this idea, the truce between the Spanish and the Dutch was approaching its end and neither party was ready to co-operate further with the other.[24]

In the end the English government decided to act alone against the corsairs. The Algerine corsairs seemed the greatest threat to England, having captured more than 400 English ships between 1609 and 1616. In 1620 a fleet of six royal warships and twelve armed merchantmen assembled at Plymouth and Sir Robert Mansell was appointed to command the force. The ships did not sail until October and reached Algiers towards the end of the year. Mansell attempted to negotiate with the Algerines but, although 40 English captives were freed, no treaty could be agreed. A Spanish squadron then appeared off Algiers, but its commander refused to assist Mansell. With sickness among his crews and running out of supplies, Mansell withdrew from Algiers. The Spanish did at least allow the English ships to replenish their supplies at the island of Majorca and the ports of Malaga and Alicante on the mainland. Next Mansell encountered a Dutch squadron patrolling off the Barbary coast, but its commander would not co-operate with him in an attack on Algiers. Having procured some vessels to use as fireships, Mansell returned to Algiers in May 1621. He tried to get his burning fireships in among the shipping inside the harbour of Algiers, but little damage was inflicted. Soon afterwards, Mansell took most of his ships back to England, and the Algerine corsairs renewed their attacks on English shipping.[25]

In 1621 the Spanish and the Dutch recommenced their war and fighting the Barbary corsairs ceased to be a priority concern of either party. During the 1620s England would be at war with both France and Spain for various periods, and its relations with the Dutch would be strained after clashes in the East Indies. A brief window of opportunity had existed between 1604 and 1621 for the main European naval powers to co-operate to resist the growing strength of the Barbary corsairs, but that opportunity had largely been wasted. What successes had been won against the corsairs were unlikely to do them any long-term damage. Busy fighting each other once again, the European maritime powers would now have to look to diplomacy rather than naval force if they wished to achieve some sort of reduction in corsair attacks on their shipping.

England, the Netherlands and France all took the view that since Algiers, Tunis and Tripoli were provinces of the Ottoman empire, the best way to curb their corsair activities was to complain to their overlord, the Ottoman sultan. However, it soon became clear that the sultan's power over his Barbary provinces was increasingly limited. This was another reason for the increase in Barbary corsair activity after 1600. The Ottoman regencies of North Africa were less and less under the control of the central government in Istanbul. On the one hand, the Ottoman rulers were distracted by foreign wars, first with Persia and then from 1593 to 1606 with the Austrian Habsburgs in Hungary. On the other, there were increasingly serious revolts in the Ottoman heartlands, especially in Anatolia, in the early seventeenth century. Curbing the activities of the Barbary corsairs was not a priority for the sultan. To please the European maritime states he might issue orders to the rulers of Algiers, Tunis and Tripoli forbidding attacks on foreign shipping, but he took little action to enforce those orders. By the 1620s it was clear to the European maritime powers that if they wanted diplomatic agreements aimed at stopping corsair attacks, they would have to deal directly with the Ottoman regencies in North Africa.[26]

Sir Thomas Roe, the English ambassador in Istanbul, reached agreement with the Ottoman government about the control of the corsairs, but no final treaty was possible until 1623 after consultation with delegations from Algiers and Tunis. A new English consul, James Frizell, was established in Algiers and he had the task of securing the release of the estimated 1,000 English captives in the city. Up to February 1624 Frizell ransomed 240 persons at a total cost of £1,800. In 1625 an ambassador from Algiers even visited England, but by the late 1620s the terms of the Roe treaty were being ignored by the Algerines, who were once more seizing English ships.[27]

Whatever England's problems with the Barbary corsairs, these were not the only predators who might attack English shipping in the Mediterranean. When Roe's period as ambassador to the Ottoman sultan ended in 1628, he took passage in the *Sampson*, a well armed Levant Company merchant ship commanded by William Rainborow, for a voyage from Istanbul to Livorno. The ship was becalmed near Malta and four galleys of the Knights of Malta made an attempt to capture it. The knights were as hostile to English Protestant heretics as they were to Muslim infidels. Far from being overwhelmed, Rainborow beat off the Maltese galleys in a prolonged battle and landed Roe and his wife safely in Italy. This incident was a clear demonstration of the superiority of the square-rigged sailing ship to the galley. In the following decade Rainborow would become a naval officer and command the English expedition against Salé in Morocco.[28]

After the Spanish–Dutch truce of 1609 the merchant ships of the Netherlands became increasingly common in the Mediterranean and began to fall victim to corsair attacks. One of those who fell victim several times to the pirates/corsairs was the young Maarten Tromp, who would later become one of the greatest Dutch admirals. In 1610, at the age of twelve, he accompanied his father on a voyage to West Africa, but his father's ship never reached that destination. It was intercepted by the ships of English pirate Peter Easton, who was using Salé in Morocco as a base. In the ensuing battle Tromp's father was killed and the boy became a prisoner, being sold into slavery at Salé. After two years young Tromp was ransomed and returned to the Netherlands. Years later, in 1621, Tromp was in the Mediterranean when he was captured by Tunisian corsairs. English renegade John Ward offered him a post in his corsair fleet, but Tromp declined the offer and within a year had been restored to freedom.[29]

Experiences like those of Maarten Tromp became increasingly common after 1609, so when the Netherlands established diplomatic relations with the Ottoman government in 1612 the Dutch asked the sultan to order the Barbary regencies not to attack their ships. Such an order was issued and the ruler of Tunis seemed inclined to obey it, but the Algerines ignored the sultan's command. Between 1613 and 1622 the corsairs of Algiers were said to have captured more than 400 Dutch merchant ships. Faced with such attacks, the Dutch sent a fleet under Admiral Lambert to put pressure on the Algerines. Lambert's greatest achievement, in association with a Spanish squadron, was to inflict a severe defeat on a fleet of Algerine corsairs in the strait of Gibraltar in 1618. Nevertheless this did not force the ruler of Algiers to make peace and the struggle continued. In 1621 war began once more between Spain and the Netherlands. The Dutch hoped this would improve relations with Algiers, since Spain was the perennial enemy of all Barbary corsairs.[30]

A peace treaty between the Dutch and Algiers was finally agreed in 1622, but many Algerine corsairs were reluctant to accept it. Attacks continued, so in 1624 Admiral Lambert took a fleet to the Barbary coast once more. After capturing some Algerine vessels, Lambert appeared before Algiers. He demanded the release of all Dutch captives and respect for the terms of the earlier treaty. If this was not done, the admiral promised to hang all his Algerine captives. The ruler of Algiers rejected this ultimatum, so Lambert executed the prisoners. The Dutch squadron then sailed away and soon took more Algerine ships and captives. Returning to Algiers, Lambert repeated his ultimatum. The prisoners aboard the Dutch ships had friends within Algiers who raised a popular outcry that forced the ruler to give in. Dutch captives were released and a new treaty was agreed between Algiers and the Dutch, although it largely repeated the terms of the earlier agreement.

The new treaty was the beginning of a period of more amicable relations between the Dutch and Algiers. A similar treaty was also agreed with Tunis. In the next few years the Dutch even allowed Algerine corsairs cruising in the English Channel to come to their ports for repairs and supplies. In 1625 the Dutch requested a commercial outpost on the Algerian coast similar to the French establishment at the Bastion of France near La Calle (now El Kala), but the Algerines refused the request. As both were at war with Spain, the Dutch were ready to sell guns, gunpowder and naval stores to the Algerines. Only after the end of the Spanish–Dutch war in 1648 did Dutch relations with the Barbary corsairs become hostile once more.[31]

As the only European Christian ally of the Ottoman empire, France might have expected especially favourable treatment from both the sultan and his supposed vassals in North Africa. Nevertheless in the early 1600s French ships were as likely to be taken by the Barbary corsairs as those of England and the Netherlands. However, the first clash between France and Algiers in the new century was not at sea. In 1604 famine conditions were gripping much of the western Mediterranean. It was at this time that French merchants at the Bastion of France, their commercial outpost on the Algerian coast, chose to export local grain to France. This caused outrage in Algiers, where the population felt the grain should have been sent to their city. In retaliation for the French action, the Algerines seized and sacked the Bastion of France. King Henry IV of France complained to the Ottoman sultan Ahmed I about this attack, and the sultan promised to order Algiers not to attack or seize any French people, property or ships. The Algerines paid no attention to the order.

Henry IV had no significant navy, so a force of French privateers under Beaulieu-Persac was sent to cruise off the Barbary coast. It had one big success, helping a Spanish squadron to burn 30 Muslim ships at La Goletta, the port of Tunis, in 1609. This did something to curb the Tunisian corsairs, but had no impact on Algiers, the main Barbary foe of the French. Later in 1609 Simon Danser left Algiers and returned to Christendom, taking up residence in Marseille. Aboard his ships were some cannon belonging to the government of Algiers. The Algerines asked for the guns to be returned by the French, but their request was ignored. Attacks on French shipping increased and in retaliation the port of Marseille sent out its own squadron of privateers under Vincheguerre to hunt the Muslim corsairs in 1616. While the French king and the Ottoman sultan remained at peace, their subjects in Marseille and Algiers were at war.[32]

As their losses rose, the merchants of Marseille demanded action by the French king. His complaints to the Ottoman government led to an order from the sultan to Algiers demanding negotiations for a peace with the French. The French crown refused on principle to engage in any direct negotiation with Algiers, a city they regarded as just a nest of pirates. The Algerines would have to negotiate at a lower level with the duke of Guise, governor of Provence and controller of the Bastion of France. By 1619 a treaty had been written and an Algerine delegation went to France to put a seal to it. Unfortunately around the same time an Algerine corsair captured a ship from Marseille and murdered the entire crew. When the news reached Marseille, the local people stormed the lodgings of the Algerine envoys and killed them all. Once news of this slaughter reached Algiers, all French people in the city were thrown into gaol and were lucky to escape death. The treaty was forgotten, attacks on French shipping increased and in 1621 the Bastion of France was once again sacked by the Algerines.[33]

By the mid-1620s Cardinal Richelieu dominated the French government. He was reluctant to negotiate directly with Algiers as this would confer recognition of its semi-independent status, but efforts to achieve anything via the Ottoman government in Istanbul had failed. In 1626 Richelieu finally had to adapt to the realities of the situation. He sent Sanson Napollon, a Corsican, to Algiers in the role of official French government negotiator. Turkish-speaking and well versed in the ways of the Muslim Mediterranean, Napollon eventually secured a peace treaty between France and Algiers in 1628. Among its terms was French agreement to return Danser's cannon to Algiers, and there was to be a release of both French and Algerine prisoners, although ransoms would be paid. Problems quickly arose, not least in relation to the Algerine prisoners in French hands. Richelieu was rebuilding the French navy and it included a galley force in the Mediterranean, in which many of the rowers were Algerine and other Muslim prisoners. The French were very reluctant to hand over young, fit Muslim rowers, and this attitude undermined hopes of peace. It was a problem which would occur again and again when

France wanted to make peace with the Barbary states during the seventeenth century.

A more immediate blow to the new peace treaty was the capture of a well-known Algerine corsair by a French warship, with the Algerine prisoners being sent to the galleys. Algerine protests were ignored, so their corsairs went back to attacking French ships. Between 1629 and 1631 the Algerines were said to have captured 80 French ships, with cargoes valued in total at five million livres, and also some 2,300 French captives. In 1633 Richelieu sent Samson le Page to Algiers to negotiate an end to the conflict, and in his party was the priest Pierre Dan, who was charged with ransoming captives. Dan would gather information about Algiers and the other Barbary corsair states that would appear in his later book *Histoire de Barbarie et des corsaires* (1637). Le Page's mission was unsuccessful, but in 1635 France went to war with Spain and, as usual, there was hope that by becoming an enemy of Spain France might win concessions from the Barbary corsairs. They were slow in coming. In 1637 France's new Mediterranean fleet appeared before Algiers and a number of Algerine ships were captured. Some of these belonged to Ali Bitchin, perhaps the most powerful corsair in the city, and in retaliation he sacked the Bastion of France, killing or capturing over 300 Frenchmen.[34]

Ali Bitchin (or Bitchnin or Pegelin) was a Christian renegade, probably of Venetian origin with a birth surname of Piccini or Piccinino. He became one of the principal corsairs of Algiers and was made head of the 'taifa', the corporate body of the city's corsair captains, in 1621. Becoming very wealthy, he built a mosque in Algiers and was said to own more than 500 Christian slaves, for whom he had a private prison constructed. Ali Bitchin seems to have been generally hostile to making peace with France, and he was glad of the opportunity to sack the Bastion of France in 1637. However, it was to be one of his last successes.[35]

In 1638 a combined squadron of Algerine and Tunisian corsair vessels collected at La Goletta near Tunis, with Ali Bitchin having overall command of the force. As the object was coastal raiding, the sixteen-ship squadron included a number of galleys. After a feint into the strait of Messina, Bitchin's force began raiding along the coast of Calabria, taking many Christian captives, before moving into the Adriatic Sea. Some sources claim Bitchin's cruise was undertaken on the orders of the Ottoman sultan, but this seems unlikely. Muslim corsairing in the

Adriatic was largely undertaken by ships from Tunis or Tripoli, or by local corsairs from Albanian and Greek ports. Nevertheless Algerine corsairs did sometimes cruise there, using the port of Valona in Albania as a forward base. Bitchin not only commanded the squadron, but owned many of the Algerine ships in it.

The Venetians had suffered particularly badly from pirate and corsair attacks in the first decades of the seventeenth century. Their ships seemed to be everybody's favourite target.[36] Despite promises from the Ottoman sultan, Venetian vessels were often attacked by Muslim corsairs, even when returning from Ottoman ports like Alexandria. From the Christian side English and Dutch pirates took many Venetian ships, while Christian corsairs like those licensed by the Knights of Malta also seized such ships if Muslim passengers or cargo were found on board. Bitchin's strike into the Adriatic in 1638 gave the Venetians a chance to hit back at their tormentors. A Venetian naval squadron under Antonio Marino Cappello set off in pursuit of the raiders, but when a storm delayed the Venetians Bitchin took his ships into the Ottoman port of Valona. Fired on by the Ottoman forts when he approached the harbour entrance, Cappello established a blockade of the port. This lasted for a month, but when Cappello learned in early August that an Ottoman naval squadron was approaching, he decided to take decisive action. The Venetians forced their way into Valona harbour and seized the sixteen Algerine and Tunisian corsair vessels. Fifteen were sunk and one sent to Venice as a prize. Many of the corsairs were killed, but Ali Bitchin and others fled ashore. The Venetians freed several thousand Christian captives, although others had already been landed in the town. The disaster at Valona was the worst blow the Algerines had suffered since their defeat in the strait of Gibraltar in 1618.[37]

Among the galley slaves in Ali Bitchin's fleet was Francis Knight, an English merchant who had been captured by Algerine corsairs in December 1631. He was one of the Christian slaves lodged ashore in Valona and he was left in his place of confinement when Bitchin and other corsairs fled inland after the Venetian attack. Later, in October, he and other slaves managed to escape at night. Knight and his group of escapees were a suitably cosmopolitan cross-section of Christian slaves held by the Barbary corsairs: four Englishmen (including Knight), a Welshman, a man from the island of Jersey, two Frenchmen, a Spaniard, a Majorcan, a Neapolitan, a Greek and a Maltese boy. Getting to the coast, they stole a boat and headed southwards along the Albanian coast until they eventually reached Venetian-held Corfu. Knight later went to Venice and got passage back to England, where he arrived in 1639. In the following year he published an account of his seven years' captivity in Algiers.[38]

Ottoman sultan Murad IV was campaigning against the Persians when news reached him of the Venetian attack on Valona. In his initial fury he wanted to declare war on Venice, but the Persian war had priority. At the end of 1638 Murad took Baghdad from the Persians and made peace with them in the following year. By then his anger against the Venetians had diminished and his advisers had all received lavish bribes from the Serene Republic to convince the sultan that it would be better to preserve peace. Murad died in 1640, but his successor Ibrahim would one day launch a war against the Venetians when he invaded their island of Crete.

Sultan Murad was not the only Muslim angered by the disaster at Valona. Ali Bitchin and other Algerine corsair captains took the view that the Ottoman forces at Valona had not given adequate protection to their ships. They wanted the Ottoman sultan to compensate them for their losses. The Ottoman government refused this request, saying that as the corsairs had not been in the sultan's service at the time of the battle, he was under no obligation to compensate them. The Barbary corsairs generally ignored most orders sent to them from Istanbul, so it seemed unreasonable of them to expect financial support from the sultan if one of their private ventures ended in disaster.

The defeat at Valona was a serious blow to the regency of Algiers and its government was now more amenable to the idea of making peace with France. A treaty was finally agreed in the summer of 1640. The French were to pay a large annual rent for the use of the Bastion of France, and that commercial outpost was to be treated as neutral ground if Algiers and France were at war. A mutual release of prisoners was promised, but it failed to take place, largely because Cardinal Richelieu decided in 1641 not to ratify the treaty. After Richelieu's death in 1642, more pragmatic French ministers recognized the need for some agreement with Algiers as soon as possible. Almost 5,000 Frenchmen were said to be captives in Algiers. Because of its other commitments, the revived French navy could only spare a few galleys to patrol off the Barbary coast, and they could have little impact on an Algerine corsair fleet said to number around 50 sailing ships and a few galleys. By the end of 1642 a treaty with Algiers had been agreed, but it largely just repeated the provisions of earlier agreements, leaving areas of dispute for the future. However, France was deeply involved in the Thirty Years War which was still ravaging Europe and relations with the Barbary corsairs were not a priority.

While Christendom was distracted by its internal wars, Sultan Ibrahim decided it would be a good opportunity to launch a war against the Venetians, aiming to take the island of Crete from them. In 1644 Maltese corsairs had captured Ottoman ships in the Aegean Sea and they went to Crete to divide up their booty. The Venetian authorities on the island were said to have colluded with the corsairs, and this was the Ottoman excuse for war. To carry out his invasion of Crete, Ibrahim would have to assemble all naval forces available to the empire. For the first time in more than half a century, the Barbary corsairs would be called upon to provide a naval contingent for the Ottoman fleet. Some corsairs were happy to do so, but Ali Bitchin was not among them. He had not forgotten his losses in the Valona disaster, and he felt the Algerine corsairs should not assist the sultan without payment. Sultan Ibrahim was angered by this response. He sent an envoy to Algiers to tell the ruling pasha to execute Bitchin. Instead Bitchin raised a revolt in the city and the pasha and the envoy went into hiding. Bitchin's revolt upset the janissaries and they drove him out of Algiers, only for him to threaten to attack the city with an army of tribesmen. Eventually a settlement was reached. Bitchin returned to Algiers, the sultan sent him presents and a new pasha was sent from Istanbul. Shortly after the pasha's arrival in 1645 Ali Bitchin died unexpectedly. He was given a lavish funeral, but there were many rumours that he had been poisoned on orders from the sultan. Certainly there were no difficulties when Algiers was called upon to send ships to assist in Ibrahim's invasion of Crete later in the year.

Despite the treaties, many Frenchmen remained in Barbary captivity and numerous Algerine prisoners still rowed in the French galleys. In French court circles Father Vincent (now known as St Vincent de Paul) expressed concern about the continued suffering of French slaves in North Africa. Exploiting royal and noble patronage, he persuaded the French government in the late 1640s to allow the priests of his Lazarist order to take over the French consulates at Algiers and Tunis. If France could not yet deploy the necessary military and naval force to curb the activities of the Barbary corsairs, at least the French prisoners in the hands of the corsairs could receive the comforts of their religion.[39]

English captives in Barbary received more direct help from their government when in 1645 the new parliamentary rulers of England ordered an envoy to Algiers specifically charged with the task of ransoming slaves. Edmund Casson did not finally reach Algiers until September 1646, but he quickly agreed a new treaty with its ruler. The Algerines promised once again not to attack English ships and offered to free English captives. Casson composed a list of all relevant captives in Algiers, and it included slaves not just from England but from all over the British Isles. He listed 650 men, women and children in Algiers, with another 100 male slaves away on board the Algerine warships serving with the Ottoman fleet at Crete. As slaves were private property, Casson could only free them by agreeing ransoms with their owners. Many drove a hard bargain and prices varied considerably.

Men went for an average of £25–30, although Thomas Thomson of London commanded a ransom of over £65. Women and children cost more. Mary Ripley of London and her two children were ransomed for over £50; Alice Hayes of Edinburgh, Scotland, for £55; Mary Bruster of Youghal, Ireland, for £70; and Elizabeth Alwin of London for £80. Such high prices meant that Casson quickly used up the funds he had brought with him. He managed to free only 242 captives and sent them back to Britain. Half of these people came from south-west England, the area which had seen the most Barbary corsair raids, while another 30 per cent came from London, England's principal port. The rest came from all over the British Isles. Casson remained in Algiers until his death in 1654. Parliament sent him its thanks for obtaining the release of captives and for negotiating a treaty with the Algerines which did something to protect English shipping.[40]

France had struggled hard to avoid negotiating treaties direct with the Barbary corsairs and had paid a high price for that reluctance. The English and Dutch had won some benefits from their treaties with the corsairs in the 1620s, but as long as all the main European maritime powers were distracted by internal or external conflicts – civil wars in the British Isles and the Thirty Years War on the continent – the Barbary corsairs could largely continue their activities undisturbed. In the first half of the seventeenth century the corsairs of Algiers enjoyed their heyday, but they were not alone. For the first and last time they found a rival in Morocco, the famous corsair port of Salé.

SALÉ: A PIRATE REPUBLIC?

Neither corsairing itself nor corsairing backed by Muslims from Spain was new to Morocco in the early seventeenth century, but their scale had not been as significant as the corsair activities carried on by the Ottoman regencies of North Africa. The city of Tetouan, linked to the Mediterranean by the river Martil, had been a significant Muslim corsair base in the late fourteenth century, leading to its destruction by vengeful Spaniards around 1400. It was slowly rebuilt during the fifteenth century, particularly late in the century by an influx of Muslims fleeing the war in Granada.

One of these Muslim refugees was Ali al-Mandari, who came from Granada to Tetouan in 1491. He built up a corsair fleet which each summer took the *jihad fil-bahr*, the 'holy war at sea', to Spain's coasts and shipping. Al-Mandari married Fatimah bint Ali Rachid, daughter of the emir of Chefchaouen, an inland Moroccan town also settled by Muslim refugees from Granada. The aged Ali al-Mandari died in 1512, but his much younger wife continued to be the *hakima* or 'governess' of the Tetouan corsairs for another 30 years. This was a rare example of a woman leading the Muslim corsairs of Barbary.[41]

Tetouan, with its position near the strait of Gibraltar and the southern coasts of Spain, remained probably the most important base for Muslim corsairs in Morocco during the sixteenth century. The activities of the Morisco corsair al-Dughali from this port during the 1560s and 1570s have already been mentioned. In 1565 the Spanish commander Álvaro de Bazán led a daring raid which sank blockships at the entrance to the river Martil, but this successful operation did not stop corsairing from Tetouan for very long. Safi and Salé were also mentioned as Moroccan corsair bases during this period, the latter being used as a forward base for the Algerine corsairs in the 1580s when they came out into the Atlantic to attack the Canary Islands.

Nevertheless Moroccan corsair vessels were neither numerous nor built for other than coastal operations before 1600. When the Moroccan ruler Ahmad al-Mansur negotiated with Queen Elizabeth I of England for a possible alliance in the period 1600–1603, he proposed an

Anglo-Moroccan expedition to attack Spanish possessions in the Caribbean. Morocco would provide the soldiers, but as the country possessed no ocean-going vessels, all the ships for the expedition would have to be provided by the English.

The event which is said to have begun the rapid rise of Salé to corsair greatness in the early seventeenth century was the arrival of the Moriscos from Hornachos in Extremadura, Spain, in 1610. In Spain they had been a lawless and aggressive group, notorious as bandits. By bribes and threats they had largely discouraged intervention by the Spanish authorities. When the expulsion of the Moriscos was decreed, the Hornacheros had sufficient influence to leave on their own terms, taking their wealth and their weapons with them. The Spanish authorities were glad to see them go, but from their exile in Morocco the Hornacheros would cause Spain more trouble than when they resided in that country.[42]

The town of Hornachos is many miles inland and it had no links with the sea. Hence the Moriscos from that place had no natural predisposition towards corsairing. At Salé they could link up with an existing corsairing tradition, reinforced by connections with the Algerine corsairs, and to which was later added the maritime skills brought by English and Dutch pirates. Also some of the later Morisco arrivals in Salé were said to have come from Spanish ports such as Sanlucar de Barrameda and Cádiz. It was from these sources that the Hornacheros could obtain the maritime skills needed for corsair activities. The Hornacheros themselves provided the wealth to finance initial corsair operations, the armed men to serve as soldiers aboard ship, and a deep hatred of the Spanish Christians.

It is usual to speak of the new Moroccan corsairs as the Salé corsairs, but this is not entirely accurate. The city of Salé (known as Sala or Sla to locals) lies on the north bank of the river Bou Regreg. In the early seventeenth century it was a commercial centre which also had a reputation for Muslim piety. Its inhabitants did not welcome the Hornacheros as fellow Muslims. They viewed them as 'bad Muslims', corrupted by Spanish and Christian ways. Thus the newcomers were forced to settle on the south bank of the Bou Regreg near an old fortress (the Kasbah) which had originally been a watchtower or 'ribat'. This proved advantageous in one way since the best harbour near the mouth of the Bou Regreg was on the south bank of the river. There was a sandbank at the mouth of the river where it flowed into the Atlantic, but this also had its uses. The corsairs became masters of how to negotiate this navigational hazard, but their enemies would have difficulty getting past it to attack the corsair harbour.

Later Morisco refugees, known as the Andalusians, also settled on the south bank of the Bou Regreg, but in area just outside the Kasbah which became known as the Medina. Relations between the Hornacheros in the Kasbah and the Andalusians in the Medina were often difficult, but both groups were on even worse terms with the inhabitants of Salé across the river. Thus the Salé corsairs were in fact based in the area which is now the city of Rabat, the present-day capital of Morocco, not in what is still known as the city of Salé. This fact has led some writers to prefer the term Rabat-Salé corsairs, but it is probably best to stick to the label used by their Christian European victims in the seventeenth century, for whom they were always the Salé corsairs. For example, the English called them the Sallee or Sally pirates or rovers, and termed the three settlements at the mouth of the Bou Regreg old Salé (Salé), the castle (Kasbah) and new Salé (Medina).[43]

At the start of the seventeenth century there were other ports along the Atlantic coast of Morocco which also played host to corsairs and pirates, both Muslim and Christian. However, the Spanish had some success in taking control of them, securing Larache in 1610 and Mamora in 1614. English and Dutch pirates forced out of the latter port naturally moved to nearby Salé, with which many of them were already familiar. The European pirates assisted the Moroccan corsairs in their transition to square-rigged sailing ships, which were capable of much longer voyages to the Christian regions of Europe bordering the Atlantic Ocean. English pirates like Peter Easton and Dutch pirates like Claes Gerritszoon Compaen regularly used Salé as a base for their operations. However, the most famous pirate/corsair using the port was probably Jan Janszoon, who had 'turned Turk' at Algiers to become Murad Reis.

Janszoon had come to Salé from Algiers in 1620 and soon made his mark, becoming leader of the corsairs in his new home. In 1622 he was cruising in the English Channel looking for prizes. As the Dutch republic had recently agreed a treaty with Morocco, Janszoon decided to take his corsair vessel, flying the Moroccan flag, into a Dutch port to get supplies. He docked at Veere in the Zeeland province of the Netherlands. While Janszoon was there, the Dutch authorities sent his wife and family, whom he had left in the Netherlands, to see him. It was hoped the sight of them might convince Janszoon to give up his career as a Muslim corsair and return to his home country. The corsair captain was unmoved. Indeed, when he left Veere, the crew of his vessel had been boosted by a number of Dutch volunteers despite official Dutch efforts to stop them getting aboard. Janszoon had another wife and family in Morocco, and his sons, known as Abraham and Anthony van Sallee, would also become corsairs. Later, however, they changed sides and became settlers in the Dutch colony of Nieuw Amsterdam (now New York City) in North America.

In 1627, as already noted, Janszoon led the corsair attack on Iceland and brought back hundreds of Christian captives. However, the prisoners were taken to Algiers, which Janszoon was once again using as his principal base in preference to Salé. It was from Algiers that Janszoon took his corsair fleet to the south coast of Ireland in 1631 and took many Christian captives at Baltimore. After years of successful raiding, Janszoon's luck ran out in 1635 when he was captured by the Knights of Malta. He was their prisoner for a number of years, but by 1640 he was free again, having either escaped or been ransomed. Janszoon returned to Morocco and he was made governor of a fortress near the port of Safi. In 1640–41 he was visited by his daughter from his Dutch family, but after 1641 his career is unknown.[44]

If input from the Moriscos and from the European pirates gave a boost to corsairing at Salé, its development was also aided by changes in the political situation within Morocco. Just as the Ottoman regencies grew as corsair centres because they were no longer under close control from Istanbul, so did Salé increase its independent power as the Moroccan central government steadily lost authority after the death of Ahmad al-Mansur in 1603. Although nominally still under the control of Moulay Zidan, Ahmad's son, the corsair port became increasingly restive. Civil war ravaged Morocco and many localities escaped from central control. In 1627 the Salé corsairs finally broke with Zidan, refusing to pay him his 10 per cent cut of their earnings from corsairing. The city state was now run by its own governing council or 'diwan', controlled by the corsair captains, and the highest official was the elected admiral. The 10 per cent previously paid to Moulay Zidan now went into the city's treasury, which was further boosted by port and customs dues.

This 'pirate republic' at Salé has been romanticized by certain writers as a bastion of democratic liberty, where free-spirited pirates/corsairs escaped the rule of sultans or kings. This picture seems most unlikely.[45] The political structure of Salé as an independent city state was very similar to that existing in Algiers. The main difference was that in the Moroccan port there was no Turkish military elite whose janissary officers could dispute control of the city with the corsair captains. Far from being suffused with any spirit of brotherhood, the 'pirate republic' was always a fragile body, with many internal divisions: between Christian renegades and Moriscos; between Moriscos and the inhabitants of old Salé; and between Hornacheros and Andalusians within the Morisco community. Most importantly, it could only continue to exist for as long as Morocco continued to be disturbed by internal political turmoil.

One of the new local rulers thrown up by the civil wars in Morocco was Muhammad al-Ayyashi, a religious ascetic who was sworn to wage jihad against the Spanish and Portuguese outposts along the coasts of northern Morocco. Mamora was a particular object of his attacks after it was taken by the Spanish. In 1627 al-Ayyashi had helped the Salé corsairs escape the rule of Moulay Zidan and in return he expected them to assist him in his attacks on the infidels. For a time the corsairs were happy to oblige, but in 1631 they avoided helping al-Ayyashi in an assault on Mamora. He suspected that the corsairs, and particularly the Hornacheros, were now in contact with the Spanish, and he was right. Some Hornacheros had been trying to negotiate a return to Spain for their people, promising to hand over the Kasbah to the Spanish and give their corsair vessels to the Spanish navy. It was rumoured in 1633 that a secret treaty had been agreed between the two sides, but no concrete actions ever resulted. Nevertheless the corsairs had now added al-Ayyashi to the list of their enemies within Morocco.[46]

Outside Morocco, the Salé corsairs soon had even more foes as their corsairs spread their activities from the shores of Iberia to the coasts of France, England and Ireland, then to Iceland, and on across the Atlantic to the Newfoundland fishery. Yet the corsair vessels themselves were not particularly impressive. At the peaks of corsairing in the mid-1620s and mid-1630s, the Salé corsairs numbered 40 to 50 ships, of which only 20 had more than twelve guns. However, the vessels were heavily manned with armed men and usually hunted in groups, making it easy for them to overwhelm single merchant ships or to launch formidable raids on land. With a shallow draft so that they could pass over the sandbank at the mouth of the Bou Regreg, this also meant the corsairs could work close inshore. The vessels were also built for speed. The French admiral Tourville said the only ship that could catch a Salé corsair was a captured Salé corsair (although he did not say how the latter might be captured). The number of Salé corsairs at sea seems to have been closely related to political conditions in the home port: if there was conflict fewer corsairs put to sea, or if they did go out, they took their prizes back to other ports, chiefly Algiers. However, when the Salé corsairs were out in force, they were a formidable threat to their Christian enemies, as the English discovered in 1625.[47]

In the days of Queen Elizabeth I the English role in privateering had been that of predator and their Spanish victims had complained bitterly about attacks by English 'pirates'. After 1600 the English had a new experience: that of becoming the prey for the Algerine and Salé corsairs who were steadily extending their operations into the northern waters of the Atlantic Ocean. In 1625, the year King Charles I came to the throne, it was the 'Sallee Rovers' who were the principal threat to England's southern coasts and shipping.

In the spring of 1625 at least 30 Salé corsairs were said to be cruising in the English Channel, off the Isles of Scilly and in the Bristol Channel. They were particularly hunting English ships setting out for Newfoundland at the start of that year's fishing season. English warships were sent to hunt the corsairs, but they were unable to catch their fast-sailing vessels. During the summer the Salé corsairs even occupied Lundy Island for a fortnight to act as a base for their operations in the Bristol Channel. In one daring raid on southern Cornwall the corsairs came ashore in Mount's Bay and seized 70 men, women and children attending Sunday service in a church. As well as land raids, the corsairs captured many English ships and by the end of 1625 there were said to be at least 1,000 English captives held in Salé.[48]

Some robust English naval response might have been expected to this series of corsair attacks, but King Charles had gone to war with Spain and hoped for Moroccan assistance in a proposed Anglo-Dutch attack on the Spanish port of Cádiz. Instead of attacking Salé, the king sent an envoy, John Harrison, to Morocco, and Harrison hoped to raise a force of Morisco soldiers for use against the Spanish. Harrison's mission was unsuccessful, just like the English attack on Cádiz, but the

English government remained reluctant to take strong action against the Salé corsairs while England was still at war with Spain.

In 1627 Harrison made another visit to Morocco. A peace treaty was agreed between Salé and the English, with Harrison providing a quantity of arms and ammunition in exchange for the release of some English captives.[49] With the end of England's war with Spain in 1629, English relations with Salé became increasingly hostile once more. In 1631 a well armed English merchant ship even captured a Salé corsair vessel. The prize was sold at Cádiz, as was its crew, who became slaves of the Spanish. Such actions caused fury among the corsairs and soon their attacks on English shipping were once more on the increase.

The European maritime states were now beginning to launch direct attacks on the port of Salé in retaliation for their losses. In 1629 Isaac de Razilly, a Knight of Malta and a French naval commander, led a French squadron which bombarded Salé and was said to have sunk three corsair vessels.[50] He made another attack in the following year and ransomed some French captives. A treaty between France and Morocco was later agreed, but since the sultan had no control over Salé, this did not solve the corsair problem, so in 1635 there was another French naval attack on Salé. Like the preceding operations, it had little long-term impact on the corsairs.

As Salé corsair attacks on English shipping increased in the mid-1630s, King Charles I began thinking about emulating the French and launching a direct attack on the corsair port. The plan of attack was drawn up by Giles Penn, whose grandson William Penn would one day establish the colony of Pennsylvania in North America. Giles Penn had 30 years of experience in the Morocco trade and he was acquainted with many of the local leaders, including Muhammad al-Ayyashi, who was known to the English as 'the Saint'. Penn first passed his plan for an expedition to the English government in the summer of 1636. At the end of that year he renewed his call for action, saying that the political situation in Salé made the success of such an attack even more likely. Not only were the Moriscos in conflict with al-Ayyashi, but they had fallen out among themselves. The Andalusians had driven the Hornacheros out of the Kasbah. If an English squadron aided 'the Saint', it seemed the Moriscos of Salé could be defeated.

Penn was insistent that an English squadron should be sent out to Morocco as early as possible in 1637. It should reach Salé before the corsairs could set out to attack English vessels leaving for the New-foundland fishery. Penn was aware of the navigational problems at the mouth of the Bou Regreg river, so he advised that the English force should take a number of small vessels, known as pinnaces, with it. They could patrol the channels around the sandbank and make a naval block-ade of the port more effective.

Penn's plans for the expedition to Salé were accepted by the English government, but his offer to command the expedition was not. Instead the command was given to William Rainborow, who as a merchant ship captain had famously beaten off an attack by the galleys of the Knights of Malta in 1628. Now an officer in the king's navy, Rainborow set off for Morocco with four men of war and the promise that two pinnaces would be sent out later.[51] Arriving off Salé in March 1637, Rainborow soon made conduct with al-Ayyashi, whose forces were besieging the Moriscos on the south bank of the river. A naval blockade of the river mouth was begun, but without the pinnaces, Rainborow could not stop corsair vessels getting through at night.

By June the pinnaces had arrived and the English naval blockade became more effective. In addition Rainborow landed men and cannon at old Salé on the north bank of the river which was held by al-Ayyashi. From there fire could be directed at the corsairs in the harbour on the south bank, doing serious damage to enemy vessels. With enemies on all sides, the Andalusians were now becoming increasingly desperate. First they tried to make a separate peace with the English, which Rainborow refused. The next proposal was for peace with both the English and al-Ayyashi, but the latter's terms were unacceptable. The Andalusians then thought of giving up their city to the Spanish, but in the end decided to offer submission to the sultan of Morocco. The English supported them in this decision, much to the annoyance of 'the Saint'. In return Rain-borow was given 300 English captives and could return to England declaring the expedition to have been a success. Although that success owed more to local Moroccan politics than the power of the English navy, Rainborow was emboldened to submit a plan for a naval expedi-tion against Algiers in 1638, but the government of Charles I had more important priorities as the political discontent within Britain increased.

In fact the sultan did not get control of Salé because his army was defeated by the Dalaiyya, a new power within Morocco. In 1641 the Dalaiyya defeated and killed al-Ayyashi. The Andalusians of Salé were now compelled to submit to the Dalaiyya, but for ten years the new rulers were content to leave the corsair port considerable autonomy as long as they received regular tribute payments. This situation ended in 1651 when a Dalaiyyan governor was installed in Salé and new policies were imposed. The corsair port was now as important for regular trade as for privateering, and Dutch and French consuls had been installed there. The Dutch were to achieve particularly close relations with the Dalaiyya during the 1650s.

Since 1600 not all Dutchmen finding their way to Morocco had been pirates and renegades. In 1610 a treaty had been agreed between the Dutch republic and Morocco, largely thanks to the work of a Moroccan Jew, Samuel Pallache.[52] Dutch trade with Morocco increased and after the Dutch returned to war with Spain in 1621, the two countries shared a common enemy. However, until some sort of order was restored in Morocco, trade relations were still difficult. The Dalaiyya seemed to have imposed this order by mid-century. The Dutch supplied guns, ammunition, naval stores and other goods to Morocco, and Moroccan corsairs were forbidden to attack their ships. However, Salé retained its links with the corsairs of Algiers, and the Algerine corsairs often sent their Dutch prizes and prisoners into Salé for sale. Dutch complaints about this were ignored by the Moroccan authorities. After 1660 the rule of the Dalaiyya was challenged within Morocco and in 1661 Salé escaped from their control, only to fall under the authority of the new power in northern Morocco, al-Khadr Ghailan, soon afterwards. In 1666 the Alawites defeated Ghailan and Salé submitted to them. The Alawites restored a strong central government to Morocco for the first time since 1603 and they were soon to take all the Moroccan corsairs under state control.[53]

During the first half of the seventeenth century, the corsairs of Morocco, like those of the Ottoman regencies in North Africa, had enjoyed a time of great power and prosperity. Largely freed from control by their overlords, their maritime strength was boosted by the new skills brought by Dutch and English pirates. While the power of Spain was beginning to wane, that of France, England and the Netherlands had not yet grown sufficiently to pose a serious challenge to the corsairs. If the French, English and Dutch had been prepared to co-operate in suppressing their common enemy, the Barbary corsairs, they might have had more impact. However, they preferred to look after their own individual interests, aiming to deflect the corsair attacks onto their rivals. As

Sir Thomas Roe said in 1624 after arranging the treaty between England and Algiers: 'It little concerns us to leave the French for prey: cormorants and wolves must have some food, else they will seize on anything.'[54] If co-operation between the maritime powers was not possible, they could only take effective action as individual states when their navies were strong enough and they had ceased fighting each other. These conditions did not begin to emerge until after 1660.

STOLEN CHRISTIANS

Perhaps the most famous Christian captive taken by the Barbary corsairs was Miguel de Cervantes Saavedra, only a humble soldier at the time of his captivity, but later to become Spain's greatest writer, the author of *Don Quixote*. He had fought as a soldier aboard one of the Christian galleys at the battle of Lepanto in 1571 and had received a number of wounds. One rendered his left hand useless, but Miguel still continued as a soldier in Don Juan of Austria's campaign for Tunis.[55]

In September 1575 Miguel Cervantes decided to return home to Spain from Italy. He embarked on the galley *Sol* at Naples, along with his brother Rodrigo, who was also a soldier. The galley was part of a four-ship squadron, under Sancho de Leyva, which was heading for Barcelona. Nearing the Spanish coast, the galleys were scattered by a sudden storm. Sailing alone, the *Sol* was attacked on 26 September 1575 by three Algerine corsair galleys under the Albanian renegade Arnaut Mami. After a fierce battle, the Spanish galley was captured. Then Leyva and the other three galleys came over the horizon and the corsairs quickly decided to flee with their prize.

After arrival at Algiers, Miguel's brother Rodrigo was one of the Christian captives reserved as booty for Ramadan Pasha, the ruler of Algiers. Miguel Cervantes became the slave of Dali Mami, a Greek renegade who was Arnaut Mami's second-in-command. Unfortunately two letters of recommendation from high Spanish officials, the duke of Sessa and Don Juan himself, were found on Miguel. They caused his new master to consider Miguel a person of some importance. His ransom was set at 500 gold escudos, which seemed to be far more than the Cervantes family could ever pay for his release.

This misapprehension about his status and the fact that his left hand was useless saved Miguel from the more onerous tasks that might be imposed on Christian slaves, such as rowing in the corsair galleys. In early 1576 Miguel and some other Christian captives tried to escape to the Spanish outpost of Oran on the North African coast, but the local Muslim who had agreed to guide them disappeared after only a few days' march. Returning to Algiers, the prisoners were lucky to escape with only beatings as punishment for their venture.

In August 1577 Rodrigo, Miguel's brother, was liberated by Mercedarian monks who had come to Algiers to ransom captives. The money they brought on behalf of the Cervantes family could only ransom one brother and Miguel decided it should be Rodrigo. However, before Rodrigo returned to Spain, he agreed to send a ship to pick up Miguel if he could escape from Algiers. The vessel was to come from Majorca and Miguel would wait for its arrival at a garden near the coast on the outskirts of Algiers. Other Christian slaves joined Miguel in his hiding place, but the expected vessel failed to appear in September 1577. Then the prisoners were betrayed to the authorities and taken back into the city. The Christian gardener who had provided them with their hiding place was tortured to death, but Miguel's punishment was to be imprisoned in chains for five months.

In March 1578 Miguel set about trying to arrange another escape. A messenger was to take a letter to the Spanish governor of Oran asking for his assistance in arranging the escape. Unfortunately the messenger was intercepted on his way to Oran and was brought back to Algiers, where he was executed by being impaled. Miguel was sentenced to receive 2,000 blows of the bastinado as his punishment. This involved being beaten with a rod on the soles of the feet or on the stomach. Such a large number of blows would usually cause the victim to die in agony. Yet Miguel never received this brutal punishment. He seems to have had protectors among some of the most important Christian renegades in Algiers, who still viewed him as an important person who was more useful kept alive.

In September 1579 Miguel organized his fourth escape attempt, arranging for a vessel to be prepared by a Christian renegade in Algiers who wished to return to Spain with the escaping captives. However, this plot was exposed and Miguel was once again threatened with death, only to escape with five months' imprisonment in chains. In this period Dali Mami sold the troublesome Miguel Cervantes to Hassan Veneziano Pasha, the ruler of Algiers, for 500 gold escudos.

Now Trinitarian monks appeared in Algiers on a mission to redeem Christian captives by paying their ransoms. They had the sum of 280 escudos earmarked for Miguel's ransom, but Hassan would not take so low a sum. He threatened to send Miguel to be sold as a slave in Istanbul, a fate much feared by Christian captives in North Africa since it severely reduced their chances of ever being ransomed. Eventually the redemptionist friars borrowed another 220 escudos from merchants in Algiers, so Hassan got rid of his captive for 500 escudos, a sum it had originally been thought Miguel could never raise. Miguel Cervantes was freed in 1580 after just over five years as a captive, and his experiences in Algiers were used in some of his later writings, including the captive's tale in *Don Quixote*. The reasons for the exceptional leniency shown to Miguel after his repeated escape attempts have bemused his various biographers, but if his captivity experience was unusual in this respect, his other sufferings in Algiers were shared with tens of thousands of other Christians who were captured by the Barbary corsairs over the years.

Estimates of the total number of Christians captured by the Barbary corsairs have always been highly speculative, even those made by contemporary European observers in the seventeenth century. One commentator claimed that between 500,000 and 600,000 Christian slaves were sold in the markets of Algiers alone between 1520 and 1660. Others claimed that all the Barbary corsairs, in ports stretching from Salé to Tripoli, captured a million Christians between 1530 and 1640. At any one time in the first half of the seventeenth century, Algiers was said to have 25–30,000 Christian slaves, with thousands of Christian renegades also in residence in the city. More recent speculative calculations have claimed that 1–1.25 million Christians were captured by the Barbary corsairs between 1530 and 1780.[56]

The period from 1580 to 1660 was probably the peak time for 'Christian stealing' by the Barbary corsairs. Greater numbers of Christians may have been taken by the fleets of Barbarossa in the first half of the sixteenth century, but these operations involved the Barbary corsairs being part of the main Ottoman fleet. Only a portion of the Christian captives seized by such expeditions would have been taken back to Barbary ports. Despite claims of 500,000 to one million Christians being taken by the Barbary corsairs during their heyday, a recent analysis has produced a much lower figure for Christians captured in the period 1574 to 1644.[57]

According to these calculations, around 140,000 Christians were captured at sea in ships during this period, while perhaps 40,000 Christians were captured ashore by corsair land raids on coastal regions. These figures would give an overall total of around 180,000 Christians taken between 1574 and 1644. However, this particular calculation is based solely on the activities of the corsairs of the Ottoman regencies of Algiers, Tunis and Tripoli. If captives taken by the Moroccan corsairs were added, using a conservative estimate of 20,000 prisoners, then the grand total would be around 200,000 Christians taken by the Barbary corsairs in the 70-year period between 1574 and 1644. While a good deal less than the more inflated estimates, this is still a significant number of Christian captives, averaging almost 3,000 enslaved every year.

Land raids by the Barbary corsairs in the first half of the seventeenth century did not bring in such large numbers of Christian captives as in the days of Barbarossa. Then thousands of men, women and children might be swept up from Christian towns and villages along the coast. A century later, the take was more likely to be numbered in the hundreds. Although the Barbary corsairs could now range far out into the Atlantic, their land raids in places like England, Ireland and Iceland were more notable for their novelty than the large numbers of captives taken. At best they might only yield a few hundred Christian slaves. Atlantic areas nearer to the home ports of the corsairs might yield better pickings. For example, in 1613 corsairs took 700 captives from the Canary Islands, while in 1619 a raid on the island of Madeira yielded 1,200 Christian captives.

Yet the Mediterranean coasts of Christendom still remained the favourite area for land raids by the Barbary corsairs. Of around 100 corsair attacks on Christian coasts known to have taken place in the period between 1574 and 1644, 75 per cent took place in the Mediterranean, with the island of Sicily as the main target (41 attacks). Other regularly visited areas were Calabria in southern Italy and the islands of Sardinia and Corsica. However, by the early 1600s much of the coastline of Christian countries in the western and central Mediterranean had been deserted by its inhabitants because of the past ravages of the corsairs. The numbers of Christians captured were often low, and when Tunisian corsairs took between 400 and 500 Christian prisoners in a land raid near Palermo in Sicily in 1619, it was regarded as a major success.[58]

The large number of Christian captives taken in ships at sea after 1600 was largely due to the steady increase of French, Dutch, and English shipping in the Mediterranean Sea in those years. The newcomers provided more and richer targets for the corsairs than the Spanish, Portuguese and Italian ships which had been their main prey in the sixteenth century. It has been calculated that the Barbary corsairs may have taken an average of 200 ships each year in the first half of the seventeenth century, while in the late sixteenth century their average take may have been only 50 ships each year. The prizes could be even greater at certain times. Dutch sources alleged that in a period of less than nine months between 17 March and 13 November 1620, the corsairs of Algiers, Tunis and Salé captured some 174 ships. Of these prizes, the flags of 106 vessels are known: 76 were Dutch, fifteen French, ten English, and five belonged to Spain or the German ports of Hamburg and Lübeck. Although the crews of most of these vessels were probably small, if one allows an average crew of ten men this would mean the Barbary corsairs took at least 1,740 Christian captives at sea in this short period.[59]

Once carried to the Barbary ports, a proportion of the Christian captives were taken by the government while the rest were sold to private buyers. The publicly owned slaves often endured the worst suffering, being used for hard labour such as rowing in galleys or working on construction projects. They were usually housed in prisons known as 'bagnios' (literally 'bathhouse', which is said to derive from such a place being used as a slave prison in Istanbul). Private slaves might be housed there too, but they were more likely to be held on the property of their owners. Private slaves might have slightly less onerous work, although the common task of doing agricultural work on the country estates of their owners was often exhausting labour.[60] Prisoners who had any skills, such as tailoring, might be allowed to work at them in the city, with most profits going to their owners. Women captives were more likely to be used for household work. Many of the new slaves, both public and private, would not survive their first year in captivity, dying of disease, starvation or ill treatment. Even when they became used to their new existence, many Christian slaves later perished in the frequent outbreaks of plague on the Barbary coast.[61]

The Christian slaves taken by the Barbary regencies did not exist in isolation. They were part of the wider slave economy of the Ottoman empire. The rulers of Algiers, Tunis and Tripoli often sent attractive young girls and boys as gifts to the Ottoman sultan. Both groups were likely to be compelled to convert to Islam. The girls would remain in the harem, while the boys might be trained in the imperial schools to become Ottoman officials. If there was a flow from west to east, there was also movement in the opposite direction. Russians and Poles captured by the Crimean Tatars might eventually end up in Algiers or Tunis. One of the most violent disputes between Christian captives in the bagnios of Algiers was between Catholic Spaniards and Orthodox Russians.[62] The various nationalities in captivity learned to converse with each other and with their masters in 'lingua franca', a Mediterranean-wide pidgin tongue largely based on Italian.

The switch from galleys to square-rigged sailing ships by the Barbary corsairs during the first half of the seventeenth century changed the maritime use of Christian slaves. Some galleys were retained, but most were not, thus reducing the demand for rowers. Christian captives still featured in the crews of Barbary corsairs, but they were fewer in number and included more skilled sailors rather than just strong men who could pull on an oar. Ali Bitchin, for example, made great efforts to build up a stock of captive Christian sailors who could man his corsairs. Equally in demand were ship's carpenters and other maritime specialists who could work in the shipyards of the corsair ports. They came under heavy pressure to convert to Islam and remain as renegades, but even if they continued to be Christians they were well rewarded for their work. The Barbary corsairs were very reluctant to give up for ransom their captured Christian sailors and shipbuilders.

Rich and powerful Christian slaves rarely remained in corsair hands for long. Their family and friends back home usually provided their ransoms quickly. Some, however, might be unlucky. Ali Bitchin in Algiers kept two captive Knights of Malta for years as an insurance policy. If he was captured by the Christians, the knights could be exchanged to secure his release. Many of the private arrangements for ransoming Christian captives were carried out via the wide-ranging merchant networks around the Mediterranean, especially those maintained by Jewish merchants. For example, Jews in Algiers might work with Jews in Livorno, Italy, to ensure the transfer of ransom for Christian captives. Although Jews had been expelled from the Spanish mainland in 1492, they remained in Spain's North African outposts for several more centuries, maintaining links with Jews in neighbouring Muslim territory to assist in ransoming captives and gathering intelligence.[63] Although the European consuls in the Barbary ports were usually involved in ransoming captives on behalf of their home governments, they also helped in private ransom deals, taking a suitable fee for their work. Those Christian captives without the means to be privately ransomed could only hope to be freed during the periodic visits to the Barbary ports by those Christian religious orders specifically charged with the task of freeing Christians from Muslim captivity.

The two principal Catholic orders were the Order of the Holy Trinity (or Trinitarians), established in 1198, and the Order of Our Lady of Mercy (or Mercedarians), established in 1218. They had a long history of freeing Christians from Muslim captivity, especially in the context of the Reconquista in Spain and Portugal. Their two main sources of money for ransoms were contributions given by families to free specific captives and general collections of alms which could be used to free any worthy Catholic captives. Once sufficient money had been collected the monks would organize a mission to one of the corsair ports, with permission from both Christian and Muslim rulers, and carry out negotiations for the release of captives. Between 1575 and 1769 at least 82 such missions to Barbary are known to have taken place, leading to the freeing of some 15,000 captives. Protestants were not held in large numbers in Barbary until the seventeenth century and, although Protestant churches made collections on their behalf, most ransoming was done by governments rather than religious organizations.[64]

When the redemptionist orders were sent to negotiate the release of Spanish captives, they were given clear guidelines by the Spanish government. Protestants, Christian renegades and military deserters were not to be freed by them. Preference was to be given to obtaining the release of government officials (civil, military and naval); persons employed in the Indies fleet (which brought back treasure from the Americas); Catholic clergy; and women and children, since the latter were thought to be particularly vulnerable to Muslim pressure forcing them to convert to Islam. Outside these particular groups, preference should be given to freeing young and fit people, not the old and sick. Naturally the Muslim authorities tried to force the friars to agree to ransom the old and sick before moving on to more youthful captives.[65]

An example of a rich catch for the Barbary corsairs was the group of passengers aboard an Indies fleet vessel captured by Algerine corsairs in the summer of 1663, when it was heading out to the Americas. Among the high officials were José de Luna y Peralta of Navarre, a member of the Council of Castile, who was going to carry out an inspection tour in Hispaniola, and Pedro de Carabajal y Vargas of Trujillo in Extremadura, also of the Council of Castile and a judge in Santo Domingo, who was travelling with his wife. They were freed in less than a year for very high ransoms. Luna y Peralta was rescued for 40,000 reales, while Carabajal and his wife were freed for 28,000 reales each. The captain of their ship, Juan de Villalobos, was freed for 24,000 reales. At this time the average ransom for a Christian captive was 1,000 to 2,000 reales. The Spanish government paid these ransoms from money collected in the New World to pay for the redemption of Christian captives held in the Old. Villalobos was an unlucky mariner. His ship was captured once more by Algerine corsairs in 1667. His ransom was again 24,000 reales, but this time only one-third of the sum came from public funds; he had to pay the rest himself.[66]

When collecting funds in Catholic Christendom, the redemptionist orders always portrayed captivity in Barbary as hell on earth, with threats to both the body and the soul of the Christian prisoner. Only Muslim brutality could compel true Christians to give up their faith and convert to Islam. The monks also cast their own visits in a heroic light, giving the impression that they were in terrible danger when visiting infidel lands. In fact they were usually quite safe. Barbary rulers welcomed them warmly because of the large cash injections they brought to the local economy. Not only did the friars have to pay for ransomed slaves, but they also had to pay the export tax on them and suitable gratuities to local government officials. However, occasionally things went wrong, and one of the worst incidents took place in Algiers in 1609.

In that year three Trinitarian friars went to Algiers and ransomed 130 captives. They were preparing to return to Spain when news reached the city that the eight-year-old daughter of a powerful citizen of Algiers was being detained in Sardinia, although her ransom from captivity had been arranged, on the grounds that she had expressed a desire to convert to Christianity. Her father persuaded the ruler of Algiers to keep the Trinitarians in the city until the girl was returned. Spanish officials pressured the church to do this, but they had no success. The girl was now said to be a Christian and so could not be sent to Algiers. Instead high-ranking Muslim captives in Spain were offered in exchange for the friars and their ransomed captives, but this offer was rejected. It seems the friars remained in Algiers and presumably died in prison there. Because of this affair the Spanish government banned all travel to Algiers. Only in 1617 did they have to alter their position. Two ships carrying 500 Spanish soldiers were captured off Cartagena by Algerine corsairs. The government now ordered the redemptionist friars to defer a planned mission to Morocco and go to Algiers instead in 1618 in an effort to ransom the captured troops.[67]

For those Christian captives not privately ransomed or freed by the efforts of the two redemptionist orders, the outlook was usually grim. A few managed to escape, but most seemed likely to spend the rest of their lives as prisoners of the Muslims. In this situation, it was only natural that some of the Christian captives should decide to 'turn Turk' by converting to Islam. Although many Christian renegades had been captured as children or teenagers and brought up as Muslims, there were also adults who, willingly or unwillingly, went over to the Muslim side. One such was Juan Rodelgas, a Spanish soldier who was one of those captured off Cartagena in 1617 by the Algerine corsairs. The troop transports had left Cartagena bound for Naples, but off Cape Palos they were intercepted by a corsair squadron under the Dutch renegade Suleiman Reis (De Veenboer). The Spanish put up a fierce fight but were eventually overwhelmed. After being sold as a slave at Algiers, Juan worked for several years on his master's estate as an agricultural labourer. He then tried to escape to Oran, but was recaptured, bastinadoed and imprisoned in chains for six months. After this experience, Juan 'turned Turk', becoming a Muslim and taking the name Mustapha.

Juan now joined the crew of an Algerine corsair commanded by Mami Reis, a Morisco who had been expelled from Granada. This ship joined a fleet of two dozen other Algerine corsairs which sailed to the strait of Gibraltar. A French ship was captured and Juan's ship was detailed to escort the prize to Tetouan in Morocco. However, near that port the prize and escort were chased by two Christian corsairs and had to be run ashore. In January 1622 Juan made his way to the corsair port of Salé and met the famous Dutch renegade Jan Janszoon, alias Murad Reis. He joined Janszoon's ship, which sailed on a corsair cruise off the Canary Islands in company with another vessel. Juan listed the crew of Janszoon's ship as nine Dutch renegades (including Janszoon), thirteen Dutch Christian slaves, eighteen Moriscos, 24 'Turks and Moors' and one Spanish renegade (himself). Three ships were captured, but since one was a Dutch vessel Janszoon only stripped it of arms and cargo before sending it on its way. The Dutch renegade then took his ships to the south coast of the island of Grand Canary and sent a party ashore to get water. Juan was among that party and took the opportunity to slip away. He surrendered to the local authorities and was sent to Las Palmas to be tried by the Inquisition of the Canaries. His trial began in October 1622. Juan claimed that he had been forced to convert, had always remained a Christian at heart, and now wished to be a Christian once more. The court took a favourable view, imposing only minor punishment, and in 1623 Juan was able to return to Spain.[68]

Although some Christian renegades took the opportunity to return to Christendom when it was offered, many more made new lives in Muslim North Africa. In detailed studies of the Canary Islands it has been established that between 1569 and 1650 more than 2,000 people were abducted in Barbary corsair raids. The careers of some 470 of these have been followed, and 234 of them are known to have become renegades (almost half), including four monks. Only a handful of the renegades ever returned to Christian territory. The friar Pierre Dan, who visited Algiers in the 1630s, claimed that the city then held around 25,000 Christian slaves and 9,000 Christian renegades, both male and female. He believed there were 10,000 Christian captives and 4,500 renegades at Tunis, while Tripoli had around 500 Christian captives and 100 renegades. Clearly many Christian captives preferred, willingly or unwillingly, to become Muslims rather than endure continued slavery.[69]

Whatever money they derived from captured Christian ships and cargoes, it was always 'Christian stealing' that was the main concern of the Barbary corsairs. Their Christian captives could either provide a valuable labour force in North Africa, be sold on within the wider slave economy of the Ottoman empire, or be ransomed for hard cash and returned to Christendom. The number of Christian captives in Barbary probably peaked in the first half of the seventeenth century, but this was never just a one-way traffic. Christians took Muslim captives as well. What became of them?

IN INFIDEL HANDS

Ahmad ibn Muhammad ibn al-Qadi was the scribe of Moulay Ahmad al-Mansur, the ruler of Morocco. In the summer of 1586 he embarked on a voyage from Tetouan to Egypt, where he intended to undertake Islamic scholarly studies. In late July the ship in which he was travelling was intercepted by Christian corsairs from Malta, and he was taken to that island as a captive. There, as al-Qadi later wrote, he was in 'great distress as a result of hunger and cold, unendurable things, beatings and other indescribable tortures'. Nevertheless the Muslim captive was permitted to write letters to his brother in Fez and to his employer Ahmad al-Mansur asking for assistance.

His brother led a family deputation to Marrakesh to put further pressure on the Moroccan ruler, but Ahmad al-Mansur needed little persuasion to take an interest in the matter. He sent letters to the governor of Tetouan and to a wealthy merchant in that city ordering them to do all in their power to secure the release of al-Qadi. Once the royal interest in the release of al-Qadi became known, the Maltese corsairs immediately raised the ransom demanded for their captive to 20,000 ounces of gold.

The emissary who took this demand to Morocco was a Spaniard who was also authorized to ask that al-Qadi should be exchanged for the man's son as part of the deal. The son had been among the defeated Christians captured at the battle of Alcazarquivir in 1578. Ahmad al-Mansur agreed to pay the ransom money demanded and the al-Qadi family took the Christian slave to Tetouan where he was handed over to his father. Al-Qadi was released in June 1587, and he was back in Marrakesh by the end of July, thanking his employer for his generosity and telling the story of his experiences during his eleven months as a captive in infidel hands.[70]

Ahmad al-Qadi was a very lucky man. He had a rich and powerful supporter in the ruler of Morocco and this ensured he was quickly ransomed from his Christian captors. Also, al-Qadi was not a member of a Muslim group that the Christians would be reluctant to send home even for ransom. Such unfortunate people included captive corsair captains and Muslim prisoners who had become experienced rowers in Christian galleys. Most Muslims who fell into Christian hands were not as fortunate as al-Qadi and spent long years as slaves. Unlike the

Christians, Muslims had no religious organizations specifically charged with the task of recovering Muslim captives from Christendom. However, it was generally accepted that Muslim rulers should make some effort to recover their lost subjects, while Muslim merchants often used their Christian trading contacts to help in ransoming captives. Even European consuls might help to recover Muslim captives if they were paid a suitable fee.[71]

Sometimes Christian countries sent back Muslim prisoners in the hope of improving relations with the Ottoman sultan or the rulers of the Barbary regencies. When Sir Francis Drake raided Spanish possessions in the Caribbean in 1585, he freed a number of Muslim slaves whose Spanish masters had taken them across the Atlantic. These men were sent to England and in late 1586 the English government hired Laurence Aldersey to take them to Istanbul in his ship. Aldersey left England in February 1587 carrying 100 freed Muslim slaves. Their arrival in Istanbul won thanks from the Ottoman sultan to the English ambassador. The Dutch took similar action. In 1604 they freed Muslim slaves from a Spanish galley captured at Sluis in Flanders. These slaves were sent, without ransom, as a gift to the ruler of Algiers. The Dutch asked him to release a similar number of Dutch captives without asking for ransom payments.[72]

These Muslim captives came into the hands of north European Christians largely by accident. Most Muslim prisoners were held in the Christian countries bordering the Mediterranean Sea. Just how many were there? In the past it was generally assumed that Muslim slaves in Christian hands were far fewer than the numbers of Christian slaves held in North Africa. Recently, however, claims have been made that much greater numbers of Muslim slaves were held by the Christians than was previously thought. It has been alleged that between 1500 and 1800 some 500,000 Muslims were brought to Italy as slaves. To this has been added the claim that a similar number of Muslims may have been enslaved in Spain and Portugal during the same period. Thus a million Muslims are supposed to have been enslaved in Italy and Iberia at the same time that a million Christians were being enslaved by the Barbary corsairs. This equivalence is a little too neat, and the new figures for Muslim slaves held by the Christians seem considerably exaggerated.[73]

Certainly large numbers of Muslims were taken prisoner during the wars between the Spanish empire and the Ottoman empire in the

Mediterranean during the sixteenth century, but the numbers captured must have fallen considerably after the end of those wars in 1580. For reasons already noted, the period between 1580 and 1660 probably saw a peak in 'Christian stealing' by the Barbary corsairs, but in this period of 'private war' rather than inter-state conflict in the Mediterranean the Christians simply could not have taken equivalent numbers of Muslim prisoners. For one thing there was a lack of Christian predators. Even if one adds together the galleys of the Knights of Malta and the Knights of St Stephen to the ships of the Christian corsairs licensed by the knights and other Christian rulers, the total in the peak period of activity would only be 50 vessels, and they would not all be at sea at the same time. Similarly, there were proportionately fewer targets for Christian predators than for Muslim corsairs. There were fewer Muslim merchant ships and the coastal populations of Muslim lands were less numerous than those of Christendom.

A more conservative view of the numbers of Muslims taken by Christians in the Mediterranean between the late sixteenth century and mid-seventeenth century gives figures which are much lower than the numbers of Christians taken by Muslims during the same period. It has been calculated that between 1568 and 1645 some 50,000 Muslims were taken captive, with perhaps 30,000 of these captives being taken by the galleys of the Knights of Malta and the Knights of St Stephen or by Christian corsairs licensed by those military religious orders. Many of the other captives would have been taken by Spanish naval galleys and Spanish corsairs. Thus 50,000 Muslims may have been captured to set against 200,000 Christians taken by the Barbary corsairs, as noted earlier for a slightly shorter period (1574–1644). If these figures are correct, then the Muslim total is only 25 per cent of the Christian total. If one applied these percentages to the whole period between 1500 and 1800, assuming a total of around one million Christians taken by the Barbary corsairs, then around 250,000 Muslims would have been taken by the Christians. This seems a more plausible figure than the claims of equivalent captures by the two sides.[74]

Although land raids by Christian maritime forces were fewer than those made by Muslim corsairs, there were a number of successful attacks in the early seventeenth century. However, these were not just confined to the Barbary coast. Christian raiders also came ashore on Muslim territory in Greece, the islands of the Aegean Sea and in Anatolia. Of the attacks in North Africa, the Knights of St Stephen had important successes, taking 1,500 Muslim captives at Bona in 1607 and 480 at Bougie in 1610. Spanish galleys from Naples, accompanied by the galleys of the Knights of Malta, raided the Kerkennah Islands off the coast of Tunisia in 1611 and took away almost 500 Muslim captives. The Christian raids were not always successful. In 1601 Spanish raiders had taken several hundred Muslim captives from Hammamet in Tunisia, but a new attack in August 1605 ended in disaster. The Spanish squadron was accompanied by galleys of the Knights of Malta, but after an initial success the landing force was driven into the sea by Muslim defenders. Over 1,000 Christians were said to have been killed or drowned, including the Spanish commander Adelantado de Castilla. In any case, land raids by Christian maritime forces seem to have declined in number after 1613. Between 1568 and 1634 the Knights of St Stephen may have captured about 14,000 Muslims, with perhaps one-third taken in land raids and two-thirds taken on captured ships.[75]

Muslim corsairs usually sought to avoid encounters with Christian warships and concentrated on capturing vulnerable and numerous Christian merchant ships. Since one of the reasons for the existence of the Christian military religious orders was to suppress Muslim corsairs, the Knights of Malta and the Knights of St Stephen had to give hunting down enemy corsair vessels at least equal status with preying on Muslim merchant shipping. This led them to concentrate on different operations in different parts of the Mediterranean. In the western and central areas of that sea Muslim merchant ships were relatively few in number, but Muslim corsairs were numerous, so they were the priority target. In the eastern Mediterranean enemy corsairs were largely absent, but there was more Muslim merchant shipping, with the regular convoys between Istanbul and Alexandria in Egypt a particularly lucrative target for Christian predators. Rich cargoes and wealthy passengers for ransom were most likely to be taken in this area. Between 1563 and 1665 the Knights of St Stephen are thought to have taken at least 300 Muslim ships in the Mediterranean, including 24 galleys and 32 galliots.[76]

Muslim passengers and sailors taken in the eastern Mediterranean were more likely to be ransomed than the Barbary corsair captains and their crews taken in the western and central parts of that sea. The Spanish in particular tried to avoid handing back corsair officers or seamen at whatever price. The pool of maritime talent in the Barbary ports was not unlimited, so this policy aimed to reduce it even further. Captured corsairs usually ended up rowing in the Christian galleys, but even this offered a possibility of being freed if the vessel was taken by a Muslim corsair. Hence Philip II of Spain ordered that captured corsair captains should be imprisoned in castles well away from the coast. As the English and the Dutch appeared in the Mediterranean in increasing numbers after 1600, they began to take Muslim captives, including corsairs. These prisoners were generally not taken to England or the Netherlands, but were sold in Christian slave markets such as those at Cádiz, Livorno and Malta.

Christian renegades found aboard corsair vessels were sometimes liable to immediate execution, but most were sent for trial before the inquisition, which had tribunals in most Mediterranean Catholic countries. These tribunals handed out widely differing punishments to renegades. Those men who had apparently been forced to convert to Islam and now expressed a sincere desire to return to Christianity might receive lenient treatment. Those who showed continued commitment to Islam were sent to the galleys or, in extreme cases, sentenced to death, which usually meant being burned at the stake. Executing corsairs, whether renegade or not, was always a risky business, since the Barbary corsairs usually retaliated by executing one of their Christian captives.

For those Muslim captives who had the option of being ransomed, prices depended largely on their age. Details of some redemption prices for Muslim captives at Malta are known for the period 1590 to 1620. Young men (under the age of 30) were the most valuable, with redemption prices starting at 200 écus de Malta and usually going much higher. Young women captives, who were much fewer in number, also commanded high ransoms. A Muslim woman known as Argentina, aged 25, was ransomed for 400 écus. The Muslim woman Aicha, originally from Cairo, went for only 48 écus, but she was 75 years of age. In 1602 Ahmed ben Abdallah, aged 70, was ransomed with his grandson, aged eighteen, for a total of 614 écus – 566 for the young man and 48 for the old man. Money was not always the medium of exchange. In 1625 some 23 Muslim slaves were swapped for a large cargo of wheat to be delivered at Malta.[77]

Unransomed Muslim captives might be used in a variety of occupations, including agricultural labour and domestic service. At the end of the sixteenth century Muslim slaves made up at least 1 per cent of the population of Sicily, being kept mainly in the towns, while on the Italian mainland Cardinal d'Este had fifty Muslim slaves working at his villa in Tivoli near Rome in 1584. Around 1600 there were said to be 5,000 Muslim captives at Malta and a similar number at Livorno, while Naples was believed to have 10,000 Muslim captives in the city. Spain's principal Mediterranean ports may have held even larger numbers of Muslim captives.[78]

As in Barbary, slaves were also likely to be used for heavy work such as construction and mining. In Spain the mercury mines at Almaden were particularly dreaded, with many slaves dying from overwork and mercury poisoning.[79] Yet it was always rowing service in the Christian galleys which seemed most significant for both sides. In 1602 the eight Spanish galleys of Sicily had 1,413 rowers, of whom 629 were Muslim slaves; in 1604 the six galleys of Tuscany (including the Knights of St Stephen) had 1,487 rowers, of whom 772 were Muslim slaves; and in 1632 the six galleys of the Knights of Malta employed 1,284 Muslim slaves as rowers.[80] Sicily and Tuscany could complete their rowing crews by using Christian convicts, but Malta was largely dependent on Muslim captives to row its galleys.[81] Muslim captives feared being sent to the galleys, while their Christian captors were reluctant to set them free once they had become experienced rowers.

In contrast to the thousands of Christian renegades in North Africa, few Muslim captives ever converted to Christianity. Even if Muslims did become Christians, it did not necessarily improve their position. If a Christian galley slave 'turned Turk', he usually escaped from the rowing bench. A Muslim galley slave who converted to Christianity usually did not. Christian renegades like Uluj Ali could have brilliant careers in the Islamic world. Muslim converts in Christendom could only expect marginal improvement in their conditions. Like the Muslims, the Christians saw young captives, male and female, as prime targets for conversion. Perhaps the most famous of these young converts was Padre Ottomano of Malta. In 1644 the galleys of the Knights of Malta captured an Ottoman ship in the eastern Mediterranean which carried some important passengers. Among the prisoners were women from the sultan's harem and a young boy with them. The Christian captors decided the boy, known as Osman, was a son of Sultan Ibrahim, although there was no real proof. When the other passengers were ransomed, the boy was kept in Malta. At first the boy resisted attempts to convert him to

Christianity, but finally he accepted baptism at the age of thirteen, with the grand master of the Knights of Malta standing as his godfather. There was some talk of returning the boy to the Ottomans if the sultan would give the island of Rhodes back to the knights, but once he became a Christian he could not be compelled to return. In 1658 the convert joined the Dominican order and became known as Padre Ottomano. Eventually becoming the head of the Dominicans in Malta, the padre died during an outbreak of plague in the island in 1675.[82]

Padre Ottomano enjoyed some European notoriety in the mid-seventeenth century, but perhaps the most famous Muslim captive to convert to Christianity was Leo Africanus in the first half of the sixteenth century. Born Hassan ibn Muhammad al-Wazzan al-Fasi in Granada, his parents fled to Morocco after the Spanish conquest. He was brought up in Fez and by 1517 he was undertaking diplomatic missions for the ruler of Morocco. In 1518 Hassan was on a voyage from Egypt to Tunis when his ship was captured by Christian corsairs. Although his captors were said to be Spanish, Hassan was taken to Rome and imprisoned there. His great knowledge of the Islamic world was appreciated by the papal court and he was presented to Pope Leo x. Eventually deciding to become a Christian, Hassan was baptized in 1520 and became known as Leo Africanus. In 1526 he completed his great work on the geography and history of Africa (meaning mainly North Africa), and Europeans were to treat it as one of the most important books on the subject well into the seventeenth century. It is said that Leo later left Italy and returned to Muslim North Africa. Although for a Muslim to convert to Christianity was usually punishable by death, Leo seems to have returned to his earlier religious allegiance without undue trouble and he probably died at Tunis in 1554.[83]

In April 1682 a released Moroccan captive accompanied the French ambassador on his journey to visit Moulay Ismail, the ruler of that country. The freed captive brought letters from Moroccan captives rowing in the French galleys. They described the great misery they suffered at the hands of 'those French dogs': hunger, nakedness, beatings, chains, curses against Islam and the Prophet, and the horrible suffering of rowing. Ismail had sent his own ambassador to France to bring back Moroccan captives, but the perfidious French had sent the galleys to sea with all the able-bodied slaves, so the ambassador could only recover some old and sick slaves left in port. The captives begged Ismail to deliver them from the 'misery of strange [lands]' and reminded him how Allah rewarded those who were charitable to the helpless and needy.[84]

Moulay Ismail was the most powerful ruler of Morocco since the death of Ahmad al-Mansur in 1603, yet even he would have trouble influencing the resurgent France of Louis xiv. In the first half of the seventeenth century the Barbary corsairs had enjoyed their heyday, with the corsairs of Salé, Algiers, Tunis and Tripoli ranging widely along the coasts of Christendom, but after 1660 the navies of France, England and the Netherlands grew in power and effectiveness. The Barbary corsairs would have to adapt to a new world in which the advantage had passed to the Christian maritime powers.

An imaginative portrayal of Father Le Vacher's execution at Algiers in 1683; engraving by Jan Luyken, 1698. (Le Vacher in fact stood in front of the cannon's muzzle and was blown to bits.)

THREE

Facing the Sea Powers
1660–1720

ALGIERS 1683

The activities of the Barbary corsairs had reached a peak in the first half of the seventeenth century. From the 1650s the corsairs had to face increasing opposition from the three rising sea powers of Christian Europe: France, England and the Netherlands. These states soon possessed large fleets of well armed warships, far more powerful than any naval forces the Barbary corsairs could deploy. Yet the corsairs would show they could stand up to the new rulers of the oceans. They could even force the Christian sea powers to accept treaties which recognized that the corsairs remained significant players in international maritime conflict.

Since France was the Christian European country with the longest record of co-operation with the Ottoman sultan, dating back to the early sixteenth century, it might be thought the French would find it easier to have good relations with the Barbary corsairs. However, this proved not to be the case. The French were at war with the Barbary regencies in the mid-seventeenth century almost as often as the Dutch and the English. Indeed in the 1680s they were to inflict more destruction on Algiers, the most powerful of the regencies, than any Christian power had previously done.

Relations between Algiers and France were strained because neither side made much effort to carry out prisoner exchanges called for in earlier treaties between them. In the 1670s at least 2,000 Muslim slaves were rowers in France's naval galleys in the Mediterranean.[1] The ruler of Algiers expected the French to return those of them who came from his territory. The French largely ignored his requests, only releasing old and sick Muslim slaves, few of whom came from Algiers. Having made peace with the Dutch in 1679 and being about to make peace with the English, the ruler of Algiers decided he could risk a declaration of war on France in late 1681 in order to force the French to meet their treaty obligations.

King Louis XIV of France was outraged that Algiers should dare to declare war on him. He was even more furious when the Algerines captured twenty French ships, including a naval frigate, in November 1681 alone. Consulting with his chief minister Colbert, Louis now decided the French navy should deliver a knockout blow to Algiers. To achieve this outcome a new weapon would be deployed, the bomb vessel.

The mortar had long been a staple of siege artillery on land, sending explosive mortar bombs over city walls to fall on the houses and other buildings within. In 1680 Colbert's protégé, Bernard Renau d'Eliçagary, a naval constructor, had proposed sending the mortar to sea for the first time. In 1681 the first such mortar-carrying vessel was launched and Louis XIV was keen to try out his new weapon in an attack on the city of Algiers.[2]

In the summer of 1682 Admiral Abraham Duquesne led a French fleet of eleven ships of the line and five of the new bomb vessels to Algiers.[3] Hadji Mohammed, the ruler of Algiers (known as the 'dey' from 1671), asked his son-in-law Baba Hassan, the real ruler of the city, to enter into negotiations with the French admiral, but Duquesne refused to parley. Instead he sent dozens of mortar bombs crashing into the city. The initial shock was considerable. Many buildings were destroyed or damaged and around 500 people were killed. An Algerine attempt to attack the bomb vessels was defeated, but it soon became clear that technical problems were limiting the bombardment. Some mortar bombs failed to reach the city, while much gunpowder was found to be of poor quality. Recovering from their initial shock, the Algerines refused to beg for mercy and Duquesne's fleet finally sailed away with little achieved.

Duquesne returned in the summer of 1683 with a fleet of thirteen ships of the line and seven bomb vessels. Baba Hassan had now replaced his father-in-law as dey of Algiers, and he sent the French consul in the city, the Lazarist priest Jean Le Vacher, to see if negotiations could be opened with the French admiral. Duquesne refused to talk and soon his bomb vessels unleashed a bombardment. Lessons had been learned from the previous attack. Each bomb vessel was now moored on a long hawser so that it could lie off during the day, avoiding Algerine gunfire, and be hauled in close at night, when most of the bombardments took place. Once again many buildings in Algiers were destroyed or damaged, but casualties were fewer than in 1682 because many of the population fled the city when the French fleet first arrived.

Baba Hassan was desperate to stop the bombardment. He freed more than 500 Christian slaves without ransom and sent them out to the French fleet. Duquesne agreed to a truce and a number of Algerine hostages were taken aboard his ships to guarantee the cessation of hostilities. In addition Duquesne now demanded that the ruler of Algiers should pay an indemnity to the French, amounting to 700,000 livres. Baba Hassan claimed he did not have that amount of money and Duquesne threatened to open fire again.

Among the hostages aboard the French fleet was Hadji Husayn, better known by his nickname of Mezzomorto (literally 'half dead'). There were many fanciful tales of how he acquired this name, but the most likely was that in a clash with the Spaniards he had been so badly wounded that he had been given up for dead, only to make an amazing recovery. Possibly a Christian renegade originally from the island of Majorca, Mezzomorto was a leading corsair captain in Algiers and headed the 'taifa', the corporate body of corsair captains in the city.

Mezzomorto convinced Duquesne that he could gather the large sum of money for the indemnity faster than Baba Hassan. The French admiral unwisely set him free and put him ashore to collect the money. Instead Mezzomorto gathered together the corsairs and some of the janissary soldiers and swiftly overthrew and killed Baba Hassan. Mezzomorto became the new dey of Algiers. He sent a message to Duquesne warning that if the bombardment was renewed, French people in Algiers would be executed. The admiral ignored the threat and soon mortar bombs were exploding within the city once more.

Father Le Vacher, old, sick and crippled, was taken from the French consulate and carried to a gun battery on the mole protecting the harbour of Algiers. For 36 years Le Vacher had worked to help and to free Christian captives in both Tunis and Algiers, winning the respect of both Christians and Muslims. Now he was placed in front of one of the cannons pointing out to sea. At a given signal, the gun was fired and Le Vacher was blown to pieces. Duquesne was not impressed. The mortar bombs continued to fall on Algiers. In reply Mezzomorto destroyed twenty more Frenchmen at the cannon's mouth.[4]

A stalemate had been reached. Bombs fell and French hostages died, but neither side showed any inclination to negotiate. Eventually, with his supply of mortar bombs almost exhausted, Duquesne sailed away, having achieved nothing but further destruction in the city of Algiers.

Any 'shock and awe' the use of the new bomb vessels might have caused at their first attack on Algiers in 1682 had been lost when they were used again in 1683. As the English consul, Philip Rycaut, observed of the Algerines in 1683: 'see how little these people value French bombs.'[5]

Louis XIV was frustrated by the failure of his new weapon to either destroy Algiers or force the Algerines to make peace on his terms. He might have ordered further attacks on the city, but the changing diplomatic situation in Europe meant that by the start of 1684 he needed peace with Algiers so he could use his fleet elsewhere. The port of Genoa was to be the first Christian target for the French bomb vessels.

In April 1684 Admiral Tourville, once a Knight of Malta and Duquesne's second in command in the bombardments of 1682 and 1683, arrived at Algiers. He was accompanied by an envoy from the Ottoman sultan, who was also keen for peace to be agreed between Algiers and France. In only a few weeks Mezzomorto agreed a treaty with France, which largely just reaffirmed the terms of earlier treaties between the two powers. There was no question of Algiers paying any indemnity to the French. However, Algiers did agree to send an ambassador to the court of Louis XIV at Versailles later in the year. The Sun King could tell his subjects that this was an act of submission by his beaten Algerine foes, but few people really believed that Algiers had been defeated.

Before the 1680s were over there would be further bloody clashes between France and Algiers, including another French bombardment of the city in 1688, and further treaties. The Algerines would be forced to recognize the superior naval power of France, promising not to attack French merchant ships, but they would only accept treaties which still allowed them to continue corsair attacks on other, lesser maritime states of Christian Europe. Louis XIV had to agree to this compromise and put away his idea of totally destroying the Barbary corsairs. In the eighteenth century Voltaire would write that the French bombardment of Algiers was one of the greatest achievements of Louis XIV's reign, but the corsairs of Algiers survived and continued with their predatory activities.

BATTLE FLEETS AND BASES

One reason the Barbary corsairs flourished in the first half of the seventeenth century was because their ships faced little opposition or distraction. On the one hand, the naval forces of Christian Europe were weak and often busy fighting each other. On the other, the Ottoman sultan was involved in no major naval conflict in the Mediterranean during this period and so he did not need to call for the support of the ships of the Barbary corsairs. Both these situations began to change from mid-century.

In 1645 Sultan Ibrahim ordered an Ottoman invasion of the island of Crete, one of the few remaining overseas possessions of Venice. At first it seemed the Ottoman conquest would be an easy one, with most of the island overrun quickly. However, the capital, Candia (now Irak-lion), held out against the invaders and was to continue to do so for the next 24 years, only surrendering in 1669. It was to be one of the longest sieges in history. That Venice could support continued resistance by the Cretan port for so long was because its navy actively disputed control of the Aegean Sea with the Ottomans. The naval struggle swung back and forth, but the Venetians usually had the advantage. However, while the Venetians won most of the battles, it was the Ottomans who in the end won the war, taking complete control of Crete in 1669.

Initial Venetian naval successes in this war owed much to the fact that the Serene Republic was ready to supplement its galley fleet with increasing numbers of armed sailing ships. Some were its own warships, but others were vessels hired from the French, the Dutch and the English. The Ottomans were slower to make sailing warships a major part of their fleet, but once they decided to do so, the support of the Barbary corsairs became even more important. By the mid-seventeenth century most corsair vessels sent out by the Barbary regencies of Algiers, Tunis and Tripoli were sailing ships and not galleys. The corsairs had fast, well armed sailing ships and much experience in their use. From 1645 the Barbary corsairs usually sent a squadron of such ships to join the main Ottoman fleet each year. The average number sent was twelve to eighteen vessels, but in 1649 it went as high as 26 ships.[6] Between the Ottoman capture of Tunis in 1574 and the invasion of Crete in 1645, the Ottoman sultan had little need to call for naval assistance from the Barbary corsairs and their ever-growing fleets could raid far and wide. Now the sultan needed their support, which necessarily led to some reduction in their corsair activities.

Another new constraint on those activities was the growing power of the navies of the main Christian European sea powers: France, England and the Netherlands. However, at first this new power was not primarily directed at Barbary. Even after its crushing defeat of the Spanish navy at the battle of the Downs in 1639, the Dutch navy remained primarily concerned with the war against Spain until a final peace between the two sides was achieved in 1648. Cardinal Richelieu had begun the rebuilding of the French navy in the 1620s, but from 1635 France was at war with Spain (until 1659) and fighting the Spanish was the first priority of the French fleet. Thus although both the Dutch and the French navies were growing in size, chasing Barbary corsairs was not their first concern. Indeed, since Spain was their principal opponent, they could even expect some support from the Barbary states for whom Spain was always the 'eternal enemy'. Only when the Dutch and the French had made peace with Spain would they take a greater interest in opposing the Barbary corsairs.

It was England, the third of the rising sea powers, that was to be the first to unleash its growing naval power on the Barbary corsairs. During the civil wars that ravaged the British Isles during the 1640s, the English navy had largely supported parliament and not the king. Once the royalists had been beaten, the new parliamentary regime went to war with its Dutch commercial rivals. The first Anglo-Dutch war (1652–4) saw a major expansion of the English navy and a number of hard-fought victories over the Dutch. To fund this naval expansion, one of the sources of finance used was a levy originally imposed on English trade by parliament to raise money to ransom English captives in the hands of the Barbary corsairs. Some £70,000 had been collected, but only £11,000 went to ransom captives; the rest was spent on building up the navy.[7]

After the war with the Dutch was concluded in 1654, Robert Blake, 'general-at-sea' and Puritan zealot, was ordered to sail to the Mediterranean with a fleet of 24 ships, the largest battle fleet England had ever sent to that region. He was to re-establish respect for the English flag among the countries of the western and central Mediterranean, whether Catholic or Muslim, and the Barbary corsairs in particular were to be forced to reaffirm earlier treaties with England. In his secret orders, Blake was told to prepare for an assault on the Spanish without declaration of war. Normally any state that was going to war with Spain could expect at least passive support from the Barbary states. However, Blake was to mismanage his mission so badly that not only did he alienate the Barbary corsairs, but he also almost provoked a war between England and the Ottoman empire, before he took any action against Spain.

Algiers, traditionally the most aggressive of the Barbary regencies, was prepared at first to have good relations with Admiral Blake, and it was with Tunis, not previously a major corsair foe of the English, that he picked a quarrel. The origins of the dispute went back to 1651 when the master of an English merchant ship had agreed to take 32 prominent Tunisians from Tunis to Smyrna (now Izmir). However, soon after leaving Tunis, the ship encountered the galleys of the Knights of Malta and the Tunisian passengers were taken captive. Indeed it was alleged that the English sea captain had sold his Muslim passengers to the knights. After the English merchants in Tunis narrowly escaped being slaughtered by an angry mob, the ruler of Tunis demanded that the English government obtain the freedom of the Tunisian captives held in Malta. Eventually the Knights of Malta agreed to ransom their prisoners, but the sum they demanded was high. In 1654 the Tunisians seized an English merchant ship as a way of putting pressure on the English government to secure the freedom of the captives in Malta. Blake had been told to obtain the release of the ship and its crew, as well as an apology from the Tunisians for their conduct.

Early in 1655 Blake brought his fleet to Tunis and entered into negotiations. These proved unsatisfactory and the admiral decided to take his ships to Sardinia to get fresh water. As he left the gulf of Tunis, Blake looked into Porto Farina. After several successful Christian attacks on La Goletta early in the century, Porto Farina had been chosen as a more secure base for the Tunisian fleet. Ships were built there and it was protected by a castle and other fortifications. When Blake visited the port, he saw nine ships fitting out, including the English prize whose release he had been ordered to obtain. This squadron of nine armed sailing ships was intended to be the contribution of Tunis to the main Ottoman fleet for this year's campaign in the war of Crete. Officially these were the sultan's ships and not Barbary corsairs about to set out on a cruise. Blake was aware of this crucial distinction, but paid it little attention.

Blake brought his fleet back to Tunis in March 1655 and engaged in further fruitless negotiations. Feeling he had been insulted and believing God's hand was guiding him, Blake decided to exceed his orders by launching an attack on the Tunisian squadron at Porto Farina. A daring attack was made and all nine ships were burned with small loss to the English attackers. The defending fortifications were silenced and it was claimed that this was the first time warships had ever defeated forts. Whether this was true or not, Blake's tactical victory was soon to turn into a strategic defeat. The ruler of Tunis was not intimidated by Blake's action. Since the ships were for the sultan's service, he would be compensated by the sultan. An angry Ottoman sultan would in turn get his compensation by a levy on the English merchants of the Levant Company who traded in his empire.[8]

It has been claimed that Blake's destruction of the Tunisian squadron helped the Venetians win an important victory over the Ottoman fleet in the Dardanelles later in 1655, but this seems unlikely. The usual rendezvous for the main Ottoman fleet, from Istanbul, and the ships from the Barbary corsairs was at the island of Chios in the Aegean Sea. The fleet from Istanbul was defeated by the Venetians before it could even reach Chios. Even had it got through, there would have been no Barbary corsair ships waiting. After Blake's attack at Tunis, both Algiers and Tunis kept all their warships at home to increase their security. No Barbary squadron aided the sultan in 1655.[9] The English ambassador in Istanbul was left to calm the sultan's rage at Blake's attack and keep him from declaring war on England.

With regard to the original cause of the dispute with Tunis, the captive Tunisians were finally released in April 1657 after the English paid their ransom to the Knights of Malta. Despite this, the ruler of Tunis was slow to release the 72 English men and women he had taken as hostages. In February 1658 Captain John Stoakes took six English warships to Tunis and secured the release of the English captives, although he still had to pay a considerable ransom for them. A treaty of peace was agreed between Tunis and England, and it included a clause that Tunisian passengers on English ships were never to be handed over to an enemy. This settlement might have been achieved in 1655 had Blake been more adroit and less aggressive. England's navy was an increasingly powerful weapon, but its first major deployment against the Barbary corsairs had a less than impressive outcome.

When England openly made war on Spain in 1656 Blake tried to intercept the treasure fleet from the New World, but failed. He then attempted to blockade the Spanish naval base at Cádiz, but found it hard to keep his fleet supplied. As Portugal was also at war with Spain, Lisbon and the Portuguese outpost of Tangier in North Africa could provide some support, but most of Blake's supplies still had to come all the way from England. The Muslim states of North Africa, the traditional foes of Spain, seem to have been unready to assist Blake after his recent actions against them. In 1657 Blake defeated a Spanish fleet at Santa Cruz in the Canaries, but he captured little treasure and died later in the year. His successors commanding the English fleet off Spain began look-ing round for a suitable base in the area that might be permanently occupied by England. Tangier seemed a possibility, while others thought Gibraltar might be taken from Spain. However, nothing was done about the suggestions. At the end of the 1650s peace was declared between England and Spain, while Captain Stoakes visited Algiers, Tunis and Tripoli to secure new treaties with the Barbary regencies. The English battle fleet then returned home. England's first use of her new naval power against the Barbary corsairs had been only a qualified success and ideas of securing a base in the region remained just ideas. After King Charles II was restored to his throne in England in 1660, things were to change rapidly.

Rulers of the Barbary states often complained that English govern-ments showed little interest in ransoming the English slaves they had captured. In part this was because most captives from the British Isles were just ordinary folk, sailors or fishermen, plus a few men, women and children picked up from raids on coastal villages. Nobody was in a hurry to find the money to set them free. Spanish or Italian aristocrats, often government officials, important churchmen and naval or military com-manders, often fell into Barbary corsair hands. Their governments and friends rushed to get them ransomed as soon as possible, willingly paying heavy ransoms. Few English aristocrats or important officials ever went to the Mediterranean, and if they did, they were conveyed in warships or heavily armed merchantmen which were largely immune to corsair attack. In 1659, for the first (and only) time, an important aristocrat from the British Isles was captured by the Barbary corsairs.

The victim was in fact Irish, not English. Murrough O'Brien, earl of Inchiquin, came from an old Irish family but had been brought up as a Protestant. When the civil wars came to Ireland in the 1640s he was a dedicated opponent of the Catholic rebels, first serving the king, then parliament, then the king again. Eventually Inchiquin became a royalist exile and served in the French army during the 1650s. In 1657 he surprised many by converting to Catholicism. In November 1659 he and his son William were sailing from France to Portugal to take up commands in the Portuguese army, but their ship was attacked by a corsair from Algiers. In the ensuing battle the Algerine ship was victorious and Inchiquin's son lost an eye. Father and son were imprisoned at Algiers, but Inchiquin was released after Charles II came to the throne in England in 1660 so as to speed the payment of the ransom for both of them. Charles II ordered the ransom to be paid quickly and before the year was out, the son rejoined his father. The O'Briens, father and son, were ransomed for a total of 7,500 dollars (3,750 dollars each). To free the 72 English captives from Tunis in 1658 Captain Stoakes had paid a total of 11,250 dollars (an average of just over 156 dollars each). Like their Spanish and Italian counterparts, aristocrats from the British Isles would not be allowed to endure Barbary captivity for very long. William O'Brien later succeeded to his father's title and returned to North Africa as governor of Tangier, the new English outpost in the region.[10]

In 1661 it was announced that King Charles II was to marry the Portuguese princess Catherine of Braganza. As part of her dowry Portugal would hand over to England the port of Bombay (now Mumbai) in India and the port of Tangier on the coast of North Africa near the strait of Gibraltar. Although it later became one of the great cities of British India, Bombay excited little interest in English government circles in 1661. It was soon out of royal hands, being passed on to England's East India Company as a trading base. Tangier, on the other hand, was thought to be a most important acquisition by the English crown.

England would now have its own base on the Atlantic entrance to the Mediterranean. Tangier would be a naval base from which an English fleet could watch Spain and France, while also taking action to curb the activities of the Barbary corsairs. It would also become a great commercial port which would bring great wealth to England. It might even be the first foothold of a land empire England would establish across North Africa. All these hopes were to prove false. Within only a few years, Tangier would become as much an expensive burden to England as North African outposts like Oran and Mazagan were to Spain and Portugal.[11]

In June 1661 Edward Montagu, earl of Sandwich, led an English fleet of seventeen ships south to the Mediterranean. He was ordered to try to agree a new treaty with Algiers; to keep an eye on a Dutch fleet under Michiel de Ruyter, also said to be going to Algiers; to take possession of Tangier for England; and to bring Princess Catherine to England to marry King Charles. Sandwich's visit to Algiers was fruitless, ending in a half-hearted English bombardment of the city. De Ruyter had better luck, agreeing a new treaty with the Algerines. Sandwich duly took possession of Tangier in January 1662; installed its new governor, the earl of Peterborough, with a garrison of 2,500 troops; and then collected Princess Catherine from Lisbon.

An English squadron was left in the Mediterranean under the command of Sir John Lawson. In late 1662 he achieved the feat of obtaining new treaties with all the three Barbary regencies, Algiers, Tunis and Tripoli, within the space of a few months. As usual the treaty with Algiers was the most important and it included a significant innovation. In future all English merchant ships coming to the Mediterranean would carry a special pass confirming their English identity. This could be shown if the ship was stopped by Algerine corsairs and according to the treaty, the corsairs would then let the ship sail on unmolested. This system of passes was to encounter various problems in the future, not least that foreign vessels often carried forged English passes. Nevertheless it remained in force until the early nineteenth century.

After its rebirth under the rule of Cardinal Richelieu, the navy of France declined once more during the 1650s. By 1660 the French navy had barely twenty ships. Then Louis xiv began his personal rule. The young monarch and his minister Colbert were to oversee a dramatic increase in French naval power, such that by the late 1680s the French navy was larger than that of the Netherlands and was the equal of that of England. What implications would this growth of French sea power have for the Barbary corsairs?

Building a large French navy required an expansion of its officer corps. Where could France obtain significant numbers of experienced sea officers? The Knights of Malta were to prove a valuable source of such men. A majority of the knights came from France and every year the knights sent out their galleys to continue the 'eternal war' against the Muslims, thus giving them unrivalled experience of maritime combat in the Mediterranean. This link between the French navy and the Knights of Malta was to last until the French Revolution in 1789 and it was to produce such great admirals as Tourville, de Grasse and Suffren. One of the first important French naval commanders to come from the ranks of the knights was Jean-Paul de Saumeur, better known as Chevalier Paul.[12] After a less than successful visit to the Barbary regencies in 1659 he called for a rapid increase in France's Mediterranean squadron, and even asked that sailors from the Atlantic coast should man it since sailors from the Mediterranean coast of France had been oppressed by the Barbary corsairs for so long that they had little faith in being able to defeat them.

After England took possession of Tangier in 1662, and de Ruyter was said to be looking for a possible Dutch base on the coast of North Africa, the French felt bound to seek such a base for themselves. It was true they already had a commercial outpost, known as the Bastion of France, on that coast near La Calle, paying an annual tribute to Algiers for its use. However, this was a vulnerable position, and the outpost had been sacked several times by the Algerines in the past. A better port, nearer to Algiers, would be useful as a French naval base.

Colbert urged Louis xiv to take aggressive action against Algiers. Chevalier Paul warned the king not to underestimate the Algerines, who had a fleet of 40–50 ships, each carrying between 25 and 40 guns. Colbert was dismissive, pointing out that Algiers had been struck by a severe outbreak of plague in 1663 which had killed many of the population and demoralized the survivors. Finally it was decided in 1664 to send an expedition to Algerine territory to seize a port on the North African coast. François de Vendôme, duc de Beaufort, sailed with fourteen ships of the line, eight galleys and other ships, carrying 5,000 troops. Seven galleys from the Knights of Malta were added to the force. It appeared a formidable force, but its command structure was somewhat confused. Chevalier Paul was Beaufort's naval adviser, but Louis xiv had written privately to Vivonne, commander of the French galleys, telling him to keep an eye on Beaufort lest the duke do something rash. In addition, the commander of the troops would not obey any naval orders with regard to their employment.

Chevalier Paul suggested the capture of the port of Bougie, which had a good harbour and a small garrison. Beaufort ignored this advice and decided instead to attack Djidjelli, which had an inferior harbour and was dominated by neighbouring hills. It seems possible Beaufort believed rumours that the local Berbers were ready to rise up against their Turkish masters in Algiers. The French troops were duly landed and easily took the town. Artillery was landed and the soldiers moved inland to take up positions in the hills. However, the local Berbers proved to be unfriendly and soon joined with forces arriving from Algiers in an attack on the invaders. The French were forced to re-embark hurriedly, leaving behind more than 40 artillery pieces and over 400 prisoners, many of whom later 'turned Turk'. To add to the misfortune, on the voyage back to France one of the troop transports capsized, drowning all on board.[13]

Djidjelli had been a humiliating defeat for the French. In 1665 Beaufort and Chevalier Paul took a French squadron along the Barbary coast and destroyed a number of Algerine ships in several engagements, but this did little to restore French prestige. In 1666 France joined the Dutch side in the second Anglo-Dutch war (1665–7) and French naval effort was moved out of the Mediterranean. The battle fleets of England, France and the Netherlands now fought in the English Channel and the Barbary corsairs were left largely undisturbed to continue their attacks on Christian shipping, including ships from the countries with which they had supposedly signed peace treaties. England might have secured a base on the North African coast at Tangier, but as yet the growing strength of the three main Christian sea powers had failed to make much lasting impression on the Barbary corsairs.

THE BATTLE WITH ALGIERS

France's duc de Beaufort somewhat redeemed his humiliating defeat at Djidjelli by finding a glorious death fighting the Turks in the last stages of the seemingly endless siege of Candia in 1669. His body, and the French force he was leading, was then returned to France. The other foreign Christian contingents, especially the knights from Malta, also departed. Finally the last Venetian commander surrendered Candia to the Ottomans on terms and went home. The war for Crete was finally over. With the Ottoman sultan finally victorious, the Barbary corsairs would no longer have to send ships every year to join his fleet, and would have more vessels available to go in pursuit of Christian merchant ships. Algiers in particular stepped up its corsairing activities, just as the European sea powers, at peace with each other once more, were sending their battle fleets back to the Mediterranean.

An English fleet under Sir Thomas Allin commenced operations against Algiers in late 1669. Allin's attempts to blockade Algiers necessitated a base much closer to the enemy city than Tangier, so he used anchorages in the Balearic Islands with the tacit approval of the Spanish. Tangier was, however, useful as a base for English warships mounting patrols in or near the strait of Gibraltar, a favourite cruising ground of the Algerine corsairs. An increasing number of corsairs were captured or driven ashore, while even large groups of them might be driven off by single English warships.

An example of the latter event occurred in December 1669. Earlier that year the famous artist and engraver Wenceslaus Hollar had been sent by King Charles II to Tangier to make drawings of the crown's newest possession. After completing his work, Hollar boarded the warship HMS *Mary Rose*, commanded by Captain John Kempthorne, for passage back to England. First Kempthorne had to convoy some merchant ships to Cádiz in Spain. Soon after the convoy left Tangier it was attacked by a force of seven Algerine corsairs. They concentrated on trying to capture the *Mary Rose*, but for many hours Kempthorne's crew beat them off. Eventually, after heavy damage had been inflicted on the Algerine flagship, the corsairs withdrew, and the *Mary Rose* and its convoy reached Cádiz safely. Kempthorne was rewarded by Charles II with a knighthood, while Hollar immortalized the event in an engraving.[14]

Despite having fought two bitter naval wars against each other, England and the Netherlands could on occasion co-operate in the fight against the Barbary corsairs. In 1670 Admiral Willem van Ghent brought a Dutch fleet of thirteen ships, drawn from the admiralties of Amsterdam, Rotterdam and Zeeland, to the Mediterranean and co-operated with Allin in the war against Algiers. An English squadron under Captain Richard Beach was detached to accompany van Ghent's ships in patrolling the strait of Gibraltar and its approaches. In mid-August 1670 the allies encountered an Algerine squadron near Cape Spartel, and in the ensuing battle they drove six enemy ships ashore, burning them, killing several noted Algerine captains and freeing 250 Christian slaves.

In September 1670 Allin handed over command of the English Mediterranean fleet to Sir Edward Spragge and returned home. Spragge continued aggressive operations against the Algerines and achieved his greatest victory over them in May 1671. Seven Algerine warships were in the harbour at Bougie, and Spragge sent in fireships which success-fully burned them all. This further heavy blow to the navy of Algiers led to a revolution in the city. The old ruler was overthrown and the new one was anxious to make peace with England, which was soon agreed. From this point onwards, the ruler of Algiers was known as the 'dey' (literally 'uncle'), a title peculiar to that city.

The English and the Dutch had inflicted notable defeats on the Barbary corsairs, and the French had also carried out lesser naval operations against them in these years. However, just as the Barbary corsairs were beginning to feel real pressure from the European sea powers, that pressure was suddenly relaxed. Louis xiv was determined to destroy the Dutch republic, and he enlisted the aid of Charles ii to launch an Anglo-French assault on the Netherlands in 1672. England would fight the Dutch until 1674, while the French continued the war against them until 1678. Once again the Barbary corsairs were left largely unopposed while the European sea powers fought among themselves.

Although the Dutch finally beat back the French invasion of 1672 which almost destroyed their country, and other states, including Spain, later joined their struggle against France, there was little doubt that this war weakened Dutch power. This was especially true in the Mediterranean. The French encouraged a revolt in Sicily against Spain, and the Dutch sent a fleet, under Admiral de Ruyter, to the Mediterranean to assist the Spanish. In a series of sea battles around the shores of Sicily in 1676 the French, under Admiral Abraham Duquesne, eventually got the better of the Dutch-Spanish fleet and the famous de Ruyter was killed in one of the encounters. The French were now masters of the western and central Mediterranean.

France and the Netherlands made peace in 1678. Dutch seaborne commerce had largely been excluded from the Mediterranean since 1672 and Dutch shipowners were desperate to regain the trade they had lost to French and English ships. Attacks by the Barbary corsairs might help those two countries in preventing a Dutch trade revival in the region. When Dutch negotiators came to the Barbary regencies in 1679 aiming to obtain new treaties from them, they came as supplicants. As usual the treaty agreed with Algiers would set the tone for those with Tunis and Tripoli. The terms the Dutch eventually agreed with Algiers were to horrify their English and French rivals. Although the Netherlands still had a significant navy and most of its merchant ships went to the Mediterranean in well protected convoys, the Dutch effectively capitulated to the Algerines.

In the treaty of 1679, ratified in 1680, the Dutch agreed, among other things, to provide what was in effect an annual tribute payment to Algiers. It did not take the form of money, but of a free gift of cannon, firearms, gunpowder and naval stores such as masts, cordage and ship-building timber. In effect the Dutch were providing the material to equip Algerine corsairs to attack the ships of other nations and in return the Algerines agreed not to attack Dutch merchant shipping. The Dutch had calculated it was cheaper to send regular tribute to Algiers than to face the cost of sending punitive naval expeditions against the corsair city. The 1679 treaty was to be the basis of Dutch relations with Algiers for the next hundred years and more.[15]

The English and the French were loud in their condemnation of what they saw as a Dutch surrender, and they resolved to bring the Barbary regencies to terms through further aggressive action by their navies. England led the way, and from 1677 to 1682 waged a fierce naval war with Algiers. However, when an English fleet, under Sir John Narbrough, returned to the Mediterranean in 1675 after King Charles II had ended his participation in France's war against the Dutch, its first target was not Algiers but Tripoli in Libya.

For most of 1675 Narbrough tried to maintain a naval blockade of Tripoli. The knights allowed him to use Malta as his forward base, but most of his supplies came from the more distant port of Livorno (called Leghorn by the English) in Tuscany, the principal base for English merchants in the central Mediterranean. Narbrough became more aggressive in the following year. In January 1676 a force of boats from the English fleet, led by Narbrough's protégé Cloudesley Shovell, entered Tripoli harbour and burned four ships of the Tripoli fleet. Soon afterwards Narbrough's ships encountered a Tripoli squadron at sea and destroyed all four vessels. After these heavy blows to his fleet, the ruler of Tripoli made peace in March 1676, freeing all his English captives and promising to pay a financial indemnity. The people of Tripoli revolted, overthrew their ruler and forced his replacement to denounce the treaty. Narborough quickly returned, threatening to bombard Tripoli unless the new ruler confirmed the treaty, which he duly did.

This success might have encouraged the other regencies to be more respectful towards England, but the Algerines were angry because so many foreign ships were using false English flags to avoid capture by their corsairs. As their complaints to the English government about this

John Seller, map of Tripoli in Barbary (now Libya) in 1675.

matter were ignored, the Algerines went to war with England in 1677. Within two years they had captured 153 English merchant ships and the number of English slaves in Algiers rose to almost 4,000. Narbrough was sent back to the Mediterranean with an English fleet which by early 1679 had risen to 34 ships, almost the same number of warships the Algerines could deploy. Despite English possession of Tangier, Narbrough preferred to use Minorca as his forward base when trying to blockade Algiers, and even when patrolling the strait of Gibraltar his ships were more likely to call at Cádiz than Tangier. Narbrough's ships had some success in capturing or destroying Algerine corsairs, but his habit of keeping most of his fleet concentrated near Algiers led to a neglect of convoys and patrolling which led to further losses of English merchant ships.[16]

Having achieved little success, Narbrough returned to England in spring 1679, leaving command of the Mediterranean fleet to Captain Arthur Herbert (later Lord Torrington), who was soon raised to the local rank of vice-admiral. Herbert had past experience of fighting the Algerines, having been wounded twice in encounters with their corsairs and having taken part in Spragge's destruction of the Algerine squadron at Bougie in 1671. Herbert was less interested in a blockade of Algiers, preferring to escort English trade convoys through the corsair danger areas, mostly in or near the strait of Gibraltar, and to mount patrols in the same areas. Not only did his ships begin to take a steady toll of Algerine vessels, captured or destroyed, but they also accounted for some Sallee rovers from Morocco as well. In the past the corsairs had always been able to outrun English warships, but since the 1660s English shipyards had produced a number of fast, well armed vessels, often of shallow draught. They were equally useful operating among the sandbanks of the North Sea off the Dutch coast or going into the shallows near headlands like Cape Gata where Barbary corsairs lurked waiting for their prey.

Although the long breakwater built by the English at Tangier was said to be almost complete by the late 1670s, it had done little to improve the city's harbour. Like his predecessors, Herbert was reluctant to make much use of Tangier as a naval base and it usually only received occasional visits from patrolling warships. This situation changed dramatically in 1680 when repeated Moroccan attacks on the defences of Tangier compelled Herbert to take the fleet there, landing sailors and cannon to assist the garrison in beating off the Moroccan assault. Nevertheless, once the danger was past, Herbert looked elsewhere for a fleet base and found it in Gibraltar. In April 1680 the Spanish gave Herbert permission to use Gibraltar as his main base and he continued to use it until his return to England in 1683.[17] Among the young officers in Herbert's fleet was George Rooke. Almost a quarter of a century later, as Admiral Rooke, he would capture Gibraltar for England in 1704.

Herbert soon began to accumulate many Muslim slaves, mostly taken from captured Algerine vessels. Like his predecessors, he was under orders not to bring them back to England. Some were used as labour in Tangier, working on the defences or constructing the breakwater. The rest were sent to the various slave markets in Christian Mediterranean countries, such as those at Cádiz and Livorno. In 1679 alone Herbert was said to have made a profit of 16,862 pieces of eight from the sale of 243 Muslim captives. Not all Muslim captives passed unresisting into slavery. At least two ships carrying Muslim slaves away from Tangier experienced revolts among the captives. The ships were seized and run ashore on the coast of North Africa.[18]

By the start of 1681 Herbert's ships were maintaining a steady rate of success against the Algerines. In March 1681 two English warships captured the noted Algerine corsair *Golden Horse*. (Algerine vessels did not have names like Christian ships, and they were usually identified by the name of their captain. When captured, they were often named after some feature of the carving at the stern of the vessel.) Some 500 Muslim crew, including the captain, a Dutch renegade, were taken prisoner and 90 Christian slaves were freed. In May history repeated itself when the warship HMS *Kingfisher* was attacked by eight Algerine corsairs near Sardinia. The ship's captain was Morgan Kempthorne, son of John Kempthorne who had found himself in a similar position in HMS *Mary Rose* in 1669. Like his father, Morgan beat off his assailants, but in the battle he was fatally wounded. In September another Algerine corsair fell to the English warships. An English renegade was found among the officers of the captured vessel. He was immediately hanged.[19]

Although Herbert was bringing increasing pressure to bear on the navy of Algiers, the city's ruler became favourable to peace with England for other reasons. Algiers had been at peace with the Dutch and the French, but at war with the English. By late 1681 the Algerines were being drawn into conflict with France. Since the traditional policy was to avoid being at war with more than one of the main European sea powers at a time, war with France meant peace would have to be agreed with the English as soon as possible. In 1682 Algiers made a peace treaty with Herbert, and this treaty was to be the basis of England's relations with Algiers until 1816.

Even before war broke out between Algiers and France in late 1681, the French had already taken action against Barbary corsairs. Admiral Abraham Duquesne had been sent with a squadron to punish the corsairs of Tripoli for their attacks on French shipping. In 1681 Duquesne chased a group of Tripoli corsairs into the harbour of the island of Chios in the Aegean Sea. The admiral called on the Ottoman governor to expel the corsairs, but he refused. Duquesne quickly tired of blockading the port. Instead he went in and destroyed the Tripoli squadron. The Ottoman sultan, Mehmed IV, was outraged by this attack on his territory, and for a time it seemed that the Ottoman empire and France, once close allies, might go to war with each other. However, after the initial fury subsided, the Ottoman government decided to preserve the peace.[20] They were perhaps encouraged in this by payments from the French merchants resident in the empire. Instead the Ottoman sultan went to war with the Austrians, eventually leading to the famous Ottoman defeat at Vienna in 1683.

France, as already noted, was determined in 1682 to destroy Algiers once and for all. Louis XIV unleashed his new weapon, the bomb vessel, on the city in the bombardments of 1682 and 1683. However, it failed to produce the dramatic results that many had expected, and in 1684 a peace treaty was agreed between the two sides. In 1685 Admiral Jean d'Estrées took the bomb vessels to intimidate Tunis and Tripoli. Here the French had better luck, both regencies coming quickly to terms, although a short bombardment did have to be inflicted on Tripoli to convince its ruler to negotiate.[21]

After England and Tripoli made peace in 1677, a new English consul, Thomas Baker, had been dispatched to the regency, although he did not manage to take up his post until 1679. Baker already had considerable experience of North Africa, and he had been an assistant to his brother Francis when he was English consul in Tunis. Baker remained in Tripoli until 1685 and left a valuable account of his service there. One of his principal tasks was to make sure that Tripoli kept the peace with England, but had bad relations, including open warfare, with the French and the Dutch. In this task he was largely successful.[22]

Tripoli was usually viewed as the least powerful of the three Barbary regencies. However, it could still send out between fifteen and twenty corsairs each year, varying in size from a small galley to a 46-gun sailing warship which was the flagship of the commander of the Tripoli fleet. The corsair captains or reis were mostly Turks or Christian renegades, chiefly Greek, but with one Frenchman. The main cruising grounds of the Tripoli corsairs were in the central Mediterranean, around the coasts of Italy and Greece.

Baker kept a careful record of the prizes taken by the corsairs during his time in Tripoli, and their successes varied from year to year. In 1679–80 the haul was five prizes, of which only a French ship was valuable. The year 1680–81 was better, with eighteen French, Venetian, Ragusan, Genoese and Maltese ships captured, and worth in total over 400,000 Spanish dollars. The year 1681–2 was poor, but things improved in the two following years, though only thanks to a rich French prize taken in each of those years. The last year of Baker's consulate, 1684–5, was particularly bad. Although sixteen Christian ships were taken, only six were carrying cargo, none of it very valuable, and some of the crews escaped ashore, so that a total of only 79 slaves were captured. Compared with the dozens of French prizes Algiers was taking in the same period, the achievements of the Tripoli corsairs did not appear that great. Nevertheless they were sufficient to bring a Dutch ambassador in 1685 keen to renew peace with Tripoli and offering the usual tribute of arms, powder and naval stores. Later in that year Admiral d'Estrées won peace with Tripoli through a short bombardment of the city.

In any case, from 1685 onwards, Tripoli, like Algiers and Tunis, would have to reduce its corsair activities because the Ottoman sultan would be calling upon the regencies to provide him with warships for a naval conflict which dragged on until 1699. After the Ottoman defeat at Vienna in 1683, the war between the Ottomans and the Austrians continued for more than fifteen years. Other Christian states joined the Austrian side to fight the infidels. One was Venice, keen to get revenge for the loss of Crete, and the republic declared war on the Ottoman sultan in 1684. The Venetians did make one failed attempt to regain Crete, but for most of the 1680s they fought (successfully) to take the Morea (now the Peloponnese) in southern Greece from the Ottomans. Then in the 1690s they began to raid widely in the Aegean Sea. The sultan was keen to have the assistance of the Barbary corsairs in opposing the Venetian naval forces.

In early 1685 the Ottoman sultan Mehmed IV sent out his first summons to the corsairs in the new war: Algiers was to provide ten warships; Tunis five; and Tripoli eight. The sultan sent cash to each regency to cover the costs of fitting out these ships. They would serve in the main Ottoman fleet without payment, but they could keep any prizes they took and if they were lost while in the sultan's service, he would pay compensation. As Baker noted, Tripoli was happy to send the requested squadron, and it was a process that was to be repeated many times in the coming years.[23]

Just as France made peace with Tripoli, its relations with Algiers began to decline once more. The old problem of French reluctance to release young and fit Algerine slaves from their galleys revived, and French warships seized a number of Algerine ships at sea. In August 1687 the ruler of Algiers, still Mezzomorto, declared war on France and his corsairs were soon bringing in French prizes once more.

In June 1688 Admiral Jean d'Estrées led a French fleet of ten ships of the line, ten bomb vessels and some galleys to Algiers. Mezzomorto, veteran of the 1683 bombardment, was no readier to give in to French threats or action than he had been in the past. D'Estrées called for negotiations, but Mezzomorto refused. Some 400 French people resident in Algiers, including the consul and the vicar-general, were rounded up for use as hostages, while much of the Muslim population fled the city in anticipation of what was to come.

On 22 June 1688 d'Estrées' bomb vessels went into action, and their mortar bombs rained down on Algiers. Many buildings in the city were destroyed or damaged, but human casualties seem to have been light. As in 1683, Mezzomorto replied to the mortar bombs with selective executions of his French hostages, with the consul and the vicar-general among those blasted away at the cannon's mouth. D'Estrées replied in turn by executing batches of the Muslim prisoners aboard his fleet and floating their bodies ashore on rafts. Mezzomorto remained unimpressed, content to wait until the supply of French bombs ran out. An English observer, Robert Cole, was keeping score, writing on 7 July 1688: 'In all, bombs fired 13,300, French murdered 49.'[24] Next day d'Estrées gave up and his fleet sailed away, leaving at least a third of Algiers in ruins, but having achieved little else.

Once again, changes in European international relations were to bring peace between Algiers and France much faster than any military action. By 1689 French king Louis XIV was facing a major war with the League of Augsburg, an alliance which would include the Netherlands, England, Austria and Spain. Louis had more important tasks for his navy than fighting the Algerines. French negotiators were sent to Algiers and in September 1689 a new peace treaty was signed. Like the treaties made with the Dutch in 1679 and the English in 1682, this 1689 treaty was to prove lasting, forming the basis for French relations with Algiers up to the French Revolution a century later.

Many Algerine corsairs were unhappy with Mezzomorto because now the merchant ships of all three main European sea powers had been granted immunity from attack. However, Mezzomorto's more immediate difficulty came from his unsuccessful land campaigns against Tunisia. These failures led the Turkish janissaries of Algiers to overthrow Mezzomorto in October 1689 and he fled abroad, eventually reaching Istanbul. Since the 1671 revolt in Algiers after Spragge's success at

Bougie Bay, the corsair captains had a large say in who became dey of Algiers, but from 1689 onwards the janissaries had the last word on who became ruler in what was essentially a military republic.

Mezzomorto had dutifully sent Algerine warships each year since 1685 to serve in the Ottoman fleet fighting the Venetians and their allies. He also seems to have offered advice on the increasing addition of sailing ships to the Ottoman navy from the early 1680s onwards.[25] As a reward for all this naval assistance, the Ottoman sultan Suleiman II was in 1689 going to give Mezzomorto the post of kapudan pasha, commander-in-chief of the Ottoman navy, following in the tradition of men like Barbarossa and Uluj Ali. However, Mezzomorto's expulsion from Algiers meant the post was given to another Ottoman official.

In 1690 Mezzomorto commanded the Ottoman ships serving on the river Danube in the war against the Austrians, and he next had a command in the Black Sea. In 1691, when Venetian naval activity in the Aegean Sea was increasing, Mezzomorto became governor of Rhodes and commander of the ships based at that island. The Venetians seized Chios in 1694, but Mezzomorto recaptured it in 1695 after defeating the Venetians in two naval battles. As a reward for regaining Chios, the Ottoman admiral was in 1695 at last made kapudan pasha. Between 1695 and 1698 Mezzomorto led the Ottoman fleet in a number of naval battles with the Venetians in the Aegean Sea. He was generally successful, but never enough to win a decisive advantage over his Christian enemy. The war ended in 1699 and Mezzomorto died in 1701, being buried in Chios.[26] Once again one of the leaders of the Barbary corsairs had played a vital naval role in the service of the Ottoman sultan.

After the Glorious Revolution in 1688 in England, King James II was driven into exile and replaced by his daughter Queen Mary and her husband King William III, who was also ruler of the Netherlands. With French encouragement, ex-King James wrote to the ruler of Algiers claiming that William and Mary were usurpers and that the Algerines could seize any English merchant ships coming to the Mediterranean carrying passes made out in their names. The Algerines very wisely ignored this attempt to embroil them in a war with both England and the Netherlands. Anglo-Algerine relations were further improved when in 1691 Thomas Baker, previously consul at Tripoli, became the English consul at Algiers. Baker seems by now to have been well known and respected in all three Barbary regencies. When he finally returned to England in 1695, Baker took home with him 45 freed English captives, all that then remained in Algiers, Tunis and Tripoli, 'except one that refused his liberty'.[27]

Just as the danger of capture by Barbary corsairs seemed to be diminishing for English seamen, they were now to face new dangers from French corsairs. The frequent Anglo-French wars between 1689 and 1815 spawned a host of privateers, with the French side being by far the most effective. Indeed the French privateer port of Dunkirk became known as 'the Algiers of the north'. The French corsairs enjoyed their heyday between 1695 and 1713, and it is useful to compare their achievements with those of the Barbary corsairs during their period of greatest success in the first half of the seventeenth century.

Between 1622 and 1642 the Barbary corsairs were estimated to have captured over 300 English vessels and taken around 7,000 English captives. Between 1695 and 1713 the French privateers captured nearly 10,000 enemy vessels, of which between 50 and 75 per cent were English/British ships. In the 1620s and 1630s, the Barbary corsairs captured an average of fifteen English ships each year. In the period 1695–1713 French privateers took an average of 600 enemy vessels each year, of which about 400 were English/British ships.[28]

Clearly English merchant ships and their crews had a much greater danger of falling victim to French privateers than to Barbary corsairs, even in the period when the Barbary states were enjoying their greatest maritime success. French privateers like Jean Bart could inflict much greater damage on the British merchant fleet than any Barbary corsair, yet it remained true that for the English sailors the risk of wartime captivity in France was never as frightening a prospect as becoming a slave in Algiers.

English sailors captured and taken to a French port by a privateer might spend only a few months in captivity if the system of prisoner exchanges between England and France was working smoothly. Even if captivity was to drag on for much longer, there was always the prospect of freedom within a definite time period. The Anglo-French wars began with declarations of war and ended with peace treaties; they were not 'eternal' like the supposedly endless conflict between Christendom and Islamic countries. Although a religious divide separated Protestant England from Catholic France, prisoners of war in either country were rarely oppressed because of their religious beliefs or pressured into converting to the alternative religion.

Captivity in the Barbary states was always a much less pleasant experience. The prisoners had no idea how long their captivity would last; they were treated as slaves, not prisoners of war; and they were always under pressure, by harsh brutality or fair promises, to give up their Christian religion and 'turn Turk'. Whatever sufferings awaited English seamen captured by French privateers, they were infinitely preferable to the hopeless misery of Barbary captivity. However, from the 1690s seizure by the Barbary corsairs was less and less likely for the merchant sailors of the main European sea powers.

By 1690 the Barbary corsairs, after 30 years of struggle, had reached some kind of understanding with the three major Christian sea powers of Europe: France, England and the Netherlands. They had peace treaties with them all by which the corsairs promised not to attack the merchant ships of those countries. In return the sea powers were happy to let the Barbary corsairs continue to prey on the shipping of the lesser maritime states of Christian Europe, and the Dutch even sent annual shipments of armaments and naval stores to better equip the Barbary corsairs for that very purpose. As in the past, these treaties might have broken down, leading to renewed war between the Barbary corsairs and the major sea powers. Certainly the English and the French consuls in the Barbary states were always trying to get the corsairs to make war on their rivals. However, the Barbary corsairs, while happy to receive the 'presents' and bribes from the rival consuls, were careful not to join the great Anglo–French wars that became such a feature of European international relations from 1689 onwards.

The corsair captains might complain about being unable to attack French, English and Dutch ships, but there were still many targets available to them: not just ships from traditional enemies like Spain, Portugal and the Italian states, but also new victims like the Danish and Swedish ships which were increasingly venturing into the Mediterranean. Nevertheless it could not be denied that income from corsairing was likely to fall, a fall further exacerbated by the need to send warships to aid the Ottoman sultan in his war that lasted until 1699.

A fall in income from corsairing did not only hit those directly involved in that activity in the Barbary regencies. It also reduced income to the governments controlled by the Turkish janissaries in those states.

Unlike the corsair captains, the janissaries could get further income by increasing their activities on land. More expeditions were sent into the interior of North Africa to wring more taxes from recalcitrant tribes, and there were more wars with neighbouring states in pursuit of booty. For example, although Algiers had fought both Morocco and Tunisia in the past, such wars were to become a more regular occurrence. Tripoli even allied with Algiers to launch attacks on Tunisia.

If the Barbary states became more distracted by land wars in North Africa, the main European sea powers were even more distracted by the wars between themselves. England (Britain from 1707) and France would be engaged in what has been called the 'Second Hundred Years War' between 1689 and 1815. As long as the Barbary corsairs kept reasonably true to their treaties with such sea powers, they could continue their attacks of the ships of the lesser maritime states of Europe. It is a measure of the naval decline of the Netherlands in the early eighteenth century that its merchant shipping was soon to become a target for Barbary corsair attacks once more.

The great European wars were also to bring more direct benefits to the Barbary states, particularly Algiers. Spain's power had declined rapidly during the second half of the seventeenth century, and by the time its last Habsburg king Charles II died in 1700 the future survival of Spain and its empire seemed problematic. Louis XIV put forward his grandson Philip's claim to the Spanish throne; the Austrian Habsburgs put forward the claim of Archduke Charles. Soon Europe was back in conflict again in the war of the Spanish succession, fought in many parts of Europe, including Spain itself.

As traditional enemies of Spain, the Barbary corsairs were indifferent about who might win the crown, but Algiers was to profit from the struggle. The English and Dutch supported Archduke Charles in his war against the French pretender to the Spanish throne. In 1704 the Anglo-Dutch fleet took control of the western Mediterranean and would continue that dominance for some years to come. The English, who had withdrawn from Tangier in 1684, now seized Gibraltar (1704) and Minorca (1708) from Spain in the belief that these places would be much better bases to support their growing power in the Mediterranean.

In the struggle the governor of Oran, the main Spanish outpost on the coast of North Africa, supported Philip, the French pretender to the Spanish throne. As the Anglo-Dutch fleet supporting Archduke Charles controlled the western Mediterranean, this made sea communications to Oran increasingly difficult. Noting the growing isolation of the Oran garrison from 1704 onwards, Mustafa ben Youssef (also called Bouchelaghem), who ruled western Algeria for the dey, began a land blockade of the outpost, but lacked the forces to undertake a regular siege. In 1707 the dey of Algiers decided to attempt the capture of Oran. He sent an army under Ozen Hassan, with siege artillery, and it was soon joined by local Berber tribesmen. From September 1707 the outer Spanish forts were stormed one after another. Then it was the turn of Oran itself, the citadel falling at the start of January 1708. Mers el Kebir continued the struggle for a little longer, but it fell in mid-April. After two centuries of Christian occupation, Oran and Mers el Kebir had been returned to Muslim rule.[29]

The warring powers of Europe scarcely noticed these events on the coast of North Africa, but the Algerines felt they had a great victory to celebrate. The struggle for Oran had been fierce and bloody, with heavy casualties on both sides, but much booty had been won and over 2,000 Christian prisoners taken, including aristocratic officers who would yield high ransoms. The dey of Algiers sent the keys of Oran to the Ottoman sultan as a token of the great victory and asked that Ozen Hassan should be made a pasha. The request was not granted. Indeed the Ottoman sultan showed little more interest in the capture of Oran than the Christian great powers had done. In the sixteenth century the Christian–Muslim battles in North Africa had been of vital concern to the Ottoman government, but now the empire faced Christian threats much closer to Istanbul and these were its first priority.

The Barbary corsairs had survived the threat posed by the rise of the great European sea powers after 1660. They might have to curb their activities in regard to French, Dutch and English shipping, but there were still plenty of Christian vessels in the Mediterranean and beyond which could be targets for their cruisers. Not only had the Barbary corsairs survived the rise of the sea powers, but the conflicts between those powers could be exploited to the benefit of the corsairs, most dramatically in the Algerine capture of Oran. Spain had been humbled by its North African enemies. Who could believe that in only a few short years, the Barbary corsairs would have to face the revival of their old Spanish enemy as a military and naval power?

MOROCCO: ISMAIL'S CORSAIRS

Although the so-called 'pirate republic' of Salé had lost its independence in the 1640s, the port continued to be a major base for corsair activities under various rulers, who took a share of the profits. Salé, like Tetouan, the other main corsair base in Morocco, also kept up its links with the Ottoman regency of Algiers for a time, allowing Algerine corsairs to use the port as their forward base on the Atlantic Ocean. In 1660 Salé came under the rule of al-Khadir Ghailan, who had secured control of much of northern Morocco. In 1662 the English took over Tangier from the Portuguese, and Ghailan sought to prove his commitment to the jihad by launching attacks on the new Christian occupants of the city. In 1664 Ghailan's forces even managed to ambush and kill Lord Teviot, the governor of Tangier, and many of his troops.

In 1666 Moulay al-Rashid, founder of the Alawite dynasty which still rules Morocco today, captured Fez and subdued northern Morocco, forcing Ghailan into exile. Salé quickly accepted the rule of Rashid, but he was killed in an accident in 1672 and his half-brother Moulay Ismail took power. Ghailan took part in a revolt in the north against Ismail in 1673, but was defeated and killed. Morocco had been wracked by political instability since the death of Ahmad al-Mansur in 1603. Moulay Ismail, a brutal and ruthless man, was now to give the country 50 years of stability and order. As he could not base his power on the unreliable Arab and Berber tribes in Morocco, Ismail created a black slave army, the Abid al-Bukhari, which was loyal only to him and which by the end of his reign had grown to 150,000 men. Distrustful of the political groups in the old capital city of Fez, Ismail built a new capital for himself at Meknes.

A variety of labour was used to build Ismail's palaces in Meknes, including men from his black army, but contemporary European writers liked to give the impression that Christian captives, taken by the Moroccan corsairs, did most of the work. It was alleged that as many as 25,000 Christian slaves laboured in appalling conditions. Such figures were absurd. In the late seventeenth century the number of Christian captives in Morocco at any one time probably did not exceed 2,000, while in the early 1700s the number was probably nearer 1,000. Most Christian slaves were Portuguese, Spanish and Italian, with only small contingents of French, English and Dutch slaves. Ismail was certainly a brutal ruler, but some of the tales told about his cruelties to Christian captives were fantastic. It was said he ordered mass executions of Christians, yet between 1684 and 1727 the records of the Franciscan monks who lived closely with the captives recorded the execution of only 127 Christian prisoners.[30]

Military power not only restored order within Morocco, but also allowed Ismail to deal with external threats. He invaded Algeria in 1679, 1682 and 1695–6 to punish the Turks of Algiers for interfering in internal Moroccan affairs, and they eventually agreed to respect Morocco's independence. Ismail also sought to remove the Christian outposts that still existed along Morocco's coasts. He had some success on the Atlantic coastline, forcing the Spanish out of Mamora in 1681, Larache in 1689 and Asilah in 1691. The Spanish outposts on the Mediterranean coast of Morocco proved more resistant to Moroccan pressure, as shown by the apparently endless Moroccan blockade of Spanish-held Ceuta. In the 1680s and 1690s, Ismail sought to get a formal alliance with France which would increase the pressure on the Spanish, but Louis XIV would not oblige.

Ismail's forces kept up some pressure on the English in Tangier during the 1670s, but he did not begin concerted attacks on the city until 1678. In early 1680 the Moroccans overran some of the outer English forts and the governor of Tangier, William O'Brien, 2nd earl of Inchiquin, who with his father had been ransomed from the Algerines in 1660, was called home in disgrace. To add to the command confusion, the lieutenant-governor, Sir Palmes Fairborne, was then killed during a sortie. Fortunately troops under Percy Kirke and sailors landed by Arthur Herbert defeated further Moroccan attacks later in the year and won back some positions. In 1681 Kirke visited Ismail and a three-year truce was agreed.

Nevertheless, Ismail's attacks had done enough to convince the English government that Tangier was a costly folly. In 1683 Lord Dartmouth, accompanied by the Admiralty official and diarist Samuel Pepys, was sent out to Tangier with secret orders to withdraw all English forces and settlers from the place. This was done at the start of 1684. Before they left, the English blew up the town, its fortifications and the famous breakwater or mole. Ismail took over a pile of ruins. In all the occupation of Tangier between 1662 and 1684 had cost the English government £2,000,000 (of which one-third was spent on building the mole), which was more than the cost of all King Charles II's other garrisons at home and overseas put together. Tangier had never come close to living up to English hopes that it would become a great commercial port and a naval base which would curb the Barbary corsairs.[31] Anglo–Moroccan relations might have improved after the withdrawal from Tangier but, as with the French, continued attacks by Moroccan corsairs made negotiating peace treaties difficult.

Having obtained a monopoly of violence on land in Morocco, it was only natural that Ismail should seek to obtain a monopoly of violence at sea as well. Between 1680 and 1700 he steadily took control of almost all Morocco's corsair vessels. As a first measure, he ordered all private corsair captains to hand over their captives to him, giving them some cash compensation in return. Then the private corsairs were to pay ever larger shares of their profits to the ruler. Soon it was easier just to sell out to Ismail, and by the start of the eighteenth century almost all Moroccan corsairs were under the control of the state. Ismail used the Christian captives his corsairs took at sea both to build the palaces at Meknes and to be pawns in his efforts to extract diplomatic and trading concessions from European states, above all France and England.

Moroccan corsairs were not particularly numerous. Salé never had more than twenty at any one time during Ismail's reign, and Tetouan somewhat fewer, but the bigger 20–40-gun frigates were swift and powerful predators which ranged widely into the Atlantic, and even made occasional forays into the Mediterranean. Christian renegades ceased to be dominant among the corsair captains. In 1671 there were twelve principal reis at Salé, of whom eight were Moroccans and four Christian renegades (two from France, one from Greece and one from Majorca).[32]

Probably the most famous Moroccan reis of the late seventeenth century was Abdallah ben Aicha (or bin Aisha) of Salé. Beginning his career in the 1670s, he narrowly escaped capture by English warships in 1684. Between 1686 and 1698 Aisha is known to have captured 33 ships. Of those whose nationality is known, fourteen were French, four English, two Portuguese, one Genoese, two Dutch and one Spanish. The prizes were taken in a variety of places: off the Atlantic coasts of Iberia; near Atlantic islands such as Madeira, the Canaries, and the Azores; and in the bay of Biscay. Eventually becoming admiral of Salé, Aicha went on a diplomatic mission to France for Moulay Ismail in 1699.[33]

Sometimes the victims had the chance to hit back. In August 1684 Thomas Phelps sailed from England as master of the ship *Success* of

London. After first visiting an Irish port, he then headed for the island of Madeira, but before he could reach it his ship was captured by a Moroccan corsair in early October. The corsair later captured two other merchant ships and then returned to Salé with its prizes. Phelps and the other captives were then marched to Meknes, where they joined 800 other Christian slaves working on Ismail's building projects in the capital city. After his attempt to be ransomed failed, Phelps decided to escape. In May 1685 he and three other Englishmen escaped from Meknes and found their way to Salé. They stole a boat and rowed out to the warship HMS *Lark*, one of three English warships attempting to blockade the corsair base. Glad of his freedom, Phelps also wanted revenge. He convinced the English naval captains that he could pilot them into the nearby port of Mamora (or Marmora) where some Salé corsairs had found refuge. The three English warships destroyed the corsairs and freed some Christian captives aboard them. Phelps later received a financial reward from his home town of Bristol 'for his good services in destroying the Sally men of Warr in Marmora'.[34]

In 1700, when Ismail learned that Louis XIV was putting forward his grandson to be the next king of Spain, he stopped trying to get a French alliance against Spain. Ismail now tried to get on better terms with the English. In 1701 Ismail agreed to release 194 English captives, including five soldiers captured at Tangier 24 years earlier, in return for a ransom of £15,000, 1,200 barrels of gunpowder and a vague promise that England would assist a Moroccan attack on Spanish-held Ceuta.[35] When it became clear the English would not attack Ceuta, Ismail unleashed his corsairs on their shipping once more.

After the English captured Gibraltar in 1704, they tried to improve relations with Morocco, and soon Tetouan was an important source of supplies for the new English outpost. By 1712 Ismail's relations with the French had deteriorated considerably, but friendship with the English was little better. In 1711 British ships and cargoes worth £100,000 were said to have been captured by Moroccan corsairs, although the two countries were supposed to be at peace with each other. In 1713 a new Anglo–Moroccan treaty was agreed, but when the 'presents' promised by the British failed to reach Ismail, he declared war in 1714.

Between 1714 and 1719 Moroccan corsairs captured 27 ships from the British Isles and New England in North America, taking 263 captives. Of these captives, 53 died in Moroccan hands and fifteen converted to Islam to escape slavery.[36] One of the latter was a Cornish teenager called Thomas Pellow, who later claimed he was ill-treated by his captors to make him become a Muslim. As a Christian renegade, Pellow was ineligible for return to England under any later Anglo–Moroccan treaty. After being trained as a soldier Pellow fought in several campaigns within Morocco. Only in 1738 did he finally manage to escape from the country, returning to England and later writing an account of his experiences.[37]

In September 1720 Commodore Charles Stewart sailed from England with a small squadron bound for Morocco. He was under orders to negotiate a treaty of peace with Moulay Ismail. Stewart's ships reached Tetouan in December and negotiations began. While acknowledging British dominance at sea, the Moroccans were conscious of the relative invulnerability of their country. The main Moroccan cities, such as Meknes, Fez and Marrakesh, were far inland. Only an invading army could threaten them. Britain's army numbered barely 30,000 men; Ismail could assemble an army of over 100,000 men with ease. The British could never pose a serious military threat to Morocco, while the new British base at Gibraltar was dependent on supplies from North Africa. If the Moroccans had advantages, they also had desires. They wanted to increase their trade with Christian Europe and good relations with Britain, already perhaps the world's greatest trading nation, were vital. Salé and Tetouan were not only Morocco's main corsair bases; they were also the main ports for the country's growing trade with the outside world. In the eighteenth century as trade increased, the activities of the corsairs declined.

In January 1721 the Anglo–Moroccan treaty of peace was agreed. Although there were to be occasional breaches by both sides in the coming years, this was to be a definitive treaty in the same way as the English treaty with Algiers in 1682. It would govern Anglo–Moroccan relations during the eighteenth century and beyond. Ismail released 296 British captives, and when they were returned to England they took part in a ceremonial parade to St Paul's in London, where there was a religious service to celebrate their release from infidel captivity. As usual, the British handed over 'presents' to Ismail, including 1,200 barrels of gunpowder and 13,500 gun locks that Ismail's armourers could use to make muskets.[38]

France and the Netherlands would not achieve treaties with Morocco until later in the 1720s, but Morocco had now reached the situation that the three Ottoman regencies had achieved by 1690. Immunity was conceded to the merchant ships of the main European sea powers in return for the great powers turning a blind eye to Moroccan corsair attacks on the shipping of lesser nations. The great powers even provided arms and gunpowder to equip Moroccan forces for that task. Like the other Barbary corsairs, the Moroccans had survived the challenge from the new sea powers and could continue their old activities on a reduced scale. Ismail's corsairs had won him the grudging respect of the British, but the much despised Spanish still held outposts on the coast of Morocco. Indeed, when Ismail died in 1727, Spanish power even seemed to be reviving.

Dennis Malone Carter, *Decatur Boarding the Tripolitan Gunboat During the Bombardment of Tripoli, 3 August 1804.*

FOUR

Decline, Revival and Extinction
1720–1830

CAPE GATA, 1815

Commodore Stephen Decatur was a man in a hurry. As he led his squadron of American warships into the Mediterranean Sea in June 1815, he felt the burdens of both duty and rivalry bear heavily upon his shoulders. Decatur's duty was to bring the war between the USA and the regency of Algiers to an early and victorious conclusion. The commodore had first made his reputation as an American naval hero during an earlier war against the regency of Tripoli. Tripoli was the weakest of the Barbary states, yet it had taken four years of conflict, from 1801 to 1805, to force its ruler to make a peace acceptable to the government of the USA.

Decatur needed success in weeks, or at most a few months. The reason for this was that his squadron was the first of two American naval forces proceeding to the Mediterranean to oppose Algiers. The second squadron was commanded by Decatur's rival, Commodore William Bainbridge. He was senior to Decatur and the latter had already declared that he would not serve under Bainbridge. Once the other commodore arrived, the two squadrons would be united under his command, and Decatur would return to America.

The war against Tripoli which had been the making of Decatur's career had almost ended that of Bainbridge. As commander of the frigate USS *Philadelphia*, Bainbridge had taken the ship too close to the shore near Tripoli in 1803 and it had run aground. He and his crew were forced to surrender, and the captured frigate was later taken to Tripoli harbour. Early in 1804 Decatur had led a daring raid which resulted in the burning of the captured vessel. Bainbridge and his men remained in captivity until the end of the conflict.

When war broke out between the USA and Britain in 1812, both Decatur and Bainbridge had initially done well. Commanding the frigate USS *United States*, Decatur took the British frigate HMS *Macedonian*. A little later, Bainbridge, in the frigate USS *Constitution*, captured another British frigate, HMS *Java*. The British blockade then much reduced the activities of the American navy. However, at the start of 1815, Decatur was determined to get his frigate USS *President* to sea. At first it seemed he might succeed, but then his ship met a superior British squadron. After a short but fierce resistance, Decatur was forced to surrender his ship. In fact a peace treaty to end the war had already been signed, but news of it only reached North America after Decatur's defeat.

Now Decatur, like Bainbridge, had lost an American frigate to the country's enemy. The commodore went to the Mediterranean determined to revive his reputation for success at sea before his rival could arrive to replace him. Given the limited time he had available, Decatur's hopes of martial success and forcing a peace on Algiers seemed vain, but good fortune was to support his efforts.

On 17 June 1815 Decatur's squadron of three frigates, two sloops and four smaller vessels was sailing eastwards along the south coast of Spain. Decatur saw what appeared to be a frigate off Cape Gata, a favourite cruising spot for Algerine corsairs on the lookout for victims. As the American ships approached, the strange ship ran up British colours. However, Decatur was not deceived. He believed the ship belonged to Algiers and he immediately closed with it. Some say Decatur also raised a British flag to confuse his opponent, but whether he did or not, the commander of the Algerine frigate seems to have believed the squadron was a British one and hence at peace with Algiers. Only when the American ships got close to the frigate did they break out American national colours. The Algerine ship immediately turned away to the south-east, heading for Algiers and putting up all possible sail. However, the American squadron was close behind and Decatur seemed certain to come up with his prey in a short time.

Unknown to the American commodore, this was not just any Algerine corsair he had come upon. It was the largest ship in the Algerine fleet, the frigate *Meshuda* (46 guns), and it was commanded by the admiral of Algiers, Hamidou Reis. The latter was not just the commander of the Algerine fleet, but also the most famous and successful of the Barbary corsairs during the period of the French Revolutionary and Napoleonic wars. By the middle of the eighteenth century the activities of the Barbary corsairs seemed to be in serious decline, even at Algiers, but after 1793 corsairing revived considerably.

Hamidou Reis was unusual not just for his exceptional seamanship and his success in taking prizes, but in his origins as well. In the past corsair captains based in Algiers had been either Turks from the Levant or Christian renegades, with few if any captains coming from the native population of the city. There is still some dispute about the family origins of Hamidou, but he certainly came from the native population of Algiers or its neighbourhood.

Originally a protégé of the governor of Oran, Hamidou came to the notice of the dey of Algiers through his corsairing successes during the 1790s. From 1797 Hamidou commanded the principal ships of the Algerine fleet, and in 1802 he captured a frigate from the Portuguese navy, enslaving the crew of nearly 300 men. After a political revolution in Algiers in 1808 Hamidou fled into exile in Beirut. However, the lack of income from his prize-taking activities impoverished the treasury of Algiers and led to further political unrest. In 1809 a new dey seized power in Algiers, recalled Hamidou and made him admiral of Algiers. In the war between Tunis and Algiers in 1810–12, Hamidou captured a Tunisian frigate, the flagship of their fleet, and brought it back in triumph to Algiers.

On his corsair cruises Hamidou Reis usually led a squadron of Algerine warships which could easily overwhelm any foreign merchant ship that might be encountered. In June 1815 Hamidou had just led such a squadron into the Atlantic on a cruise, but when he returned through the strait of Gibraltar, he lost touch with the other ships of his force. Now the Algerine corsair found himself alone and under fire from a much superior American squadron.

Hamidou was wounded by wood splinters produced by the impact of American cannonballs. Refusing to go below to have his wounds tended, he had a chair brought up on deck so he could sit there and continue to give orders. Seeing he could not outrun the American warships, Hamidou changed course and headed his ship towards the Spanish coast, hoping to find refuge in neutral waters.

Decatur's flagship, the frigate USS *Guerriere* (44 guns), now blocked the *Meshuda*'s way, assisted by the sloop USS *Ontario*. The *Guerriere*'s broadsides smashed into the Algerine ship and Hamidou Reis was cut in two by a cannonball. Most of his remaining crew fled below deck and

Decatur assumed the enemy ship would surrender. However, the Algerines continued to fight. It was only after the sloop uss *Epervier* fired
nine more broadsides into the Algerine frigate that the *Meshuda*'s colours
were finally hauled down.

Hamidou and about 30 of his men had been killed. Just over 400
Algerines were taken prisoner, many being wounded. Decatur's squadron
had lost only a handful of men killed and wounded. The frigate uss
Macedonian escorted the *Meshuda* to Cartagena in Spain as a war prize,
while the rest of the squadron continued on their journey towards
Algiers. On 19 June the Americans came upon another Algerine warship, the brigantine *Estedio* (22 guns), off Cape Palos and captured it
after a short fight, killing 23 of the enemy and taking 80 prisoners.

When Decatur's squadron reached Algiers on 28 June, the commodore and the diplomat William Shaler sent word ashore of the American successes. Omar, the recently installed dey of Algiers, was like most
of his people unwilling to believe that the Americans could have inflicted
so much damage on the Algerine navy so quickly. Some of the captured
Algerines were sent ashore by Decatur so that they could swear to the
truth of his claims. In a state of shock, Omar agreed on 3 July to the
peace terms that Decatur and Shaler offered. Their only concession to
the ruler of Algiers was to promise the return not only of Algerine
prisoners, but also of the two captured Algerine warships. Omar feared
that if he did not get this promise he would be overthrown. The
Americans wanted a quick agreement and wanted to avoid any political
turmoil in Algiers that might throw up a less compliant ruler.

The Algerines would no longer demand any tribute from the Americans to ensure the safety of their merchant ships from corsair attack. This
concession lifted the usa out of the ranks of the lesser tribute-paying
maritime states like Denmark and Sweden and put the country on a par
with Britain and France, countries that never paid tribute to the Barbary corsairs. The sailors of the single American merchant ship that had
been taken by the Algerines were released without payment of ransom,
and compensation had to be paid for the ship and its cargo. William
Shaler was to become the American consul to the Barbary states, being
based in Algiers.

Although it was not required by his orders, Commodore Decatur
now took his squadron on visits to Tunis and Tripoli. The rulers of those
Barbary regencies were only too happy to renew their treaties with the

USA and pay compensation for what Decatur claimed were past misdeeds. Early in August Decatur met Bainbridge's newly arrived squadron at Gibraltar. Handing over command of the combined force, Decatur sailed for home having triumphantly carried out his aim to defeat Algiers before Bainbridge arrived. It had taken four years to force Tripoli to make a peace acceptable to the USA. Decatur had forced Algiers to make peace in less than four weeks.[1]

The American success against Algiers in the war of 1815 was to mark the end of the revival of Barbary corsairing which had taken place in the previous two decades. The impact of Decatur's victory would be reinforced in the following year when the Anglo-Dutch fleet under Admiral Lord Exmouth bombarded Algiers and destroyed the remaining ships of the Algerine navy. The Barbary corsairs never recovered from these blows and they faced final extinction after the French conquest of Algiers in 1830. Stephen Decatur did not live to hear of that event. In 1820 he was wounded in a duel with another American naval officer and died shortly afterwards.

SPANISH REVIVAL

In the treaties which ended the war of Spanish succession in 1713–14, Louis XIV's grandson was accepted as the new Bourbon king of Spain, becoming Philip V. However, to appease the enemies of the French and Spanish Bourbons, Spain had to make many concessions. One was to give up most of its Italian possessions, including Sardinia, Sicily and Naples. These losses were not accepted by Philip V's Italian wife Elizabeth Farnese, nor by his chief minister Giulio Alberoni, another Italian. They looked for an early opportunity for Spain to regain its lost Italian territories.

Any reconquest would require the deployment of effective Spanish military and naval forces, but during the recent war the Spanish armed forces seemed to have reached a new low point after half a century of decline. This made their swift revival after 1714 all the more surprising. The Bourbons brought more effective administrative methods from France, but these would have had little impact if there had not been able Spaniards, above all José Patiño, willing to adopt them.

As preparation for action in Italy, the Spanish king sought to win the favour of the pope, Clement XI. Venice was once again at war with the Ottomans and an Ottoman landing on the island of Corfu seemed to pose a threat to Italy as well. In 1716 Spanish warships and galleys were sent to assist the Venetians in driving the Ottomans from Corfu. This was successfully accomplished, and as a reward the pope made Alberoni a cardinal.

In 1717 Philip v ordered Patiño to collect a fleet and army at Barcelona, giving out the story that these forces were to be sent against the Ottoman Turks as in the previous year. In August the expedition sailed, but it was not to attack the Muslim foe. Instead troops under the marquis of Lede were landed on Sardinia, and by the end of the year the island had been returned to Spanish rule. The following year an even larger Spanish expedition was sent against Sicily, quickly overrunning the island. The other great powers of Europe were angry that Spain was trying to overturn the settlement of 1713–14 and prepared to take military action. Britain struck first, with its Mediterranean fleet destroying a Spanish squadron off Cape Passero in Sicily in August 1718. Austria joined the coalition against Spain, and in early 1720 Spanish forces were withdrawn from Sicily and Sardinia.

The Spanish had eventually been forced to give in to superior force, but their actions between 1716 and 1720 had shown striking evidence that Spanish military and naval forces were experiencing a significant revival. To underline this change, no sooner had Spanish forces returned from Sicily and Sardinia than a new expedition was being prepared by the indefatigable Patiño. The target was the Moroccan army that had been besieging the Spanish-held port of Ceuta on the North African coast for some years. The Spanish squadron, under Carlos Grillo, sailed from Cádiz in October 1720 carrying 16,000 troops under the marquis of Lede. The army was landed at Ceuta soon afterwards and quickly drove the Moroccans back. By the end of the year the Moroccans had given up their attempt to capture Ceuta.

If Spain could not recover Sicily and Sardinia, perhaps it might have better luck trying to recover Gibraltar and Minorca which it had been forced to cede to Britain. In 1727 the Spanish went to war with the British and tried to recapture Gibraltar. They failed and the war soon ended. In peacetime the Spanish still tried to keep up pressure on the British garrisons in Gibraltar and Minorca by restrictive measures. However, the British turned to North Africa for most of their supplies. Tetouan in Morocco supplied Gibraltar, while Algiers supplied Minorca. The Spanish were not happy about these links and accused the British of allowing Algerine corsairs to find shelter in the waters around Minorca. The Algerines could be equally suspicious, warning the British not to sell on to Spain wheat which had been supplied to Minorca from Algiers. In the new Mediterranean empire of Protestant Britain, the principal enemies were Catholic Europeans, while most support for the British outposts came from Muslim North Africans.[2]

Even more than Gibraltar and Minorca, the Spanish wanted to retake Oran, lost to the Algerines in 1708 after two centuries of Spanish rule. In 1732 the Spanish began assembling powerful naval and military forces at Cádiz, Alicante and Barcelona, and other countries anxiously speculated about the intended destination of the expedition. The fleet was commanded by Francisco Cornejo and the troops by José Carrillo de Albornoz, count of Montemar. On 6 June 1732 Philip v published a manifesto declaring that the objective of the expedition was to recapture Oran. The expedition sailed on 15 June and appeared off Oran ten days later. After an unopposed landing, the Spanish swiftly routed the local Algerine forces. Mers el Kebir fell to the Spanish first, and then on 5 July the count of Montemar entered Oran as its conqueror. On his return to Spain Montemar received the Order of the Golden Fleece, as did José Patiño, the 'organizer of victory'.

After their initial confusion, the Algerines collected their forces and launched strong counterattacks during August 1732. Reinforcements were rushed from Spain, and after a bitter struggle the Algerine assault on the main fort overlooking Oran was finally repulsed. As a distraction, a Spanish naval force under Blas de Lezo raided the nearby port of Mostaganem. The Spanish gained considerable prestige from their reconquest of Mers el Kebir and Oran, but soon these outposts on the North African coast were as much a burden to the Spanish exchequer as they had been in former centuries.[3]

Building on his success at Oran, Montemar went on to win new victories in Italy when Spain took part in the conflict known as the war of Polish succession (1733–5). By 1735 the Spanish had won back Sicily and Naples. In 1736 José Patiño, the 'Spanish Colbert', died. When he had begun his career in Spanish state service in 1717 the navy of Spain barely existed, but when he died it consisted of more than 30 ships of the line, a dozen frigates and twenty lesser warships. It was a force that would stand comparison with the fleets of Britain and France, and it was a major threat to the Barbary corsairs.

Spain's military and naval revival had led to significant successes in Italy, but the other powers once again placed limits of that success. The mainland kingdom of Naples and the island kingdom of Sicily would be united in a state to be called the kingdom of the Two Sicilies (but more commonly known as the kingdom of Naples), but the new kingdom would not be part of the dominions of Spain. A member of the Spanish Bourbon royal house would rule the new state, but it could not be part of the Spanish empire.

One result of these arrangements was that the new kingdom of Naples would not enjoy the protection of the Spanish armed forces. Not only would Naples be vulnerable to pressure from the great powers, for example as exercised by the Mediterranean fleets of France and Britain, but it would find itself insufficiently strong to deal with the threat from the three Ottoman regencies of North Africa. The navies of Algiers, Tunis and Tripoli were not large in size, at barely twenty vessels each, but neither was the Neapolitan fleet. A zone of naval vulnerability now existed for the Christian states of the central Mediterranean. Individually the naval forces of Sardinia, Tuscany, the papal states and Naples were barely a match for the Barbary corsair fleets. Nor could they turn for assistance to Venice, for its navy went into considerable decline during the eighteenth century. Unless the French, Spanish or British navies were willing to provide support, the navies of the Italian states could not be sure of any superiority over the Barbary corsairs. Only the Knights of Malta remained as a constant support to any Christian state fighting the infidel, but even they were finding it hard to meet the cost of their small fleet, newly converted from galleys to sailing warships.[4]

Nevertheless this new area of weakness was not immediately apparent because the Spanish navy remained strong and continued to be active against the Barbary corsairs. The Spanish fleet performed reasonably well in the war with Britain from 1739 to 1748, and in the 1750s further naval and military reforms were carried out by the marquis of Ensenada. One change in the navy was the steady reduction in the number of galleys serving with the Spanish fleet. This was a general trend among the Mediterranean navies, France laying up its last galleys in 1748. If there were to be no more galleys, there was no more need for Muslim galley slaves, and this change had a significant impact on the process of freeing Christian captives from the Barbary states.

Previously Spanish captives in the hands of the Barbary corsairs had usually been redeemed for cash, but from the 1730s onwards, there was an increasing tendency to exchange man for man, Christian captive for Muslim captive. With the declining importance of galleys, the Spanish crown was more willing to give up Muslim galley slaves for such exchanges. The first such exchange was in 1739. The Mercedarian friars paid cash ransoms for 350 Spanish captives in Algiers, but also exchanged 50 Algerine slaves chosen by the ruler of Algiers for 50 Spanish captives chosen by the Spanish crown.

Now the Moroccans decided that no further redemptions of Spanish captives would take place unless they included a direct exchange of captives. In 1740 the governor of Tangier told the Mercedarians not to come to his city without such an arrangement. King Philip V agreed to this, and in 1741 the friars went to Tangier with 60 Muslim slaves from the Spanish galleys, whom they traded for an equal number of Spaniards. Another exchange took place at Tangier in 1759, with 88 Spaniards rescued, of whom 36 were obtained for one Muslim slave and 550 pesos each.[5]

The Algerine attitude to this new policy of direct exchange was always ambivalent. Freeing Muslim slaves from the Christians would win the ruler of Algiers much popular acclaim in his city, but if it was done on a man for man exchange, it would not bring him any cash ransom. The revenue of the government of Algiers derived from corsairing had been steadily declining since 1700 and the government preferred to get cash for its Christian captives if it could.

The last great Spanish religious redemption of Christian slaves in Algiers was in 1768–9. Negotiations for it had begun in 1766 and from early on the Algerine government made it clear that it wanted only cash in return for its Christian captives. However, news of this attitude leaked out and popular unrest in Algiers compelled the ruler of the city to agree that some Christian captives would be swapped for Muslim slaves held by the Spanish. The Algerines wanted corsair captains included in the Muslim captives for exchange. Traditionally the Spanish had been very reluctant to give up captured corsair captains, but eventually they agreed to their inclusion in this exchange.

The Spanish aim was to rescue all legitimate Spanish captives remaining in Algiers, as well as Catholics of other nationalities who had been taken prisoner under the Spanish flag, for example, Irish Catholic soldiers in Spanish service. Soldiers who had deserted from the Spanish outposts in North Africa would not be rescued, nor would Spaniards who had converted to Islam and become renegades. Although many of the captives would be ransomed for cash, direct exchange would be an important part of the deal.

The redemptionist friars arrived in Algiers in Spanish warships, bringing 1,246 Algerine slaves for exchange. This was a much larger number than the government of Algiers had been expecting. The Mercedarians were told by the dey of Algiers that he 'did not want Moors, but money'. However, the population of the city became restless and threatening, so the Algerine government began the direct exchange. The 26 corsair captains among the Algerine captives were exchanged for the same number of Spanish naval officers and captains of merchant ships. The other Muslim slaves were exchanged at a rate of two Algerines for one Spaniard.

During the course of the redemption, the Algerine government repeatedly tried to revise arrangements so that they could get as many cash ransoms as possible. When the process was completed, a total of 631 Christian captives had been exchanged for 1,236 Algerines, and 819 Christian captives had been ransomed for cash. The total amount of the cash ransoms was 694,463 pesos.[6]

The Spanish redemption at Algiers of 1768–9 took place during the reign of King Charles III. Formerly ruler of the new kingdom of Naples, Charles had succeeded to the throne of Spain in 1759. Anti-British and pro-French, he unwisely involved Spain in the later stages of the Seven Years War. Havana in Cuba and Manila in the Philippines were lost to British attacks. These places were returned to Spain at the peace in 1763, but Spain had to hand over Florida to the British. The French gave Louisiana to the Spanish as compensation for this loss. Charles III continued to build up his forces in anticipation of a new war with Britain, and as he did so he was willing to take a more conciliatory line towards some of the Barbary corsairs. The redemption at Algiers was part of this policy, and Spain also signed a peace treaty with Morocco in 1767.

However, Spain still had no intention of giving up any of its outposts on the North African coast and they remained a provocation to the local Muslims. Possibly with British encouragement, Mohammed ben Abdallah (Mohammed III), ruler of Morocco, decided to attack the Spanish outpost of Melilla in 1774. Assisted by Algerine forces, the Moroccans set up siege lines outside Melilla in December 1774 and began a bombardment of the city. The Spanish governor, Irish-born Juan Sherlock, kept up a determined resistance, while a small Spanish garrison under Florencio Moreno likewise resisted a Moroccan attack on Vélez de la Gomera. Then in March 1775 a Spanish squadron brought troop reinforcements to Melilla and the Moroccan and Algerine attackers were forced to abandon the siege.[7]

The Algerine involvement in the attack on Melilla encouraged the Spanish to take further action against Algiers. Preparations were made for a major expedition against the city, but they were ill-organized and little intelligence was gathered about the target. The Algerines soon learned of what the Spanish were doing, so they made their own preparations to resist the Spanish assault. Irish-born Alejandro O'Reilly, previously a highly successful soldier in Spain and also a favourite of King Charles III, was given command of the Spanish troops, while Pedro González de Castejón commanded the fleet.

The Spanish expedition arrived off Algiers at the start of July 1775. It consisted of seven ships of the line, twelve frigates, seven galleys, 30 gunboats and 20 other warships, with over 200 transports, carrying 20,000 troops. Like Emperor Charles V back in 1541, the Spanish commanders chose to land their troops on beaches east of Algiers on 8 July. There was little Algerine resistance and the first two waves of troops came ashore without any trouble. Then artillery started to come ashore, only to get bogged down as it was dragged across the sand dunes. Lulled into a false sense of security, the Spanish did not build adequate field works from which they might resist an Algerine counterattack. Suddenly the Algerine forces, supported by thousands of Berber tribesmen from the mountains, swept down upon the disordered Spanish troops. In a desperate struggle, the Spaniards retreated to the water's edge, and they were lucky that most of the soldiers were picked up and taken back to the fleet. Nevertheless it was a serious defeat for Spanish arms.

In all 500 Spaniards were killed, 2,000 wounded and 2,000 were taken prisoner by the Algerines. Some fifteen artillery pieces fell into the hands of the victors. As the defeated troops returned to Spain, popular outrage erupted in Madrid and elsewhere. It was the most humiliating Spanish defeat of the century, and it seemed to undermine the country's naval and military revival that had been going on since 1714. Only the support of Charles III saved O'Reilly from a worse fate than just public hostility.[8] Nevertheless the king retained faith in his armed forces, and in 1779 he chose to commit them to the French and American side in the war of American independence. Although a three-year siege of Gibraltar ended in failure, Spanish forces did take Florida and Minorca from Britain, and they remained in Spanish hands at the peace in 1783.

When the peace was concluded in 1783, Spain had been about to send an army and fleet to join the French in a combined assault on the British island of Jamaica in the West Indies. Charles III saw no reason to waste such preparations. Instead of Jamaica, the target would be Algiers, and the Spanish hoped to exact some revenge for their defeat at that city in 1775. A fleet under Antonio Barcelo bombarded Algiers for eight days in August 1783, but no troops were landed and it was decided to postpone further action until the following year. In a gesture of defiance, five Algerine corsairs came out in September 1783 and captured two Spanish merchant ships near Palamos.

For the attack in 1784, the Spanish fleet was to be joined by ships from such traditional enemies of Algiers as Naples, Portugal and the Knights of Malta. In all Antonio Barcelo had a combined fleet of nine ships of the line, eleven frigates, five galleys and almost 80 smaller warships, chiefly gunboats and bomb vessels. The bombardment of Algiers began on 12 July 1784 and continued for many days. Barcelo was directing operations from a small warship when it was sunk by a lucky shot from the Algerine side. He was pulled from the water unharmed. An attack by Algerine gunboats on the Christian fleet was repulsed with loss, and as the days passed most of the Algerine vessels were sunk in harbour and the city was badly damaged. Nevertheless the government of Algiers refused to open negotiations for peace with the Christian fleet. With his munitions running low, Barcelo decided to end the attack on 21 July. The combined fleet had lost only 53 killed and 64 wounded, but Algerine casualties must have been considerably greater.[9]

Undeterred by the comparative lack of success achieved by the bombardments of 1783 and 1784, the Spanish intended to send another fleet, under José de Mazarredo, against Algiers in 1785. However, it was not required. The Algerines had suffered sufficient loss and damage to make them willing to enter into negotiations for a peace treaty with the Spanish in 1785. This was a major concession on their part. Since the creation of the corsair state of Algiers by the Barbarossa brothers in the early sixteenth century, there had never been a peace treaty between Algiers and

Spain. They had in theory been at war with each other for almost 270 years. Now both sides were finally ready to find a way to a peace settlement.

The negotiations proceeded surprisingly smoothly. Spain was now ready to withdraw from Oran and Mers el Kebir, although it wanted to retain a trading post at the latter port. In return the Algerines would cease all attacks on Spanish shipping. With the prospect of the return of Oran, the Algerines were happy to concede a trading post on the same terms that the French held their trading post at the Bastion of France, an annual tribute payment to Algiers. The treaty of 1786 might be acceptable to the Spanish government, but the Spanish public took a different view. Popular outrage at the terms of the treaty caused the Spanish government to delay carrying out those terms. In particular, the Spanish seemed in no hurry to leave Oran. Charles III died in 1788 and the French revolution broke out the following year. The new king, Charles IV, had more to think about than the fate of Oran.

The dey of Algiers became increasingly impatient with Spanish procrastination. By the end of 1789 he had begun a new blockade of Oran, and in 1790 he began to assemble his forces for a formal siege. Then nature took a hand. In October 1790 a violent earthquake struck Oran and did considerable damage to the town and its defences. The Algerines saw their opportunity and launched an immediate assault. However, the Spanish could still assemble enough forces to fight back, and the attack was repulsed. Now the Algerines began to besiege Oran more closely. New negotiations were opened between the two sides and in late 1791 a new treaty was agreed, though it largely confirmed the terms of the earlier one.

On the last day of February 1792 the Algerines took possession of Oran. The Ottoman sultan in Istanbul sent his congratulations that the city had been returned to Muslim and Turkish rule. Three hundred years earlier the Catholic Monarchs, Ferdinand and Isabella, had taken possession of the city of Granada, ending the last Muslim state in Spain. Now Spain's most important possession on the coast of North Africa had been handed back to the Muslims. Although a few Spanish outposts remained (and remain even today), the Algerines might well feel that after a struggle of three centuries they had finally defeated Christian attempts at expansion in Muslim North Africa.[10]

Spanish military and naval power had revived greatly during the eighteenth century, but the Algerines had not only survived that revival:

they had even inflicted an important defeat on the Spanish, both actual and symbolic. Lost once more to the Christians in 1732, Oran had been won back for Islam in 1792. However, the world was changing. Holy warriors, whether Christian or Muslim, were becoming increasingly irrelevant in international affairs. The Europe that would emerge from the French revolution and the wars it produced would be a greater threat to Muslim North Africa than the Catholic Monarchs of the past. In the nineteenth century Christian Europeans would take not just a few cities on the northern shores of Africa; they would take the entire continent.

TREATIES, TRIBUTE AND TRIBULATIONS

During the eighteenth century corsairing was to decline as an activity pursued by the three Ottoman regencies of Algiers, Tunis and Tripoli for both internal and external reasons. Externally the steady extension of treaties of immunity to almost all the main European maritime states naturally reduced the number of potential targets. However, regular tribute payments in cash or goods from lesser maritime states seemed increasingly preferable to the lottery which corsairing had become. A few ships took valuable prizes, but most did not. Another external change was the decline in the Ottoman sultan's need for naval help from the Barbary corsairs. Between 1718 and 1770 the Ottomans faced no naval war in the Mediterranean and so had no need for corsair assistance. When a Russian fleet came into the Mediterranean intent on attacking the Ottomans in 1770, the naval forces of the Barbary regencies were so depleted that they were irrelevant to the struggle. Internally, the regencies, and especially Tunisia, began to see foreign trade as a more lucrative occupation than corsairing. The trade was not only with other parts of the Ottoman empire, but increasingly with European countries, particularly France.

From 1714 onwards the relations between the Ottoman regencies and the main sea powers of Europe were largely peaceful, despite occasional disputes. Britain found the North African states a useful source of supplies for its Mediterranean garrisons and squadrons in both peace and war. France became an important trading partner of the regencies, but this did not prevent several short outbreaks of hostilities. In 1728 Admiral Nicolas de Grandpré was sent with a small squadron to Tripoli after French ships were taken by its corsairs. After a short bombardment and a blockade, the ruler of Tripoli came to terms and met French demands.[11] In the late 1760s France was to have a similar short war with Tunis in a dispute over Corsica.

The island of Corsica, ruled by the republic of Genoa, had suffered many raids by the Barbary corsairs over the preceding two centuries, and a number of Corsicans had become Christian renegades who rose to be important corsair captains. In 1768 the Genoese sold Corsica to France. In future Corsicans could claim the protection offered by France's treaties with the Ottoman regencies, and the corsairs were denied valuable targets. The ruler of Tunis was particularly angered by this new restriction and tried to obtain British help to dispute the French acquisition of Corsica. The British were not interested, while the French dispatched a squadron under Captain de Broves to intimidate the Tunisians. Assisted by some ships from the Knights of Malta, the French force bombarded the ports of Bizerta and Sousse in 1770, quickly forcing the ruler of Tunis to accept the new reality.[12]

The Netherlands had previously been ranked among the principal naval powers of Europe but, after the end of the war of Spanish succession, the country's navy was increasingly neglected. As the Dutch merchant fleet remained large and vulnerable, this weakening of naval power was an unwelcome development. Like all predators, the Barbary corsairs were ever alert to signs of weakness among their potential prey, and they began attacks on Dutch shipping. Between 1714 and 1720 the Algerines captured some 40 Dutch ships and 900 Dutch sailors. In 1723 and 1724 a Dutch frigate captain, Cornelis Schrijver, took several Algerine corsairs, but it was clear that diplomacy, not naval action, would be the only way to bring peace.

The Dutch were already the only major naval power which paid tribute to Algiers (under the 1679 treaty) and the only way they could win peace was by offering an increase in such tribute. Algiers agreed to peace in 1726, and the Dutch also made new treaties with Tunis and Tripoli. In 1730 Cornelis Schrijver visited Algiers not to make war, but to deliver the tribute and redeem Dutch captives. Some 256 were freed, including one unfortunate Dutchman who had fallen into Algerine captivity as long ago as 1690.

By mid-century it was clear that the Netherlands had slipped out of the ranks of the main European sea powers and would in future be on a par with the tributary lesser maritime states. The Dutch relationship with the Barbary regencies usually involved a diligent adherence to the terms of the treaties, sending tribute of arms, gunpowder and naval stores almost every year. In 1783 the Dutch tribute to Algiers included 44,000 pounds of gunpowder, which the Algerines found very useful for resisting the Spanish attacks on their city in that year and the next. Occasionally, if the demands of the Barbary corsairs became too excessive, the Dutch would fight back. They were at war with Algiers from 1755 to 1757 and 1792 to 1794, and with Tripoli from 1789 to 1791. However, in the end peace would once more be concluded. Payment of tribute was always cheaper than maintaining a naval squadron in the Mediterranean for years on end.[13]

Among the lesser maritime states which the Dutch now joined were the kingdoms of Denmark (then including Norway) and of Sweden (then including Finland). Their merchant fleets grew considerably during the eighteenth century, largely because the two countries remained neutral during the major naval wars between Britain and France in the period. Danish and Swedish vessels became more common in the Mediterranean and picked up much lucrative trade.

The Swedes had originally found protection from the Barbary corsairs by sending their ships along with Dutch convoys bound for the Mediterranean. After the Dutch peace with Algiers in 1726, foreign ships were not allowed to accompany such convoys. The Swedes would have to negotiate directly with the Algerines about the future safety of their shipping. George Logie, a Scotsman resident in Algiers, helped arrange the first treaty between Sweden and Algiers in 1729. In return for regular tribute, Swedish ships, which were to carry special passes, would be granted immunity from attack. Appointed as the first Swedish consul in Algiers as a reward for his work, Logie went on to negotiate Swedish treaties with Tunis in 1736 and Tripoli in 1741, all on terms similar to the Algiers treaty.

The Danes did not negotiate their first treaty with Algiers until 1746, and it had the usual provisions that tribute would be paid and Danish ships would carry special passes. Between 1735 and 1746 the Swedes paid tribute amounting to 68,000 rixdollars to Algiers. In 1766 the ruler of Algiers threatened to go to war with Sweden unless its tribute was increased and paid more regularly. The Swedes quickly agreed. The Danes were less obliging, and between 1769 and 1772 they were at war with Algiers, even undertaking a not very effective attempt to bombard the city in 1770. Despite this protest in arms, the Danes finally had to give in and accept payment of higher tribute to the corsairs.

After 1790 the Barbary regencies began to demand even larger tribute payments. Finding the Swedes initially unresponsive, Algiers declared war in 1791. When peace was restored the following year, Sweden agreed to pay an enhanced tribute of 175,000 rixdollars. Even the Swedes eventually tired of these endless demands. They increased their naval presence in the Mediterranean from 1798, and in 1801 they went to war with the regency of Tripoli. Around the same time the USA was beginning its own war with Tripoli, and initially the Americans co-ordinated their attempt to blockade Tripoli with the activities of a force of four Swedish frigates under Olof Rudolf Cedeström. However, the Swedish government soon decided that paying tribute was cheaper than war. Much to the disgust of the Americans, the Swedes agreed a peace treaty with Tripoli in October 1802 which raised their tribute payment to 650,000 rixdollars.[14]

The older treaties with Britain and France, together with the newer agreements with the Dutch, the Swedes and the Danes, meant that much of the Christian merchant shipping in the Mediterranean was now immune to attack by the Barbary regencies. Occasional 'presents' from the major sea powers and regular tribute from the lesser ones meant a steady stream of revenue to the regency governments, but it was still necessary to be at war with some Christian states otherwise the corsairs would cease to be a credible threat and so would lose their power to blackmail potential prey. By the 1760s the main remaining targets for the corsairs of the Ottoman regencies were the ships of nations which had been their principal enemies since the sixteenth century: Spain, Portugal, Naples, Venice, Genoa and other Italian states. However, they provided few prizes of any great value. After making peace with the Ottomans in 1718, Venice pursued a policy of strict neutrality in all Mediterranean naval wars. As a consequence, like Denmark and Sweden, Venice saw its merchant fleet expand considerably. This growing number of ships naturally attracted the attention of the Barbary corsairs and for a time Venice continued to battle the corsairs. Then, in 1764–5, Venice took a new path, making peace treaties with Algiers, Tunis and Tripoli. The Serene Republic was now ready to provide tribute of 60,000 ducats a year for the right to sail unmolested through seas it had once dominated.

The new arrangement soon broke down, and by the 1780s Venetian naval forces under Angelo Emo were active against the Barbary corsairs. Emo, the last great admiral of Venice, tried to reform the republic's navy in the light of practices in the British and French navies, but with only limited success. Nevertheless, he did strike some blows against the corsairs, in particular bringing the ruler of Tunis to terms by 1785. Yet by the time of Emo's death in 1792 Venice had given in to the corsairs once more, being prepared to pay an annual tribute in return for immunity for its ships. Soon even Spain was looking to reach a settlement with the corsairs. The treaty between Spain and Algiers in 1786 was a first step, and by the early 1790s Portugal too had begun to negotiate with the Barbary corsairs. It seemed the Ottoman regencies might soon have no Christian enemy left whose ships they could attack.[15]

This might not matter to some of the regencies, especially Tunis, where maritime trade was steadily becoming more important than corsairing. Trade considerations were also beginning to put pressure on both Muslim and Christian sides to bring the 'eternal war' at sea in the Mediterranean to a close. As early as 1697 the Knights of Malta had agreed not to allow their own ships or the Maltese corsairs they licensed to take Muslim prizes in waters close to the coast of Palestine. This was because of Ottoman threats to disrupt the Christian pilgrim trade to Jerusalem in retaliation.

During the eighteenth century, France, close ally and major trading partner of the Ottoman empire, put increasing pressure on the Knights of Malta and other Christian states sending out corsairs against Muslim shipping not to operate in the eastern Mediterranean. Just as Barbary corsairing was declining due to treaties of immunity with most Christian maritime states, so Christian corsairs found their activities steadily reduced by limitations imposed by France and other states active in trade with the Ottoman empire. Soon the only Muslim ships the Knights of Malta and the remaining Christian corsairs could attack were those belonging to the Barbary states, which were few in number and rarely carried valuable cargoes. The knights saw a drop in their income just as they needed more money to support their new fleet of ships of the line and frigates. At least the shift to sailing warships and the decline of their galley fleet meant the Knights of Malta had less need of Muslim galley slaves. Conscious that most Italian maritime states remained vulnerable to corsair attacks because of their weak navies, the Knights of Malta now sought to justify their continued existence by stressing their role as maritime policemen of the central Mediterranean.[16]

If the Knights of Malta were finding it increasingly hard to justify their role as Christian 'holy warriors', the Barbary corsairs had similar problems. Once the vanguard of a powerful and expanding Ottoman empire, the world's most powerful Muslim state, the corsairs had by the mid-eighteenth century sunk to a minor role in the struggle between Islam and Christianity. Although the religious justification for their activities was still seen as important, the Barbary corsairs were now more likely to trade with the Christian Europeans than attack their ships. Nor were the corsairs any longer an important naval auxiliary for the Ottoman sultan.

The Ottomans made peace with Venice in 1718 and with the Knights of Malta in 1723, although neither treaty included the Barbary regencies. Of the other main naval powers in the Mediterranean, France was an ally of the Ottomans and the British were generally friendly, although they did assist the Russians when they sent a fleet to the Mediterranean in 1770 to fight the Ottomans. Apart from the episode at Corfu in 1716, the revival of Spanish naval power posed no threat to the Ottomans, and in 1782 the two states signed a wide-ranging treaty. Thus between 1718 and 1770 there was no naval conflict in the Mediterranean which might lead the Ottoman sultan to ask for aid from the Barbary regencies. In addition by the mid-eighteenth century the main Ottoman navy was being developed on European lines. The Ottomans were more likely to ask for naval advice from France than from the Barbary corsairs who had given such assistance in the sixteenth and seventeenth centuries.

When the Russian fleet came to the Mediterranean in 1770 and crushed the Ottoman fleet at the battle of Chesme, the Barbary corsairs were largely irrelevant to the naval struggle. After the victory the Russian naval forces could operate in the eastern Mediterranean largely unopposed until the peace of 1774. When the Ottoman navy was rebuilt after the war, naval assistance was provided by France not the Barbary regencies. Indeed this new Ottoman fleet was to become a threat to the autonomy of those states. In the 1780s the Ottoman government used naval pressure to bring wayward provinces like Egypt back under central control. It seemed this policy would next be extended to the Barbary regencies, especially Tripoli and Tunis. However, a new war broke out with the Russians in 1787 and the Ottoman fleet was sent to the Black Sea instead. In this war (which lasted to 1792) no Russian squadron came to the Mediterranean. Barbary aid to the Ottomans in this struggle was muted and indirect. For example, when Sweden joined the war against Russia between 1788 and 1790, Algiers generously waived the tribute that country was due to pay to the corsairs in those years.

If the Barbary regencies no longer gave much assistance to the Ottomans in naval matters, this was just a reflection of the growing estrangement between the two sides that had begun in the early eighteenth century. In 1705 Husain bin Ali seized power in Tunis and established a dynasty that would last until 1957. In 1711 Ahmed Karamanli took similar action in Tripoli and his dynasty would rule there until 1835. Also in 1711, the dey of Algiers added the title of pasha to his own and refused to accept any more pashas appointed by Istanbul. The Ottoman sultan had few ways of exerting pressure on the regencies. One way was to forbid them to recruit new Turkish corsairs and janissaries in the heartlands of the empire such as Anatolia. However, such a threat was no longer as important as in the past. In Tunis and Tripoli both soldiers and sailors increasingly came from the local population rather than being imported from outside. For Algiers the recruitment of Turkish janissaries from Anatolia and elsewhere still remained important, but even here by the latter years of the century local recruits were as important among the corsair captains as Turks or Christian renegades.

By the late 1780s the Barbary regencies had attained a kind of stability. Receiving occasional 'presents' from the great European maritime states and regular tribute from the smaller ones, they still maintained small corsair fleets (around twenty vessels each, few with more than eighteen guns) whose threat was sufficient to keep up the maritime blackmail. The regencies still maintained some links with the Ottoman sultan, but these imposed few obligations on them and seemed to be declining. As their corsairing activities diminished, the rulers of Algiers, Tunis and Tripoli took a greater interest in maritime trade both within the Ottoman empire and with Christian Europe. This stability was, however, to prove short-lived. The wars which followed the French revolution of 1789 were to destroy completely the old European international system. In an effort to adjust to the new realities, the Barbary regencies would return to their old corsair activities in a big way, and this in turn would provoke a European reaction which would end those activities forever.

MOROCCO: CORSAIRS AND DIPLOMACY

In September 1753 a Moroccan sailor called Hamet appeared before the governor of Tetouan and the British consul in that city, William Pettigrew. Hamet had a strange story to tell. In 1736 he had been part of the crew of a Moroccan vessel taking a cargo of corn from Salé to Mogador (now Essaouira) in southern Morocco. The vessel was intercepted and captured by a Portuguese frigate. The prize was taken to Mazagan (now El Jadida), the last Portuguese outpost on the coast of Morocco. Hamet and another man escaped and went to a British merchant ship in the harbour. Although the two men did not speak English, they seem to have known that under the treaties between Britain and Morocco, the British had agreed to assist escaped Moroccan slaves in getting home. Hamet and his companion hoped they might be returned to Morocco via England. The British ship put to sea, but went not to England, but to the British colonies in North America. At Charleston, South Carolina, the two Moroccans were sold as slaves to a plantation owner. They were taken to a plantation some 150 miles from Charleston. For the next fifteen years they remained there, spending much of their time grinding corn to feed the plantation's black slave labour force.

Hamet and his companion were saved when the plantation owner went bankrupt. They had by now learned enough English to tell the creditors who they were. The Moroccans were allowed to present their case to James Glen, the governor of South Carolina, and he agreed to send them back to Morocco. After Hamet told his story to the governor and the consul in 1753, the British representative agreed to give the two Moroccans over £30 in compensation, a large sum for two sailors in those times. Pettigrew accepted Hamet's knowledge of English as corroborating his story. The consul's generous compensation reflected British sensitivity to a breach of their treaties with Morocco. It also showed a willingness to view Muslim slaves as being different to black African ones. Moroccans made a similar distinction between Christian slaves and black slaves, and by the 1750s they were using Christian captives brought in by their corsairs as a diplomatic lever to get commercial and other concessions from the European maritime states.[17]

After the death of Moulay Ismail in 1727, instability returned to Moroccan politics. The black slave army made and unmade rulers. By the early 1750s some normality had been restored. Abdallah was nominal ruler, but his son Mohammed was the real power in the government. Mohammed sought to appease the black army by reducing taxes within the country, but this was only possible if government revenue could be made up from other sources. An expansion of corsairing might well lead to open war with the major European sea powers. Instead corsair activities would be carried on at such a level that they put pressure on the European states, but did not lead to war. In return for Morocco curbing the corsairs, the larger European powers would make commercial concessions that would boost Morocco's foreign trade. Taxes on that trade would provide the revenue lost through tax reductions elsewhere. Lesser European maritime states could be forced not just to make trade concessions, but also to pay regular tribute to avoid corsair attacks.

To assist in the expansion of foreign trade, Mohammed wanted more foreign consuls to be established in Morocco. In the spring of 1756 a British naval officer, Captain Hyde Parker, visited Morocco to renew the treaties between the two countries. Mohammed requested the appointment of a British consul in Morocco and a gift of a cargo of naval stores. Parker had been ordered to refuse both requests, and he did so in a way that left Mohammed feeling he had been personally insulted. The rude captain got away unscathed, but in August 1756, Mohammed sent out the Moroccan corsairs to seize British ships and so put pressure on the British government.

Several British merchant ships were captured almost immediately, including the *Ann*, which was on a voyage from Gibraltar to England. Among the passengers on board was a young woman called Elizabeth Marsh. She was not the first British woman to fall into the hands of Barbary corsairs, but she was the only one to produce an account of her short captivity, which was published in 1769. Taken first to Salé and then to Marrakesh, now once again the capital of Morocco, Elizabeth even had an interview with Mohammed. In return for British promises to consider his earlier requests, Mohammed released Elizabeth and other British captives in November 1756. However, there was no progress in negotiations, so the Moroccan corsairs returned to sea. They had further successes and by 1758 the Moroccans held almost 400 British captives.

Deeply involved in the Seven Years War, Britain could do without this Moroccan distraction. In addition, it needed free access to Moroccan resources to get supplies for its Gibraltar garrison and its Mediterranean fleet. The easiest course seemed to be to give in to the wishes of

Mohammed ben Abdallah (Mohammed III), who had become official ruler of Morocco in 1757. In 1758 the British government apologized to him for Captain Parker's bad manners, paid 200,000 Spanish dollars for the release of the British captives, and agreed to have a British consul in place in Morocco by 1760 to encourage trade relations between the two countries.[18]

During the 1760s Mohammed made a number of treaties of friendship and commerce with European states. The less powerful countries, such as Denmark, Sweden and Venice, not only made trade concessions but also had to promise regular tribute payments to Morocco in return for immunity from corsair attack. Because of its heavy naval losses in the Seven Years War, even a major power like France might appear vulnerable to Moroccan pressure. After increasing losses to Moroccan corsairs, the French sent a naval expedition to Morocco in 1765.

Duchaffault de Besné in a 50-gun ship led a force of 15 frigates, bomb vessels and other warships to Salé. Among the commanders in this squadron were two Knights of Malta who would one day become famous French admirals: de Grasse and Suffren. In the first half of June 1765 the French bombarded the port of Salé for nine days. They then moved on to Larache, which was bombarded for several days toward the end of the month. Next a group of French boats under Captain Latouche Beauregarde was sent into the Loukkos river to burn Moroccan ships moored there. Unfortunately the French force fell into a Moroccan ambush. Some 200 French were killed, 48 captured and only nine got back to their squadron. Despite this disaster, French hostilities with Morocco continued until 1767, when a peace treaty was signed and the French captives were released.[19]

Some of those prisoners had spent their time in captivity doing building work on the new port city Mohammed was creating at Mogador. All the foreign trade of southern Morocco was to be concentrated there, and by 1770 many European merchants had taken up residence. While creating new coastal cities, Mohammed was also trying to remove the last European outposts along Moroccan shores. In 1769 the Portuguese finally gave up Mazagan, and this meant there were no major foreign-held ports left on the Atlantic coast of Morocco. In 1774–5 Mohammed launched attacks on Ceuta, Vélez and Melilla, the last Spanish-held outposts on the Mediterranean coast of Morocco, but all these assaults were repulsed. In 1780 and 1785 Mohammed made treaties with Spain.

By the 1770s Morocco's corsair fleet had fallen to barely twenty ships, of which only half were fast, well armed frigates. Nor was this fleet always successful. In 1773 a frigate from Tuscany's small navy encountered five Moroccan corsairs and managed to capture three of them. As all the corsairs were now state-owned, it might be better to see them as the Moroccan navy rather than a corsair force. Most of the captains were Moroccans, but there were still a few Christian renegades, including a Dane called Georg Høst who later wrote his memoirs.[20]

In 1777 Mohammed became the first foreign ruler to recognize the new USA, and he opened Moroccan ports to American ships. Once American independence had finally been secured in 1783, Mohammed expected the Americans to open up diplomatic and commercial relations with Morocco. When the young republic was slow to do this, Mohammed sent his corsairs against American shipping, leading to the capture of the *Betsey* in October 1783. The American government took notice and diplomatic negotiations were soon opened. The ship was released in 1785 and a treaty between Morocco and the USA was agreed in 1786. The question of tribute was studiously ignored by the Americans, but the Moroccans would later claim that as a lesser maritime state the USA should make some payment.[21]

Although the corsairs were still sometimes sent to sea, the Moroccans were now getting many of their Christian captives by enslaving the survivors of European ships which were wrecked on their coasts. One such victim was James Irving, a Scotsman active in the African slave trade from the port of Liverpool in England. In May 1789, outward bound from Liverpool to West Africa, his ship, the *Anna*, was wrecked on the coast of Morocco and it was he who became a slave. Irving eventually managed to contact British consular officials at Mogador and Tangier, and he was finally freed in the autumn of 1790. Irving seems never to have appreciated the irony of his position, the slave trader become a slave. He complained bitterly of being 'a slave to a savage race who despised and hated me for my [Christian] belief', but he did not change his occupation once he regained his freedom. In April 1791 Irving was back in West Africa, buying more than 300 black slaves on the Gold Coast for transport to the Caribbean.[22]

Christians were not the only ones active in freeing captives. Mohammed made considerable efforts during the 1780s to free Muslim slaves held by the Christians. His concern was not just for Moroccans but for all Muslims. Not only was redeeming slaves a religious duty, but Mohammed also saw political advantages in his policy. If successful, it would add to Mohammed's prestige, not just in North Africa, but in the wider Muslim world. In particular he hoped it would bring closer relations with the Ottoman sultan. Mohammed concentrated his efforts on the large number of Muslim slaves still held by the Knights of Malta. After seventeen months of negotiations, Mohammed managed in 1789 to ransom some 600 Muslim slaves at a cost per head of 400 riyals or Spanish piastres. On 3 July 1789 57 Moroccans and seven other North Africans sailed from Malta bound for Tangier, and on 20 August 536 Muslims left Malta for Istanbul, being carried in a Ragusan ship and two French vessels.[23]

Mohammed ben Abdallah died in 1790 and Morocco once again experienced political instability. His son Sulayman came to the throne in 1792, but he did not completely establish his power across the whole country until 1798. When war broke out between the USA and the Ottoman regency of Tripoli in 1801, Sulayman was sympathetic to the Muslim side and by 1803 he was considering sending out his corsairs against American shipping. The American squadron off Tripoli had already seized a Moroccan vessel which tried to slip through their blockade.

In the summer of 1803 Captain William Bainbridge, who was bringing the frigate USS *Philadelphia* to join the American squadron in the Mediterranean, met a Moroccan corsair near the Atlantic entrance to the strait of Gibraltar. The corsair, the *Mirboka*, had an American prize, the *Celia* of Boston, with it and they were heading towards Tangier. Bainbridge took the two ships to Gibraltar instead, and when the Moroccan corsair was searched an order was found for attacks on all American shipping. Bainbridge passed this document on to Commodore Edward Preble, commander of the US Mediterranean squadron, when he arrived at Gibraltar in the frigate USS *Constitution*.

Preble did not wish to add a war with Morocco to the existing conflict with Tripoli, but he could hardly ignore the Moroccan provocation. In October 1803 Preble took three American frigates to Tangier as a show of force and sought to negotiate with the Moroccan authorities. Purely by chance, Sulayman was visiting the Tangier area and Preble was able to meet him personally. Sulayman claimed there had been an unfortunate misunderstanding and that he had issued no orders to attack American ships. The 1786 treaty was reaffirmed, and the American commodore made it clear that the USA would never pay tribute to Morocco. Sulayman asked that as a goodwill gesture the Americans should release the two Moroccan ships they had captured, and Preble reluctantly agreed.[24]

If the USA seemed too strong for the Moroccans to harass with their corsairs, Sulayman thought he had found a much weaker adversary in Austria. Before 1797 the port of Trieste had been Austria's only significant outlet to the Adriatic and Mediterranean seas, and the Austrian government took little interest in maritime matters. In 1797 Napoleon Bonaparte passed the Venetian republic, his recent conquest, on to Austria as part of the peace settlement between the two sides. Suddenly Austria had a significant (ex-Venetian) merchant fleet to defend and it was compelled to start developing a navy. When the Moroccan corsairs began to attack Austrian ships in 1803, the Austrians were forced to react. They sent a force of two naval brigs, under the French émigré Count Charles Mogniat de Pouilly, to the Moroccan coast and the ships patrolled with little success while the diplomats negotiated. Peace between the two sides was finally agreed in November 1805.

When the Napoleonic wars were over and Sulayman witnessed the American, British and Dutch attacks on Algiers in 1815–16, he decided it was time for Morocco to give up corsairing. He made an announcement to that effect in 1818, four years before his death. However, the Moroccans still wanted to receive tribute from states like Denmark, Sweden and Naples, so it was necessary to keep some corsairs ready as a threat. Abderrahman came to the throne in 1822 and was soon tempted to restart corsairing. In 1828 he abrogated the 1805 treaty with Austria and a Moroccan corsair captured an Austrian merchant ship. A small Austrian squadron under Francesco Bandiera arrived off Morocco at the start of 1829 and attempted to impose a blockade on Moroccan ports. A daring raid freed the crew of the captured ship, and in July 1829 the Austrians bombarded Larache. The Austrian government then reminded Bandiera of the essentially defensive nature of his mission, but it did send him further warships. In March 1830 Bandiera agreed a peace settlement with the Moroccans, and the captured Austrian ship was returned.[25]

The French conquest of Algiers in the summer of 1830 led to further Moroccan protestations that they had given up corsairing and the taking of Christian captives. However, the Moroccan government was still extorting tribute from the smaller European maritime states. A visit from a Neapolitan squadron in 1834 led to a reduction in the amount of tribute paid by Naples, but did not end it. In 1840 Denmark and Sweden-Norway asked the Moroccans for a reduction in their tribute payments, but the Moroccans refused. Finally, in 1844, Britain and France threatened hostile action against Morocco unless the tribute system came to an end. In the following year Morocco agreed to this, provided all arrears of tribute were paid. Official sponsorship of Moroccan corsairing was at an end. Although there would be a few instances of piracy in Morocco later in the century, such as an attack on a French ship in 1851 which led to a French bombardment of Salé, these were private actions. When Morocco gave up taking tributes in 1845 the age of the Barbary corsairs finally came to an end.[26]

REVOLUTION, WAR AND THE CORSAIR REVIVAL

The French revolution of 1789 had few immediate effects on the Ottoman regencies. Only when Britain and France went to war in early 1793 did the conflict provoked by the revolution start to have adverse effects on the Barbary states. France had been their principal foreign trading partner in peacetime. Now direct contact with ports such as Marseille was cut off by the British naval blockade. Attempts to continue trade via neutral ports such as Genoa had only limited success. Revenue from the taxes levied on the regencies' external trade began to decline.

In addition to this, several maritime states ceased to pay any more tribute. The Netherlands came under French control from 1795 and Venice was conquered by France in 1797, only to be passed on to Austria when peace was made. Both the Dutch and the Venetians ceased to pay tribute to the Barbary states. Napoleon Bonaparte's campaign in Italy in 1796–7 did much to disrupt the political and economic status quo in the peninsula. The Ottoman regencies found it more difficult to trade with ports such as Genoa and Livorno. Any territory which was occupied by the French or fell under their control was quick to claim the immunity from tribute guaranteed by the treaties between France and the regencies.

Faced with this growing loss of revenue from trade taxes and tribute, the Ottoman regencies began to consider a return to full-scale corsairing in an effort to boost their income. One obstacle to such a revival of corsair activities was removed in June 1798. Napoleon Bonaparte had decided to take a French army to invade Egypt, and on the way he seized the island of Malta, ending the rule of the knights that had lasted a little over 260 years. Hoping to win favour in the Islamic world, Napoleon released the last 2,000 Muslim slaves held on the island without asking for ransom.[27]

After a mid-century slump, the Knights of Malta had revived their own operations against the Barbary corsairs after 1770, and they had also assisted other states such as Spain and Venice in attacks on the corsairs and their bases. During the 1790s the knights took 32 prizes, mostly in Tunisian waters, and secured 468 Muslim captives. Their last prize was a Tunisian vessel taken after a short fight on 26 April 1798. Some 30 Tunisians were killed, including the captain, and 95 taken as captives. The holy war at sea which the Knights of St John had begun at Rhodes in the early fourteenth century now ended with the fall of Malta in the last years of the eighteenth century. The naval defenders of Christendom were gone and the Barbary corsairs no longer faced their most implacable enemy.[28]

If one obstacle to corsairing had been removed by Napoleon, his invasion of Egypt in 1798 seemed to promise a wealth of new prizes for the corsairs to attack. For two and a half centuries, despite occasional clashes, France and the Ottoman empire had basically been on good terms, and on occasion were close allies. Although the Ottoman sultan, Selim III, was a Francophile, he could hardly ignore Napoleon's invasion of Egypt, one of the Ottoman empire's richest provinces. The Ottomans embarked on a war with France that would last until 1802. The Ottoman sultan called on his Barbary provinces to begin corsair attacks on French shipping immediately.

The Barbary corsairs proved distinctly reluctant to do the sultan's bidding. They still had links with French merchants and shipowners, and in any case the British fleet in the Mediterranean was blockading the French coast. Instead the corsairs of Algiers, Tunis and Tripoli preferred to direct their attacks against Venetian ships which had recently been declared to be Austrian. Between 1798 and 1799 around 40 such vessels were taken, with the six richest cargoes said to have a combined value of some two million florins. It was not just ex-Venetian ships that suffered. Austrian ships from Trieste were also attacked, and their owners claimed they had suffered losses of one and a quarter million florins at the hands of the Algerines alone. With regard to the ex-Venetian ships, the

Austrian government had already informed the Ottoman sultan that the ships had changed nationality and were now covered by the treaties between Austria and the Ottoman empire. This did not impress the Barbary corsairs. They claimed to have received no notice of the change of flag. They considered the ships to be Venetian, and since Venice had ceased paying tribute they were legitimate targets. Also the Austrians lacked any warships capable of disputing this interpretation. Eventually the Ottoman sultan pressured the corsairs into making some restitution to the Austrians, but generally the Barbary states had done well out of the affair.[29]

The revival of corsairing in the 1790s led to a transformation in the fleets of the Ottoman regencies. In the 1780s those fleets had reached a new low. Algiers had only thirteen ships, the largest mounting 34 guns. Tunis had 38 vessels, but most were small and the largest had only eighteen guns. Tripoli followed Tunis with fourteen small vessels mounting relatively few guns. These fleets reflected a more circumscribed world for corsair operations. Algiers retained some larger ships because its cruisers operated off the Mediterranean coasts and islands of Spain, with occasional voyages through the strait of Gibraltar into the Atlantic. Tunis and Tripoli were largely restricted to operations around Sardinia, Sicily and southern Italy, so smaller vessels were more suitable for those tasks.

Between 1790 and 1815 the composition of the fleets changed considerably. By the latter date Algiers had five frigates (40–50 guns), four corvettes (20–30 guns), three brigs, two schooners, a half-galley and 20–30 gunboats. Tunis had three frigates (all 48 guns), two corvettes (20–28 guns), five xebecs, a brig, two schooners, two feluccas, a galliot, and four gunboats. In addition there were 24 small corsair vessels owned by individuals. Tripoli had one frigate of 40 guns, one corvette of 20 guns, three polacres, three xebecs, one galliot and fifteen gunboats. Although these were small fleets when compared to the great navies of Britain or France, the regency fleets had been substantially strengthened since the 1780s and could easily overwhelm their merchant ship prey.[30]

The first Algerine frigate, with 44 guns, was built at Algiers in 1791 under the direction of a Spaniard. Tunis got its first frigate in 1796 and Tripoli its first such vessel in 1799. The Algerines also pioneered the use of gunboats. They had been impressed by the Spanish use of such craft in the bombardments of Algiers in 1783 and 1784, and decided to develop their own fleet for operations close inshore. The new gunboats were not just a defence against future Christian attack. They were also used by Algiers in its conflicts with the neighbouring regency of Tunis. Indeed, in addition to the expansion of corsairing, the increase in fleets was also encouraged by a local naval construction race, chiefly between Algiers and Tunis. By 1815 the 'capital ship' of the regency navies was the frigate of 40–50 guns built to the same design as in European navies.

In both Algiers and Tripoli, as in Morocco, the corsairs were now controlled by the local government and not by private individuals. Tunisia was unusual in retaining a mixed system. Between 1798 and 1805, most Tunisian corsairs were sent out by private individuals, but between 1806 and 1815, only 20–30 per cent of those corsairs were private concerns. Even the private corsairs still had to pay a percentage of their prize money to the state. In all the regencies a small share of prize takings was paid to Islamic religious foundations, a tradition that went back to the age of the Barbarossas and beyond.

Tunis was also unusual in the widespread nature of corsairing within the country. By this time most corsairing was concentrated at Algiers, with few other ports in the regency making a contribution as they had done in the past. Tripoli had always been the principal corsairing port in that regency. In Tunisia there were seven main ports sending out corsairs: La Goletta (the port of Tunis), Bizerta, Djerba, Monastir, Porto Farina, Sfax and Sousse. This was partly due to the fact that many corsairs were sent out by local governors. For example, of 98 corsairs sent out by Mahmoud Gelluli, 75 left from Sfax, where he was governor, 12 from Sousse, where he also became governor, and 17 from La Goletta.

Of the corsair captains, the reis, an increasing number were local people rather than Turkish imports or Christian renegades. As already noted, perhaps the greatest Barbary corsair of this period, Hamidou Reis, was a native of Algiers, not a member of the Turkish elite in that city. In Tripoli at this period only a quarter of corsair captains came from the Ottoman heartlands of Anatolia, the Balkans and the Levant; most of the other reis were North African Arabs. Tunis also had a preponderance of captains drawn from the local population, although the larger corsair vessels were usually commanded by Turkish reis from Albania, Greece, and elsewhere. Despite the success of Hamidou Reis, perhaps half of Algerine corsair captains were still Turkish, but this was still a contrast to the janissary garrison in Algiers whose recruits were all still drawn from the Ottoman heartlands. The contrast between Algiers on the one side and Tunis and Tripoli on the other clearly reflects the different government systems. In both Tunis and Tripoli dynasties had ruled for almost a century. They had started out Turkish, but had been steadily 'nativized' as the years passed. Only Algiers preserved rule by a Turkish military elite.

Christian renegades were now a dwindling minority among the Barbary corsair captains. Algiers at this time may have had only one, a Maltese. There were still a few at Tripoli, and one of them, the Scotsman Peter Lyle, was probably the last famous Christian renegade among the Barbary corsairs. In 1793 Lyle had been part of the crew of a British vessel visiting Tripoli. After being accused of theft, he jumped ship and converted to Islam, taking the name Murad Reis. He was to have a successful career in Tripoli, marrying the ruler's daughter and becoming admiral of the Tripoli fleet. The Christian renegades who had been such an important part of the Barbary corsairs in the sixteenth and seventeenth centuries were now only a tiny handful.[31]

Most corsair captains seem to have gone out on only a few cruises, and most of the captains did not have long careers. Hamidou Reis was the most notable captain at Algiers, but there were others. Ahmed el-Haddad of Algiers participated in the capture of eleven European ships between 1798 and 1815. Peter Lyle alias Murad Reis was the most famous captain at Tripoli, but Mohammed Arnaout and Omar Chelly also had long careers, commanding corsair ships from the late 1790s to 1815. In Tunisia at least five reis went on between 17 and 24 cruises each over a similar period, with Ramadan Arnaout making the most cruises, some 24, between 1797 and 1815.

Judged by the number of corsair cruises from Algiers, Tunis, and Tripoli, the main period of the corsair revival was between 1793 and 1805, with a peak around 1798. Tripoli was under American blockade from 1801 to 1805 which reduced corsair sailings. Algiers has the best records of prizes taken. Between 1783 and 1792 the Algerines captured 67 prizes, but between 1793 and 1802 the number soared to 172 captures, with 1798 as the best year with 42 prizes taken. Some 60 prizes were taken between 1803 and 1813, then 17 in 1814 and eight in 1815.

Although the fleets of the Barbary corsairs had more ships of a more heavily gunned type, their cruising grounds remained much the same. Algiers concentrated on the Mediterranean coasts of Spain and offshore islands with occasional forays into the Atlantic; Tunis and Tripoli concentrated on Sardinia, Sicily and southern Italy. There was some cross over, with Algerine corsairs sometimes cruising near Sicily and Tunisian ones off the coast of Catalonia. One change was the increasing use of Malta as a port of call. After the French garrison of Valletta surrendered to British and Maltese besiegers in 1800, the island came under British control. The British largely took an indulgent attitude towards the corsairs of the Barbary regencies. Between 1801 and 1816 some 66 corsairs visited Malta, with four from Algiers, 38 from Tunisia and 24 from Tripoli. Just over half these visits took place in the period 1801–5. The corsairs mostly came to get supplies and water, or to repair storm damage. Sometimes they came with a prize and the British raised no objections.[32]

The revival of corsairing not only led to more attacks on ships at sea, but also to an increase in raids on land. Such land raids had become steadily more uncommon during the eighteenth century, but now they increased once more. The principal targets were villages in Sardinia, Sicily and Calabria. Ciro in Calabria was attacked each year from 1803 to 1805, while the Italian Adriatic coast between Pescara and Brindisi was attacked eleven times between May and November 1815. One of the most notorious raids was the attack on Carloforte, on the island of San Pietro off Sardinia, in September 1798. Almost 1,000 Tunisian corsairs in ten ships landed on the island, quickly overcame local resistance, and then took away almost 900 Christian men, women and children. Tunisian attempts to repeat this success at other places in 1799 were defeated, but much later, in October 1815, the Tunisians successfully raided Sant'Antioco (on the island of the same name off Sardinia) and took away 150 Christian captives.

There are no 'typical' corsair cruises, but the following examples give some idea of what went on and what could go wrong. In September 1805 a felucca, carrying four cannon and a crew of 40 men, under Hassan Lazoghlu Reis of Monastir, left Tunis and went to cruise off Calabria and Sardinia. A Sicilian vessel and a Genoese vessel were captured and sent back to Tunis with prize crews. As the felucca had oars as well as sails, it could work close inshore, leading to the capture of several fishing boats. Then in December the Tunisian vessel was struck by a storm and driven ashore in Neapolitan territory. The captain and crew ended their cruise in a Neapolitan gaol. Somewhat more fortunate was the xebec of Mohammed Karabak Reis which left Tripoli in October 1815. The vessel, carrying 10 guns and 70 crew, went to cruise off Calabria. It stopped five ships to inspect their papers. Three were Ottoman ships and two were under the British flag, so all had to be released unharmed. Then the Tripoli corsair managed to capture two Neapolitan ships, one in ballast and the other carrying grain. The crew of one vessel escaped ashore in the ship's boat, but the crew of the other ship became captives. The two captures were sent to Tripoli with prize crews. Damaged by a storm in early December, the xebec went to Malta to make repairs, then returned to Tripoli without taking any further prizes.

It has been estimated that between 1798 and 1816 the corsairs of Algiers, Tunis and Tripoli probably took around 500 prizes, roughly in the proportion 200 by Algiers, 200 by Tunis, and 100 by Tripoli. Spanish, Portuguese and Italian vessels predominated, and only a few were of significant value. Rich prizes were the Austrian (mostly ex-Venetian) ships taken in 1798–9 and the occasional Swedish, Danish or American ship when the corsairs were in dispute with those nations. Vessels from Napoleon's empire or from territories enjoying British protection usually passed untouched. The same could usually be said for Ottoman ships, but when prizes grew scarce, the corsairs sometimes seized Greek merchant ships sailing under the Ottoman flag, much to the annoyance of the sultan.

More ships taken usually meant more Christian captives in corsair hands. Although the numbers involved could hardly compare with those in the sixteenth and seventeenth centuries, there was a definite increase in their numbers. In 1795 there were 630 Christian slaves in Algiers and the number peaked at 1,645 in 1813. Tunis probably had numbers slightly below those of Algiers, while Tripoli had only around half the Algerine figures. In the 1790s slaves were mostly Spanish, Portuguese and Italian, but by 1815 the two former groups featured less and Italians, particularly from Neapolitan territories, made up the largest group. Austrians, Americans and Dutch were also captives for certain periods according to the changes in international affairs.

That the Barbary corsairs could operate so freely was largely due to the indulgence shown them by the British navy which dominated the Mediterranean for most of the period 1793–1815. This did not sit well with many British naval officers, including the most famous of them all, Admiral Horatio Nelson. An angry Nelson observed in 1799: 'My blood boils that I cannot chastise these pirates. They could not show themselves in the Mediterranean did not our country permit. Never let us talk of the cruelty of the African slave trade while we permit such a horrid war.'[33] Yet, like all the rest, Nelson, when commander-in-chief in the Mediterranean, had to do his best to appease the rulers of the Barbary states in order to keep local supplies flowing to his fleet. Nelson died heroically at Trafalgar in 1805 and his second-in-command at that battle, Admiral Cuthbert Collingwood, took over the Mediterranean command (to 1810). After 1807 Napoleon's continental system sought to end all British commercial links with Europe, making the support of the Ottoman regencies even more important to the British. Supplies were needed for garrisons in places like Gibraltar, Sicily, Malta and the Ionian Islands; for the ships of the fleet; and later for the British armies in Portugal and Spain. Collingwood and his successors had to continue the tradition of appeasing the Barbary corsairs, including allowing them to use Malta as a support base.

What led to some slackening of the Barbary corsair revival after 1806 was not the actions of opponents, but the opening up of new commercial opportunities. The British blockade and the French continental system meant that neutral shippers bringing goods into Europe, whether legally or illegally, could make a fortune. Greek shipowners in the Ottoman empire were soon expanding their fleets as this neutral trade boomed. It was only natural for Barbary merchants to want a share of this lucrative trade, which promised a large and regular income in contrast to the lottery of corsairing.[34] However, this was only a wartime phenomenon. With the return of peace in 1814, European merchants regained their trade, and the merchants of Barbary began to look once more at corsairing.

Usually such a strong revival of Barbary corsair activities would have provoked violent retaliation from the European maritime powers. However, on this occasion they were too busy fighting each other to have forces to spare for punitive expeditions against Barbary ports. The only country that was willing and able to fight the corsairs was the new USA, and even the young republic had initially preferred paying tribute to dispatching warships to the Mediterranean. Independence had meant that American ships lost the protection afforded by the Royal Navy and Britain's treaties with the Barbary states. As the USA had no navy it was in a particularly vulnerable position in the 1780s. Like all predators, the corsairs were quick to spot and attack weak prey. By the end of 1793 the Algerines had taken a dozen American prizes and held over 100 Americans as captives.

Some Americans wanted their government to buy immunity by paying tribute to the corsairs as the Danes and the Swedes did. Others wanted the USA to build a navy and fight the corsairs. Although the foundations of the US Navy were laid by the decision in 1794 to build six frigates, in the short term the Americans were forced to make tribute treaties with the corsair states. A treaty was agreed with Algiers in 1796 and the 88 Americans still alive out of the original 119 taken were ransomed for a payment of 650,000 dollars. Similar treaties were made with Tripoli in 1796 and Tunis in 1797.

In 1801 Thomas Jefferson, the new American president, decided his country should stand up to the corsairs and ordered the preparation of a naval squadron to be sent to the Mediterranean. By coincidence, just as the president made his decision, one of the Barbary states had decided to declare war on America. Yusuf Karamanli, ruler of Tripoli, felt he should receive the same tribute from the Americans as that given to Algiers and Tunis, but the American consul said this was not possible. In retaliation Yusuf sent out his corsairs to attack American shipping. An American squadron of three frigates and a sloop, under Commodore Richard Dale, appeared off Tripoli in July 1801 and began to blockade the port. In August a warship from Tripoli was captured by the Americans after a short action, but as the USA was not formally at war with Tripoli, the vessel could only be stripped of its armament and released.[35]

Congress still refused the president a formal declaration of war on Tripoli, and he had to be content with a resolution allowing US warships to take military action to defend American merchant shipping. In 1802 command of the American squadron in the Mediterranean passed to Commodore Richard Morris, who proved even more ineffective than his predecessor. The Americans co-operated for a time with Swedish warships in enforcing the blockade since that country was also at war with Tripoli. However, the Swedes soon tired of this, made peace with Tripoli and returned to paying tribute. The Americans had the use of the British bases at Gibraltar and Malta, but bad feeling produced by the desertion of British sailors to American ships made this arrangement increasingly difficult. The financial terms offered by Yusuf Karamanli for a new peace were unacceptable to the Americans, so the blockade dragged on, with occasional clashes between the two sides.

In 1803 Commodore Edward Preble was sent to command in the Mediterranean, and he was to prove more aggressive than either Morris or Dale. As already noted, Preble managed to avoid a new war with Morocco, combining a show of force with successful negotiations at Tangier. Before he moved on from Gibraltar to Tripoli, he learned that a major misfortune had befallen his squadron. On the last day of October 1803 the frigate USS *Philadelphia*, commanded by William Bainbridge, went too close inshore near the entrance to Tripoli harbour and struck a reef. Unable to get off, the ship was soon surrounded by gunboats and compelled to surrender. Bainbridge and his crew of over 300 men became captives, while the *Philadelphia* was later refloated and taken into Tripoli as a prize. Not only was this affair a humiliation for the Americans, but Yusuf now had a new frigate to add to his fleet and the large number of American captives strengthened his hand in any negotiations.

Preble now set up a supply base for his squadron at Syracuse in Sicily and set about considering what to do about the captured frigate. In February 1804 he sent Lt Stephen Decatur on a daring mission into Tripoli harbour which led to the burning of the *Philadelphia*. This was a great success, but the Americans were still no nearer forcing Yusuf to make peace. In addition, Preble was once again faced with the possibility of a new war breaking out. A Tunisian vessel had been seized while trying to run the American blockade, and the ruler of Tunis was threatening to open hostilities. Fortunately the offer of generous financial compensation by the Americans bought further peace with Tunis in April. In the following month Preble consulted with Sir John Acton, the prime minister of the kingdom of Naples, about getting naval cooperation against Tripoli. A French-born English Catholic, Acton had originally served in the navy of Tuscany, taking part in the ill-fated Spanish attack on Algiers in 1775. Then he had joined the Neapolitan service, reorganizing the navy before going on to higher political office. Acton agreed to lend the Americans six gunboats and two bomb vessels for an attack on Tripoli.[36]

In August 1804 Preble launched a bombardment of Tripoli, during which his gunboats clashed with those sent out by the corsairs. Stephen Decatur again distinguished himself, capturing three enemy gunboats, but his brother was killed in the fighting. Preble now learned that a new commodore, Samuel Barron, was coming from America to replace him, so he redoubled his attacks on Tripoli in the hope of forcing Yusuf to make peace before Barron arrived. He even sent a vessel packed with explosives towards Tripoli harbour, hoping its explosion would create such chaos that the American captives might escape in the confusion. It was a last desperate throw of the dice, and it failed. The vessel blew up prematurely before it reached the harbour, killing all the Americans on board.

It seemed that after years of effort, the Americans were still no nearer to forcing Yusuf Karamanli to sue for peace. Now a new approach was tried. William Eaton, who had been American consul in Tunis, proposed encouraging Hamid, the exiled elder brother of Yusuf Karamanli, to return to the regency of Tripoli and raise a revolt against his brother. President Jefferson gave his support to this project. In March 1805 Eaton and Hamid invaded Libya from Egypt with a force of mercenary troops and a handful of us marines. In April they seized the port of Derna and then repulsed a counterattack by Yusuf's forces. All seemed to be going well when Eaton received word that the war was over. Hamid's cause was quickly dropped and the Americans withdrew from Derna.

Although Eaton's invasion of his territory caused no immediate threat to Yusuf Karamanli, it was unsettling and made him more willing to make peace. Commodore Barron and American envoy Tobias Lear soon reached a peace deal with him. The us would pay 60,000 dollars for the release of all American prisoners, but it refused to pay Tripoli any further tribute. Of the 307 crew of the *Philadelphia*, 296 were released, six had died in captivity, and five had 'turned Turk'. Barron was now taken ill, and command of the squadron passed to Captain John Rodgers, who took the opportunity to visit Tunis and compel its government to agree terms acceptable to the USA. After that, most of the American ships returned home.

Although this war had been a success for the USA, it had taken a very long time and its cost consumed a large amount of money. As already noted, when the USA embarked on another war against the Barbary corsairs in 1815, it was a model of brevity. Commodore Stephen Decatur achieved decisive success against Algiers in weeks not years. These two Barbary wars had not cost the Americans much blood, with a total of only 35 sailors and marines killed and 64 wounded, but the financial costs were heavy. The war against Tripoli alone had cost over 3 million dollars at a time when the entire annual expenditure of the us government was barely 10 million dollars. From a pragmatic viewpoint, the USA would have found it cheaper simply to pay off the Barbary corsairs. However, a new state seeking to make its mark on the world had at some point to fight for its rights. The challenge of the Barbary corsairs led to the creation of the US Navy, and it was that navy which humbled the Ottoman regencies.

THE CONQUEST OF ALGIERS

In late 1814 the great powers of Europe were meeting in the Congress of Vienna to re-order international affairs after the end of the war against Napoleonic France. The British, who were proud of their abolition of the black slave trade in 1807, were particularly keen that all maritime states should agree to the suppression of that trade. However, not all Britons at Vienna were convinced that priority should be given to this anti-slavery measure. A maverick British admiral, Sir Sydney Smith, thought that more attention and urgency should be given to the final suppression of the taking of white Christian captives by the Barbary corsairs.[37]

There had already been proposals that the Knights of St John might be re-established in Malta so that they could resume their centuries-old struggle against the Barbary corsairs. Smith put forward the idea of a multinational naval squadron in the Mediterranean which would perform a similar task, and he generously offered to be its commander. Unfortunately Sir Sydney Smith was widely distrusted in British government circles. His great achievement had been to assist in the defeat of Napoleon at the siege of Acre on the Palestinian coast in 1799, but since then the British navy had been reluctant to employ him. The predominant British view was that Algiers and the other Ottoman regencies had largely observed their treaties with Britain, avoiding all attacks on British-protected shipping, and so there was no reason to take hostile action against them.

Nevertheless, such a narrow nationalistic view could not survive for long. British diplomats were well aware that their country was open to charges of hypocrisy for seeking an end to the transatlantic trade in black slaves while ignoring the plight of white Christian slaves in North Africa. While Napoleon's Hundred Days unfolded during the summer of 1815, ending in defeat at Waterloo, the American commodore Stephen Decatur was winning his lightning war against Algiers. In October 1815 some 150 Christian men, women and children were abducted from the island of Sant'Antioco off Sardinia by Tunisian corsairs. This only increased the growing outrage in Christian Europe at the continued activities of the Barbary corsairs. Would Britain, the world's dominant naval power, ever do anything to suppress them?

Edward Pellew, Lord Exmouth, was the admiral commanding Britain's Mediterranean fleet. In the spring of 1816 he took his five ships of the line and seven frigates to visit Algiers, Tunis and Tripoli. Despite this show of force, Exmouth's orders gave him tasks both bizarre and trivial. He was to inform the rulers of the Ottoman regencies that the Ionian Islands were now a British colony and so its inhabitants and their vessels were under British protection. Similarly, the German state of Hanover, still linked to the British crown, had enhanced its maritime interests by acquiring the port of Emden under the peace treaties. Hanoverian ships were to be treated as British. Exmouth was also to arrange peace treaties with the three Barbary states for the recently created kingdom of Piedmont-Sardinia, which had absorbed the republic of Genoa, and the kingdom of the Two Sicilies, usually just known as the kingdom of Naples. Treaties were arranged, but both these states still had to pay tribute to the corsairs. Also, Exmouth had the humiliating task of haggling with the corsairs about the ransoms to be paid for slaves from those two states currently held by the corsair states. These were hardly the duties a naval commander in the world's most powerful navy might expect to perform.[38]

Having made his visits to the three ports, arranged the treaties and freed hundreds of Italian slaves, Exmouth then received orders to return to Algiers and obtain a declaration from the dey that he would no longer enslave Christians. The dey was unwilling to do this and claimed he would first have to consult with his master, the Ottoman sultan. This was clearly a delaying tactic, since the rulers of the Ottoman regencies only acknowledged their subordination to Istanbul when it suited them. The dey said it might take six months to get the sultan's opinion, and Exmouth meekly agreed to this delay. However, the admiral was less submissive when it seemed popular disturbances might endanger British naval officers and the British consul Hugh McDonell, who came of an American loyalist family.[39] Exmouth's threats to the dey, Omar, led to the latter issuing orders for the arrest of British people throughout the regency. The quarrel was largely patched up before Exmouth's departure, but consul McDonell remained under house arrest in Algiers. The admiral even provided a British frigate to carry Omar's emissary to Istanbul and escort a ship carrying presents from Omar to his nominal overlord, the Ottoman sultan. Exmouth did not know that among those presents were 40 Austrian Christian slaves.

Lord Exmouth returned to England in late June 1816. He found himself decidedly unpopular, although he had only carried out his orders. It seemed to many people that he had humiliated Britain by negotiating with a gang of pirates. Then dissatisfaction turned to outrage when news reached Britain of a massacre on the Algerian coast. Some years earlier Britain had been given the right to run a coral fishery on that coast, although nearly all the fishermen were Sicilians. When Omar sent out his order to arrest British people, the local officials believed this order included the Sicilians. In carrying out the order they met resistance, so several hundred Sicilians were massacred and the rest put in prison. Christian Europe was outraged, and Britain was made to look weak and cowardly. The government ordered a squadron be prepared for dispatch to Algiers. Sir Sydney Smith made a hopeful plea that he might be its commander, but Exmouth was to be allowed to return to Algiers to restore his reputation. His orders were simple. The dey was to give in to all British demands or Algiers would be bombarded. As an officer on HMS *Albion* wrote: 'We are to be one of the ships employed in the holy war, or crusade, to proceed against the infidels of Algiers to abolish Christian slavery and to chastise those barbarians for the outrages they have been committing in the Mediterranean.'[40]

At Gibraltar Exmouth's fleet acquired an ally. The Netherlands had ceased paying tribute to the Barbary corsairs while it was under French domination after 1795, but once French hegemony ended in 1814 the corsairs wanted a resumption of Dutch tribute payments. The Dutch government was unwilling to comply and had sent warships to the Mediterranean to defend its interests. A squadron of Dutch frigates under Admiral Theodorus van Capellan was at Gibraltar and Exmouth agreed to a Dutch request to join his fleet. The admiral now had a British force of five ships of the line, a 50-gun ship, four frigates, five sloops and four bomb vessels, along with a Dutch force of four frigates and one corvette.

Arriving off Algiers in the second half of August, Exmouth found the dey unwilling to give way to British demands, so preparations were begun to open a bombardment. Exmouth would concentrate his attack on the fortifications along the seashore and on the Algerine fleet, including five frigates and four corvettes, moored in the harbour, largely avoiding the

Nicolaas Baur, *The Anglo–Dutch Fleet in the Bay of Algiers, 26 August 1816*, 1818.

city itself. The bombardment began on the afternoon of 27 August 1816 and went on for almost ten hours, ending around midnight. The Algerine fleet was destroyed and heavy damage inflicted on the fortifications.[41] The British lost 128 killed and 690 wounded; the Dutch 13 killed and 52 wounded; and the Algerine casualties were estimated at between 2,000 and 5,000. Although his men had fought heroically and stood to their guns hour after hour, Omar was depressed at the damage inflicted on Algiers and considered fleeing the city. On the other side Exmouth was aware that his forces had used up nearly all their ammunition and the bombardment could not be renewed. Thus it was a bluff when the British admiral demanded on the following day that Omar give in to all his demands on pain of further attacks. Omar was not to know this and immediately complied. Consul McDonell and other British hostages were released unharmed while all remaining Christian slaves, over 1,600 in number and two-thirds Neapolitans and Sicilians, were freed without ransom. Omar agreed that Algiers would no longer take Christian slaves and that the Dutch need not pay any more tribute. Having lost to the Americans in 1815 and the British and the Dutch in 1816, Omar seemed doomed, but widespread bribery temporarily appeased his troops. Only in 1817 did the janissaries kill Omar and install a new dey of Algiers.

However, before his murder, Omar had begun rebuilding the fortifications of Algiers and its fleet. In 1817 Algiers received one vessel as a
present from the ruler of Tripoli, while four other replacement vessels were
bought in Italy, two at Livorno and two at Naples. In 1818 Algiers
received a 46-gun frigate as a present from the Ottoman sultan Mahmud
II and a 36-gun frigate as a present from the ruler of Morocco. This
Muslim solidarity was not joined by Tunisia, which had been glad to see
its recent enemy Algiers humbled by the Christian fleet. A new 32-gun
frigate was built at Algiers. By 1820 the Algerine fleet had largely been
restored to the state it had been in before Lord Exmouth made his attack.[42]

Despite the treaties of 1816, some corsairing continued. In 1818 the
European powers met at the Congress of Aix-la-Chapelle (now
Aachen). Among the topics considered was the maritime situation in
the Mediterranean. It was decided to send a diplomatic note to the three
Ottoman regencies telling them to renounce their 'system of piracy' and
turn to peaceful commerce. The note was delivered at Algiers, Tunis and
Tripoli in 1819 by a combined British and French naval squadron under
Admiral Sir Thomas Fremantle and Admiral Pierre Jurien de la Gravière.
The rulers of the Barbary states were unimpressed, especially as since
1814 the Mediterranean Christian states had been placing restrictions on
the peaceful commerce of Barbary merchants and shipping.

In 1821 there was a major revolt in Greece against Ottoman rule.
When the European powers eventually intervened to back the Christian
Greeks, this would finally lead to an independent Greek state in 1832.
However, in the early years of the revolt the Greeks fought largely alone
and it seemed the Ottomans might suppress them. As well as land forces,
the Greeks had active squadrons in the Aegean Sea and for the first time
in many years the Ottoman sultan called on the Barbary states to send
him naval assistance. Thanks to the revival of corsairing after 1793, those
states now had some significant vessels to send, especially well armed
frigates. In 1821 Algiers sent eight ships, a large part of its fleet, and they
did not return from service in the sultan's fleet until the autumn of
1823.[43] When they did so, the ruler of Algiers was in dispute with the
consuls, especially British consul McDonell, and he was also considering hostile action against the shipping of Spain and the Netherlands.
Now his ships had returned, he could launch such action.

In January 1824 a British merchant ship arrived at Algiers from
Smyrna carrying 60 Turkish recruits for the janissaries who controlled

the city. Although the recruits were welcome, the Algerine authorities threatened to seize the vessel. In the same month Algerine corsairs were sent out to attack Spanish shipping, and soon a captured ship was sent in and the Spanish captives on board were declared to be slaves, contrary to the 1816 treaty. After the British consul complained, he was threatened with arrest. Finally he left the city in a British warship and soon afterwards an Algerine corsair clashed with a British frigate. Algiers and Britain were once again at war.[44]

During the spring and summer of 1824 Admiral Sir Harry Neale maintained a blockade of Algiers, but it was not very effective due to a lack of ships in his squadron. One novelty was that the squadron included a steamship, HMS *Lightning*, the first such vessel used in British naval operations. Its role was to tow sailing warships into position to bombard Algiers if there was no wind to fill their sails. In late July Neale decided to bombard Algiers even though his squadron numbered only one ship of the line, three frigates, three bomb vessels and a dozen smaller vessels, including the paddle steamer. After some desultory fire from both sides, the dey requested further negotiations. Eventually terms were agreed, with the dey giving in to most British demands. The Spanish prisoners would be freed and a British consul would return to Algiers. However, it would not be Hugh McDonell. The dey claimed he was hated by the populace and would be in danger, so Neale gave way on that point.[45]

After the hostilities between Britain and Algiers in 1824, which excited very little interest in Britain, the Algerines could return to assisting the Ottoman sultan in the following year. Since 1805 Mohammad Ali had created a semi-independent state in Egypt, with European advisers building up his armed forces. After some defeats at the hands of the Greeks, the Ottoman sultan, Mahmud II, was forced to call on his nominal vassal in Egypt for military assistance. In 1824 Mohammad Ali's son Ibrahim took an Egyptian fleet and army to Greece to aid the Ottoman forces. In May 1825 a convoy left Alexandria bound for Greece taking supplies and reinforcements for Ibrahim. It had a large naval escort, mostly Ottoman and Egyptian warships, but also including five from Algiers (two frigates, two corvettes and a schooner) and four from Tripoli (a corvette, a brig and two schooners).[46]

While Britain had clashed with Algiers, for the first half of the 1820s France had generally had good relations with the regency. This situation changed dramatically on 30 April 1827. In an angry meeting with the French consul, Pierre Deval, the dey, Hussein, had struck the diplomat with a fly swatter. After such an insult, Deval left the city and the French government sent an ultimatum to the dey demanding an apology. Hussein refused to give one, and in June 1827 France declared a blockade of the Algerian coastline, sending warships to enforce it. For the first time since the 1680s serious hostilities had broken out between France and Algiers.

The original dispute between Deval and Hussein involved two issues. First, Deval's nephew, Alexandre Deval, French vice-consul in Bona, had been fortifying French commercial establishments there and at La Calle contrary to treaty. (The French were evacuated from these outposts before the naval blockade was imposed.) Second, the dey believed that the French government owed him a large sum of money. Between 1793 and 1798 the French army had purchased Algerian wheat through two Jewish merchant families, Bakri and Bushnaq, but payment was delayed. Those merchant families owed money to the Algerian government and said it could not be paid until the French paid them first. After much delay, the French government offered a settlement in 1820 to the merchants, but did not mention money owed to the dey although his claim had been formally lodged. Hussein suspected that Deval had been collaborating with Jacob Bakri to thwart the dey's claims.

Because of the French blockade, the Algerines could not send a squadron to aid the Ottoman sultan in his war against the Greek rebels in 1827. This was probably just as well, since the Greek war was reaching a new level of international involvement. A combined British-French-Russian fleet, under the overall command of British admiral Sir Edward Codrington, had been sent to shadow the Ottoman-Egyptian fleet in Greek waters. The Muslim fleet took refuge in the bay of Navarino (now Pylos), and when, on 20 October 1827, Codrington tried to lead his ships into the same anchorage, he was fired on. A battle resulted and most of the Ottoman-Egyptian fleet was destroyed. The only Barbary vessels present were three Tunisian frigates, but they do not seem to have seen much action and in November Codrington allowed them to leave Navarino.[47] The battle of Navarino was a blow not just to Ottoman sultan Mahmud II and his over-mighty vassal Mohammad Ali of Egypt, but to all Muslims in the Mediterranean. However, the Algerines were determined to stand firm in their conflict with France.

Taking advice from Captain Abel Dupetit-Thouars, who had carried out regular patrols along the Algerian coast during the 1820s, the French government began preparing plans for an expedition against Algiers. These were well advanced by the start of 1828, but then a new government came to power in Paris and showed less interest in taking such direct action. Instead the naval blockade was intensified and several clashes took place between French and Algerine ships. The blockade of the Algerian coast began to inconvenience French merchants more than the Algerines. The merchants of Marseille, whose trade in the eastern Mediterranean had already been disrupted by the Greek war, complained that the loss of North African trade was further increasing their losses. At first they supported the idea of a settlement with the dey but, as the disruption dragged on, many came round to the view that the best solution would be for France to seize Algiers and possibly the rest of the regency as well.

In 1829 new incidents strengthened French resolve and made a major French expedition against Algiers seem more likely. In June the boats from two French frigates were sent to raid the Algerian coast, but their occupants fell into an ambush, losing at least 23 men killed. As the dey had offered money for the head of any Frenchman, the heads of those slain were immediately sent to Algiers so that the reward could be collected. A month later a French ship of the line was allowed into Algiers under a flag of truce to see if peace negotiations could be commenced. This was not possible and as the ship left Algiers, still flying a flag of truce, it was fired on by the Algerine batteries. Fortunately the ship escaped unscathed, but this outrage only added to calls for more aggressive French action against Algiers.[48]

The French government now began to view its conflict with Algiers in a wider context. In the autumn of 1829 the French prime minister, the prince of Polignac, opened discussions with Mohammad Ali of Egypt, a close ally of France. First Mohammad Ali was to be offered a loan and the gift of four ships of the line, to make up for his losses at the battle of Navarino, if he would attack Algiers. Then Polignac suggested that the Egyptian ruler should occupy all the three Ottoman regencies in North Africa. There would then be a strong Muslim state along the southern shores of the Mediterranean which was linked to France. Mohammad Ali was willing to consider the idea, but then the French changed their plan. Now France would take over the regency of

Algiers, leaving Tunis and Tripoli to be occupied by forces from Egypt. Mohammad Ali could only reject this plan. If he was seen to be aiding French expansion into Muslim territory it would damage his reputation in the wider Islamic world. Although the discussions came to nothing, rumours of them alarmed not only the ruler of Algiers but also those of Tunis and Tripoli.

Within France the government of King Charles x was facing an increasing challenge from the liberal opposition. An election was to occur in 1830 and the government feared that the liberals would become dominant in the assembly. The royalist ministers decided that a successful foreign adventure like the conquest of Algiers would win new support for the Bourbon king and perhaps turn back the liberal tide. In March 1830 the French government decided to launch an attack on Algiers, and the war minister, the count of Bourmont, was given command of the military contingent which would be sent. Admiral Guy-Victor Duperré would command the fleet.

An event in May 1830 further inflamed French sentiment against the Algerines and ensured public support for an attack on Algiers. Two French naval brigs patrolling the Algerian coast were wrecked after losing their way in fog. The survivors were immediately attacked by local people. Some 109 French sailors were killed and 73 taken prisoner, including the two commanders of the brigs. The prisoners and the heads of the slain men were immediately dispatched to Algiers, where they were received with popular rejoicing and payment from the dey. French anger at this event would soon be translated into action.[49]

Napoleon had on one occasion during his imperial rule considered launching an attack on Algiers as part of his wider scheme to break up the Ottoman empire. Vincent-Yves Boutin, an officer of engineers, was sent to Algiers in 1808 with secret orders to survey the city and its defences and draw up a plan of attack. Boutin completed his mission, but Napoleon had been distracted by other events.[50] Nevertheless the invasion plan was kept in the war ministry files. Boutin's plan was radically different to the previous, failed attacks on Algiers by Christian European states. On those occasions the invaders always landed on beaches within the bay of Algiers to the east of the city. Boutin proposed that the next invasion should come ashore at Sidi Ferruch to the west of Algiers. The invaders would then move towards the city and seize the high ground which dominated it. In particular they would aim to capture the Emperor's Fort. This fortification was built on the supposed site of Emperor Charles v's camp during his unsuccessful 1541 attack on Algiers. Once the fort was taken, the invaders would control the heights overlooking Algiers and could mount a successful assault on the city itself. By the 1820s this plan seems to have become well known. US consul William Shaler outlined it as the best way to take the city in his book on Algiers, which was published in 1826.[51]

Bourmont collected more than 35,000 troops for the expedition, along with over 80 pieces of artillery, including large siege guns. In May Duperré sailed from Toulon with a naval force of four ships of the line and seventeen frigates fully armed; eight of the line and seven frigates with some guns removed to allow carriage of troops; and over fifty smaller naval vessels, including two paddle steamers. In addition over 600 transport ships, in two waves, also joined the invasion force. Keeping this vast amount of shipping in order was not easy, especially as a first attempt to reach Algiers was disrupted by a storm. However, most of the expeditionary force reassembled at Majorca and then set out for Algiers once more.

The delay robbed the French of any element of surprise in their attack, but the dey had already received details of the French plans from his agents in Marseille and Toulon. Hussein now had more time to collect his forces. His governors in Oran and Constantine sent over 30,000 men, mostly cavalry, to Algiers. In the city itself there were about 12,000 men, but only half were Turkish soldiers. Even these Turks, the backbone of the Algerine army, had their deficiencies. Many were elderly and no new Turkish recruits had come from Anatolia since 1827 because of the French naval blockade. In total the dey had an army of over 40,000 men, but relatively few were disciplined troops. Hussein had been warned that Sidi Ferruch was the likely landing place, so he sent a force of 12,000 men to the bay, but most of these troops were cavalry.

On 14 June 1830 the French army came ashore at Sidi Ferruch, despite gunfire from Algerine batteries, and quickly drove back the defending Algerine forces. Unlike previous invaders, the French immediately began to entrench and build field fortifications. The Algerines soon launched an attack on the French positions, but they were repulsed. Then the French advanced and captured the Algerine camp at Staoueli after a fierce battle. Beating off an Algerine counter-attack at Sidi Khalif, the French advanced steadily and by the end of the month they were preparing to besiege the Emperor's Fort. As a distraction, Duperré carried out several largely ineffective naval bombardments of the seaward defences of Algiers. Once the French began their bombardment of the fort, its garrison withdrew to Algiers, blowing up the magazine as they left.

The French were now ready to attack Algiers itself, but further military action proved unnecessary. On 5 July 1830 the dey of Algiers capitulated, surrendering not just the city but the whole regency of Algiers to the French. The French took possession of Algiers without any looting or other excesses. The treasury of Algiers yielded over 48 million francs, which was enough to pay the cost of the expedition and to give prize money to members of the victorious French forces. As part of the terms of surrender, the French provided Hussein with a ship to take him into exile in Naples, but he was not permitted to take much money with him. By the end of July all the Turks in Algiers had been expelled, the French providing transport to Smyrna for most of them. In addition to Algiers, French forces had occupied Oran, Bona and Bougie, but the rest of the regency was still outside their control.[52]

In taking Algiers the French had lost 400 dead and almost 2,000 wounded. Bourmont had taken his four sons along on the expedition and, shortly after the general's victory, one of them died of his wounds. The Algerines had lost perhaps 2,000 dead, with many more wounded. In their well prepared invasion, the French had shown boldness and determination. The Algerine defenders had shown undisciplined courage, which all too easily degenerated into confusion. Bourmont was proud of his army's achievement and he told his men: 'Twenty days have been sufficient to destroy the state whose existence has wearied Europe for three centuries.'[53]

One of the reasons for the expedition to Algiers was to influence political developments within France in favour of the royalist government. In this aim it was a complete failure. The liberals had won the election, and attempts by the Bourbon government to suppress constitutional liberties quickly led to a revolution in late July 1830. Louis Philippe, from the Orléanist branch of the French royal family, replaced Charles x as king in a new liberal monarchy. As a supporter of Charles x, the count of Bourmont sought to collect his army at Algiers and take it back to France to oust the new king. Oran, Bona and Bougie were evacuated. However, it soon became clear that the army would not support Bourmont, so he went into exile in Spain. The conquest of Algiers, a Christian dream for more than three centuries, had been achieved, but the conqueror followed the defeated dey into exile only a few weeks later.

Now the French had Algiers, what were they going to do with it? Leave with the loot after appointing a client Muslim ruler? Directly occupy it as an isolated outpost like the Spanish presidios or England's Tangier in an earlier time? Or would they use it as a base from which to launch the conquest of the whole of the regency of Algiers? Because of the political turmoil in France, there were no clear guidelines from Paris and much was left to the decision of the new military commander in Algiers, General Bertrand Clauzel. The Tunisians had not been sorry to see the downfall of the dey of Algiers. They opened negotiations with Clauzel, and there was talk of Tunisian princes ruling Oran and Constantine as vassals of France. Algiers would remain in French hands, and Clauzel began the process of French colonization in and around the city. It was the beginning of a twenty-year war of conquest, at the end of which the French would have control of most of Algeria.

After the conquest of Algiers, a French naval squadron under Admiral de Rosamel visited both Tunis and Tripoli to compel their rulers to sign new treaties favourable to France and make a definitive promise to end all corsairing and white slavery. Tunis, already favourable to the French presence in Algiers, went so far as to agree to a French demand that land should be set aside where a memorial to St Louis, the French king who had died leading a crusade against Tunis in 1270, could be set up.

Tripoli had enjoyed some success in resisting the lesser European maritime states during the 1820s. In particular, a Neapolitan fleet had been sent in 1828 to demand an end to tribute payments, but the fleet's bombardment of Tripoli was ineffective and when peace was finally restored, the Neapolitans still had to pay tribute to avoid attack by the Tripoli corsairs. Yusuf Karamanli, who was still the ruler, had less success in handling the major powers of Britain and France. Hanmer George Warrington had become British consul at Tripoli in 1814 and soon began to establish a close, even dominant, relationship with Yusuf.[54] After a time Yusuf came to resent Warrington's dictates and looked for support from the French consul. By signing a treaty favourable to France in 1830, Yusuf only increased Warrington's hostility to him. When there were tribal revolts against Yusuf soon afterwards, Warrington was suspected of encouraging them. However, a new power was to intervene in the affairs of the regency of Tripoli.

Although the Ottoman sultan had little direct control of affairs in the regencies of Algiers, Tunis and Tripoli, it was a great blow to have Algiers removed from even nominal membership of his empire by a Christian European power. Russia and Austria had already taken Ottoman lands. Was France now to do the same? Although there was no direct confrontation between France and the Ottoman empire, the resistance within Algeria of Ahmed, ruler of Constantine, which lasted until 1837, was undertaken in the name of the Ottoman sultan. The Ottomans soon had to accept that Algeria was lost, but they were determined not to give up their claims on Tripoli and Tunis. As revolts against Yusuf Karamanli increased, an Ottoman fleet and army arrived in the country in 1835. The Karamanli dynasty was overthrown and Tripoli was once again brought under direct Ottoman control, a situation that would continue until the Italian invasion in 1911. After their success at Tripoli the Ottomans tried to force Tunis to accept direct Ottoman rule in 1836, but the French stepped in to preserve the semi-independent status of Tunisia.[55] To preserve this position the Tunisians had to balance between France and the Ottoman sultan. They cut off supplies to Ahmed, thus assisting the French conquest of Constantine, but during the Crimean war of 1853–6 they sent troops to join the Ottoman sultan's army. The balancing act could not last forever, and in 1881 the French declared a protectorate over Tunisia and took control of the country.

William Shaler had been installed as US consul at Algiers after Decatur's victory in the short war of 1815. The consul was exasperated by what he saw as the weak European response, even by Britain and France, to the challenge still posed by the Barbary corsairs. In 1826 Shaler wrote angrily: 'that while the great maritime powers of Europe were establishing colonies, at a vast expense of human life and of treasure, at the utmost extremities of the earth, a mere handful of mischevious banditti has been left in the quiet enjoyment of the fairest portion of the globe, at their very threshold, and receiving from them submission, little short of homage'.[56] Within four years this centuries-old situation was ended, and with it the age of the Barbary corsairs. Then, slowly but surely,

Algeria, Tunisia, Tripoli and Morocco were brought under the colonial rule of the European Christian powers. The dream of Ferdinand and Isabella had become a reality.

The American destroyer USS *Bainbridge* on anti-piracy patrol off Somalia in September 2007.

Conclusion:
A New Barbary?

The president had given the order, and the commander of the destroyer had passed it on to the snipers deployed at the ship's stern. If the three pirates threatened the life of their hostage, the snipers were to open fire. The pirates raised their AK47 assault rifles. The prisoner might die at any moment. The snipers from the US Navy's SEAL commandos opened fire. Three Somali pirates were killed, and Captain Richard Phillips of the *Maersk Alabama* was freed unharmed. A fourth Somali pirate became a prisoner aboard the destroyer. The date was 12 April 2009.

The fire order from Commander Frank Castellano on the destroyer USS *Bainbridge* brought to an end the last act in a drama which had begun with the first seizure of an American-flag merchant ship by pirates since the early nineteenth century. Somali pirates had got onboard the *Maersk Alabama* on 8 April and seemed likely to capture the ship quickly. However, the crew fought back, and in the confusion they captured one pirate while Captain Phillips was taken by the other attackers. An exchange was agreed, but while the pirate was released by the crew, Captain Phillips was not freed by the pirates. Instead they fled from the *Maersk Alabama* in the ship's lifeboat, taking the captain with them as a hostage. Then American warships reached the scene and after attempts at negotiation, the affair was concluded by three shots from the SEAL snipers.[1]

This incident included a link between the Barbary corsairs of old and the Somali pirates of today. Commander Castellano's destroyer was named after William Bainbridge, the US Navy captain who had lost a frigate to the corsairs of Tripoli in the first Barbary war (1801–5), but had redeemed himself by capturing a British frigate during the war of 1812. This link was purely coincidental, and despite fears by some commentators that Somalia is becoming 'a new Barbary', the pirates from that country cannot be considered as the heirs of the Barbary corsairs. Nevertheless there are parallels between the two groups and it is worthwhile to consider what similarities and differences there are when the story of the Barbary corsairs is compared with the modern Somali pirate menace.

The chief reason the Barbary corsairs had such an impact in the sixteenth century was because they were closely linked to the Ottoman Turkish empire, the most powerful Islamic state of that time. The Ottomans were steadily pushing back the frontiers of Christendom, and the Barbary corsairs were their vanguard in the central and western Mediterranean. No such Islamic superpower exists today, but repeated attempts have been made to link the phenomenon of Somali piracy with the threat from Islamist terrorism.

As yet no such link has been clearly established. Indeed, the Islamist militants in Somalia claim to be strongly opposed to piracy. The Somali pirates may be Muslims, but the motivation for their activities is that of mercenary criminals, not religious zealots. Since piracy is the only lucrative economic activity in Somalia today, it is inevitable that most local political groups should seek to derive some financial benefit from it. Some pirates may make payments to Islamist militants, but so far there is no sign of the pirates adopting their political/religious agenda. This situation may change, but as yet there is little sign of it.

The Barbary corsairs enjoyed their heyday in the first half of the seventeenth century largely because of a crisis of political authority both among their nominal Ottoman overlords and their Christian enemies. Internal revolts weakened the authority of the Ottoman central government, allowing the regencies of Algiers, Tunis and Tripoli to become semi-autonomous city states. A comparable collapse of central power in Morocco allowed its corsairs to achieve a similar status. On the other, Christian side, Spain and Portugal were losing political power and authority, but the new powers of France, England and the Netherlands were not yet strong enough to replace them and stand up to the Muslim corsairs. Also, the Christian powers were distracted by the wars between them, above all the Thirty Years War.

Today's Somali pirates certainly benefit from a collapse of political authority within Somalia. The country has had no functioning national government since 1991, leading to the rise of regional authorities. Most of the Somali pirates are based in the semi-autonomous region of Puntland, but the government of that area cannot or will not take effective measures to curb their criminal activities. The clan-based Somali pirates thrive because there are no government authorities within Somalia ready to oppose them. Outside Somalia, many countries have come forward to contribute warships to the anti-piracy fleet currently patrolling off the coast of Somalia, but problems of divided authority and legal loopholes have prevented a co-ordinated response that might curb the growth in Somali piracy.

The success of the Barbary corsairs was also related to the advantages conferred by their geographical position. During the sixteenth century the Ottoman empire took control of almost all the southern shore of the Mediterranean Sea, exposing many Christian maritime trade routes to Muslim corsair attack. Also, the Barbary corsairs dominated important 'choke points' like the strait of the Gibraltar and the Sicilian narrows, the channel between that island and North Africa. Technological change allowed the Barbary corsairs to extend their cruising grounds into the Atlantic Ocean in the early decades of the seventeenth century. Today's Somali pirates also have geographical advantages. They are close to major maritime trade routes in the Indian Ocean and the Red Sea, while the gulf of Aden, a favourite hunting ground, leads to the choke point of the Bab al Mandab strait between Yemen and Africa. The multinational anti-piracy fleet has had some success in reducing the number of pirate attacks in the gulf of Aden, but this has merely led to the Somali pirates extending their operations further across the Indian Ocean.

In the second half of the seventeenth century the Barbary corsairs had to face the full power of the growing navies of France, England and the Netherlands. Resistance to the Christian sea powers eventually proved futile and the corsairs agreed not to attack the merchant ships of those states. However, the European great powers were not unhappy for the Barbary corsairs to continue operations against the shipping of the lesser Christian maritime states. In this way the merchant fleets of those states could be prevented from becoming serious rivals to the French, English and Dutch merchant fleets. The international shipping industry is very different in the twenty-first century and the Somali pirates have learned to take advantage of this difference.

The Barbary corsairs lived in a time of emerging European nation states. A French merchant ship, for example, was French-owned, flew the French flag and had a French crew. To capture it was to invite retaliation from the French government and its navy. Today the world-wide shipping industry presents a totally different picture. In the age of globalization a merchant ship may be owned in one country, fly the flag of another and have a crew drawn from any number of countries. It might be said that this modern diversity is reflected in the multinational composition of the anti-piracy fleet of warships now assembled off Somalia, but the multiplicity of national interests involved in vessels captured by the pirates is a source of weakness not strength.

The *Maersk Alabama* incident in 2009 was very much the exception which proves the rule. To have an American warship save the all-American crew of an American-flag merchant ship was an echo of an earlier, simpler time. Generally merchant ships captured by the Somali pirates cause as many international complications as does the successful interception of suspected pirate craft by warships on anti-piracy patrol.

The Ottoman regencies of Algiers, Tunis and Tripoli had made lasting treaties with the main European maritime states by 1690, and Morocco did the same in the 1720s. Optimists hoped that the Barbary states would now turn away from predatory activities and take up peaceful maritime trade. However, corsairing was to continue at varying levels of intensity for another hundred years and more. This was largely due to the fact that the two most powerful maritime states in Christian Europe, England/Britain and France, were to spend most of the period 1689–1815 fighting each other in the so-called 'Second Hundred Years War'. Crushing the last remnants of the Barbary corsairs was not a high priority for those powers as long as the corsairs did not attack British or French shipping. Indeed in wartime the two contending sides were likely to be found trying to bribe the Barbary corsairs to attack their opponents. The corsairs wisely took the bribes but stayed out of the wars.

Today's Somali pirates are not a high priority concern of the USA and its allies, whatever the rhetoric coming from the US State Department or the European Union. Events like the *Maersk Alabama* affair in 2009 and the tragic killing of an American yacht crew in February 2011 may temporarily focus American attention on the Somali pirates, but in general US interest has been concentrated on events in countries like Iraq, Afghanistan and Pakistan. If a link between the Somali pirates and Islamist terrorism could be clearly established, then the USA would undoubtedly take a greater, and more aggressive, interest in those pirates. Similarly, if the great Arab revolt of 2011 should reduce Yemen to a state of chaos, such unrest may lead to the growth of piracy in that country, threatening the Bab al Mandab choke point and the gulf of Aden. The USA and its allies would then be forced to increase their anti-piracy activities. Until such events occur, it seems likely that as long as the Somali pirates remain just 'ordinary criminals', there will be no effective international effort to end their activities.

What finally ended corsairing from the Barbary states after three centuries was the conquest of North Africa by European imperialists which began with the French seizure of Algiers in 1830. It is already received wisdom that Somali piracy can only be finally ended by action on land rather than at sea. Such land action clearly cannot be foreign conquest. With memories of the 'Black Hawk Down' incident of 1993 still fresh, the USA is unlikely to want to put its troops on the ground again in Somalia in the near future. In any case, yet another Western invasion of a Muslim country would not go down well in the wider Islamic world.

This leaves only one option for re-establishing some sort of state power on land within Somalia. The current attempt at a revived national government, the UN-backed Somali Transitional Federal Government, barely controls more than a section of the capital, Mogadishu. A more realistic approach to ending the power vacuum in Somalia would be to work with the functioning regional governments in that country. These are in the self-declared independent state of Somaliland and the semi-autonomous region of Puntland. The government of the latter is particularly important since Puntland contains most of the Somali pirate bases. Western assistance can help to strengthen the Puntland government so that it is strong enough to suppress the Somali pirates, but any such process is unlikely to be completed quickly.

Thus while the realm of the Somali pirates is unlikely to become a new Barbary, there are significant parallels between the pirates and the Barbary corsairs, highlighting both differences and similarities. It took European and American states more than three centuries to defeat the Barbary corsairs. One can only hope that today's international community will end the activities of the Somali pirates in a rather shorter period of time.

GLOSSARY OF PLACE NAME CHANGES

PAST	PRESENT
Alcazarquivir	Ksar el Kebir (Morocco)
Bizerta	Bizerte (Tunisia)
Bombay	Mumbai (India)
Bona, Bône	Annaba (Algeria)
Bougie, Bugia	Bejaia (Algeria)
Candia	Iraklion (Greece)
Cape Matifou	Bordj El Bahri (Algeria)
Constantinople	Istanbul (Turkey)
Coron	Koroni (Greece)
Djidjelli, Gigery	Jijel (Algeria)
Famagusta	Gazimagusa (Northern Cyprus)
La Calle	El Kala (Algeria)
La Goletta	La Goulette (Tunisia)
Leghorn	Livorno (Italy)
Lepanto	Nafpaktos (Greece)
Mamora, Marmora	Mehdya (Morocco)
Mazagan	El Jadida (Morocco)
Modon	Methoni (Greece)
Mogador	Essaouira (Morocco)
Morea, the	Peloponnese, the (Greece)
Navarino	Pylos (Greece)
Negroponte	Euboea, Evvia (Greece)
Persia	Iran
Porto Farina	Ghar al Melh (Tunisia)
Ragusa	Dubrovnik (Croatia)
Smyrna	Izmir (Turkey)
Tripoli	Tarabulus (Libya)
Valona	Vlore (Albania)

1415   Portuguese capture Ceuta in North Africa
1453   Ottoman Turks capture Constantinople. End of Byzantine empire
1471   Portuguese capture Tangier
1482   Start of war to conquer kingdom of Granada, last Muslim state
        in Iberia
1487   Ottoman sultan sends Kemal Reis to give naval assistance to Granada
1491   Ali al-Mandari comes to Tetouan, Morocco, from Granada and
        starts building up a corsair fleet
1492   Final surrender of Granada to the 'Catholic Monarchs'
1497   Spanish capture Melilla
1499   Muslim revolt in Granada (lasts until 1501)
1500   Turkish corsairs Aruj and Khizr (Barbarossa brothers) arrive at
        La Goletta, Tunisia
1501   All Muslims in Castile ordered to convert to Christianity or leave.
        Converts known as Moriscos (similar order not made in Aragon
        until 1526)
1505   Spanish capture Mers el Kebir
1508   Spanish capture Velez de la Gomera. Turkish corsair Kurtoglu Reis
        arrives at Bizerta, Tunisia
1509   Spanish conquest of Oran by Cardinal Cisneros and Pedro Navarro
1510   January: Navarro captures Bougie. Algiers submits to Spanish, who
        put garrison on offshore island. July: Navarro captures Tripoli in
        Libya. August: Navarro's attack on island of Djerba repulsed.
        Barbarossa brothers based in Djerba and assist in repulse of Navarro
1512   Genoese squadron under Andrea Doria destroys Barbarossa ships
        at La Goletta, Tunisia
1516   Ottoman sultan Selim I summons Kurtoglu Reis to command
        Ottoman ships in campaign to conquer Egypt (completed 1517).
        Barbarossa brothers take control of Algiers
1517   Aruj Barbarossa takes possession of Tlemcen
1518   Spanish drive Aruj out of Tlemcen and kill him in a skirmish. Khizr

now sole ruler of Algiers and holder of name Barbarossa. Barbarossa submits to Ottoman sultan Selim I and his possessions become an Ottoman province. Christian corsairs capture Leo Africanus

1519 Spanish attack on Algiers repulsed

1520 Local Muslim revolt forces Barbarossa out of Algiers (he returns in 1525)

1522 Ottoman sultan Suleiman the Magnificent besieges Knights of St John in Rhodes. Knights surrender and are permitted to leave (January 1523)

1528 Andrea Doria and the Genoese change sides, in future serving Spain not France

1529 Barbarossa captures Spanish fortress on offshore island near Algiers. Algerine corsairs defeat a Spanish squadron off island of Formentera

1530 Knights of St John take possession of island of Malta and Tripoli in Libya, given to them by Emperor Charles V. Andrea Doria's attack on Cherchell ends in failure

1533 Sultan Suleiman summons Barbarossa to Istanbul to take command of Ottoman fleet as kapudan pasha

1534 Barbarossa seizes Tunis from its pro-Spanish Muslim ruler

1535 Emperor Charles V drives Barbarossa out of Tunis, returns Muslim puppet ruler, and leaves Spanish garrison at La Goletta. Barbarossa raids Mahon on island of Minorca

1536 Alliance between France and the Ottoman empire is openly proclaimed

1538 Holy League formed to resist Ottoman aggression. September: Barbarossa defeats Holy League fleet under Andrea Doria at Preveza

1541 Emperor Charles V's attack on Algiers ends in defeat

1543 Barbarossa's fleet joins French and aids in capture of Nice. Ottoman fleet spends winter of 1543–4 at Toulon, France

1544 Barbarossa ransoms Turgut Reis from Genoa

1546 Barbarossa dies at Istanbul

1550 Turgut Reis captures Mahdia in Tunisia. Spanish take Mahdia and attack Djerba. Turgut Reis has narrow escape

1551 Turgut Reis and Sinan Pasha raid Malta and Gozo, before going on to besiege and capture Tripoli

1552 Turgut Reis and Sinan Pasha defeat Andrea Doria's squadron off Ponza

1553 Turgut Reis and Ottoman fleet assist in French invasion of Corsica

1555 Salih Reis from Algiers takes Bougie from the Spanish

1556 Turgut Reis becomes ruler of Tripoli in Libya

1558 Turgut Reis and Piyale Pasha seize Ciutadella in Minorca and threaten coast of Spain. Spanish army from Oran defeated by the Algerines near Mostaganem

1560	Spanish expedition is destroyed at the island of Djerba by Piyale Pasha and Turgut Reis
1561	Spanish squadron defeated by Turgut Reis near Lipari Islands
1562	Spanish galleys lost in a storm at Malaga
1563	Algerine attack on Mers el Kebir and Oran is repulsed
1564	Spanish expedition recaptures Vélez de la Gomera
1565	March: Alvaro de Bazan sinks blockships in river leading to Moroccan corsair port of Tetouan. May: Ottoman invasion of Malta. June: Turgut Reis killed during assault on Fort St Elmo. September: Relief force lands on Malta and Ottoman forces leave the island
1568	Uluj Ali becomes ruler of Algiers. December: Start of Morisco revolt in Granada (lasts until 1570)
1570	January: Uluj Ali seizes Tunis, but unable to remove Spanish garrison in La Goletta. July: Uluj Ali destroys galley squadron of Knights of Malta off Sicily. Ottoman invasion of Ventian-held island of Cyprus
1571	May: New Holy League formed by papacy, Spain, and Venice. August: Fall of Famagusta, last Christian outpost in Cyprus. October: Battle of Lepanto. Holy League fleet under Don Juan destroys Ottoman fleet. Uluj Ali escapes with surviving Ottoman ships to Istanbul. Uluj Ali made kapudan pasha and rebuilds Ottoman fleet
1573	Don Juan captures Tunis
1574	Uluj Ali and Koca Sinan Pasha recapture Tunis
1575	Cervantes captured by Algerine corsairs
1576	Abd al-Malik takes control of Morocco with Ottoman support
1578	King Sebastian of Portugal invades Morocco. Defeated and killed at battle of Alcazarquivir. Ahmad al-Mansur becomes ruler of Morocco (to 1603)
1580	Truce between Spain and Ottoman empire in the Mediterranean. Cervantes ransomed from captivity in Algiers
1585	Algerine corsairs raid Lanzarote in the Canary Islands
1587	Death of Uluj Ali in Istanbul
1601	Spanish expedition against Algiers disrupted by a storm
1606	English pirate John Ward arrives in Tunis. Attack by Spanish and Knights of Malta on Hammamet, Tunisia, repulsed
1607	Knights of St Stephen seize many captives in raid on Bona
1609	Beginning of expulsion of Moriscos from Spain (concluded in 1614). Franco-Spanish squadron destroys corsair ships at La Goletta, Tunisia
1610	Spanish take possession of Larache in Morocco. Moriscos from Hornachos, Spain, arrive in Salé, Morocco
1611	Former renegade Simon Danser visits Algiers and is executed
1614	Spanish capture Mamora in Morocco
1617	First Barbary corsair raids on Galicia (north-west Spain) on Spanish Atlantic coast
1618	After raiding the Canary Islands, a corsair squadron returning to

	Algiers is intercepted in strait of Gibraltar by a Dutch-Spanish fleet and suffers heavy losses
1620	Dutch renegade Suleiman Reis from Algiers dies in battle with Christian ships near Cartagena. Admiral Mansell leads English fleet against Algiers. After little success, he returns to England in 1621
1621	Ali Bitchin becomes head of corsair corporation in Algiers
1622	First treaty between Algiers and the Netherlands
1623	Death of Yusuf Reis (John Ward) in Tunis. First treaty between England and Algiers
1624	Admiral Lambert leads a Dutch expedition against Algiers
1625	Raids by Salé corsairs on south-west England
1627	Corsairs under renegade Murad Reis raid Iceland. Salé corsairs break free from rule of sultan of Morocco. Treaty between England and Salé
1628	First French treaty with Algiers
1629	French fleet under de Razilly bombards Salé
1631	Corsairs under renegade Murad Reis raid Baltimore, Ireland
1637	French fleet sent to Algiers. Ali Bitchin sacks the Bastion of France. English fleet under Rainborow sails to Salé and frees some captives
1638	Algerine-Tunisian squadron destroyed by Venetians in Ottoman port of Valona in Albania
1641	Salé loses its independence and submits to the Dalaiyya
1645	Ottoman invasion of Venetian-held island of Crete. Resulting war lasts until 1669. Death of Ali Bitchin in Algiers
1655	Admiral Blake's English fleet destroys a Tunisian squadron at Porto Farina
1658	England makes peace with Tunis and Algiers
1659	Lord Inchiquin and his son captured by Algerine corsairs (ransomed in 1660)
1662	Portugal passes possession of Tangier in Morocco to England
1664	French attack on Djidjelli ends in defeat
1666	Salé comes under the control of the Alawites
1669	English fleet sent to Mediterranean to fight Algerines
1670	Dutch fleet under Van Ghent and English ships under Beach defeat Algerine squadron off Cape Spartel
1671	English fleet under Spragge uses fireships to destroy Algerine ships in port of Bougie
1675	English fleet under Narbrough sent against Tripoli
1676	After English successes, Tripoli agrees peace treaty with England
1677	Algiers and England go to war. Narbrough returns to Mediterranean
1679	Treaty between Algiers and the Netherlands. Herbert takes over from Narbrough as commander of English fleet in Mediterranean
1680	English garrison and fleet repulse Moroccan attacks on Tangier
1681	French squadron under Duquesne destroys corsairs from Tripoli taking refuge in harbour of Ottoman island of Chios. Algiers declares

war on France. Moulay Ismail, ruler of Morocco, takes Mamora from the Spanish.

1682   French squadron under Duquesne bombards Algiers, using bomb vessels for first time. Peace treaty between England and Algiers

1683   Duquesne bombards Algiers once again. Execution of Father Le Vacher. Mezzomorto seizes power in Algiers

1684   France and Algiers make peace. English withdraw from Tangier and Moroccans take possession

1685   French squadron under d'Estrées bombards Tripoli. English warships destroy Moroccan corsairs at Mamora

1686–98 Moroccan corsair Abdallah ben Aicha captures 33 Christian ships

1687   Algiers declares war on France

1688   French fleet under d'Estrées bombards Algiers

1689   Peace treaty between France and Algiers

        Mezzomorto overthrown in Algiers and flees to Istanbul

        Moulay Ismail takes Larache in Morocco from the Spanish

1691   Moulay Ismail regains Asilah

1695   Mezzomorto leads Ottoman forces which recapture Chios from Venetians. Mezzomorto is made kapudan pasha of Ottoman fleet

1701   Death of Mezzomorto

1704   English capture Gibraltar

1708   British capture Minorca. Algerines take Mers el Kebir and Oran from the Spanish

1715   Young Englishman Thomas Pellow captured by Moroccan corsairs. Became a renegade and did not return to England until 1738

1720   Peace treaty between Morocco and England. Spanish end Moroccan siege of Ceuta

1726   Dutch treaties with Algiers, Tunis, and Tripoli

1728   French squadron under Grandpré bombards Tripoli

1729   First treaty between Sweden and Algiers (with Tunis 1726; with Tripoli 1741)

1732   Spanish recapture Mers el Kebir and Oran from the Algerines

1746   First treaty between Denmark and Algiers

1756   Morocco launches corsair attacks on British merchant ships

1758   Britain agrees peace settlement with Morocco

1764–5 Venetian treaties with Algiers, Tunis, and Tripoli

1765   French squadron bombards Salé and Larache in Morocco, but a boat attack at Larache ends in defeat

1767   France and Morocco reach peace agreement

1768   Last Spanish religious redemption mission to Algiers. France takes possession of Corsica

1769   Portugal hands over Mazagan to Morocco

1770   French warships bombard Bizerta and Sousse in Tunisia. Danish warships bombard Algiers. Russian fleet destroys Ottoman fleet at

Chesme in Aegean Sea

1773	Tuscan frigate captures three Moroccan corsairs
1774	Spanish repulse Moroccan attack on Melilla
1775	Spanish expedition under O'Reilly sent to take Algiers, but ends in defeat
1783	Spanish fleet under Barcelo bombards Algiers
1784	Barcelo repeats bombardment of Algiers
1785	Venetian squadron under Angelo Emo forces Tunis to make peace
1786	First treaty between Spain and Algiers. First treaty between USA and Morocco
1789	Ruler of Morocco ransoms 600 Muslim slaves held at Malta
1790	Earthquake at Oran. Algerine attempt to take city repulsed by Spanish garrison
1791	New treaty between Spain and Algiers
1792	Spain hands over Mers el Kebir and Oran to the Algerines
1796	First treaty between USA and Algiers (with Tripoli 1796; with Tunis 1797)
1797	French conquer Venetian republic, then pass territory on to the Austrians
1798	French conquer Malta and end rule of Knights of Malta. French invade Ottoman province of Egypt. Ottoman sultan declares war on France (lasts to 1802). Tunisian corsairs take 900 Christian captives from Carloforte, Sardinia
1798–9	Barbary corsairs attack Austrian (ex-Venetian) shipping
1800	Surrender of French garrison on Malta. Island now ruled by Britain
1801–5	America's first Barbary war (USA against Tripoli)
1802	Algerine corsair Hamidou Reis captures a Portuguese frigate
1802–3	Hostilities between USA and Morocco
1803	US frigate runs aground and is captured off Tripoli. Naval conflict between Morocco and Austrian empire to 1805
1804	Captured frigate burned at Tripoli by US naval raiders. American squadron bombards Tripoli several times
1805	American expedition to Derna. Tripoli makes peace with USA
1809	Hamidou Reis becomes admiral of Algiers
1815	America's second Barbary war (USA against Algiers). Hamidou Reis killed in action off Cape Gata. Algerines give in to US demands. Tunisian corsairs take 150 captives from Sant'Antioco, Sardinia
1816	British fleet under Lord Exmouth and Dutch squadron bombard Algiers. Algiers, Tunis and Tripoli promise to give up corsair activity and taking of Christian captives
1819	An Anglo-French naval squadron visits Algiers, Tunis and Tripoli delivering diplomatic note demanding end to corsairing and taking of captives
1821	Outbreak of Greek war of independence. Algeria, Tunis and Tripoli

	send ships to aid Ottoman sultan against Greek rebels
1824	Algerines seize Spanish ship and enslave crew. In retaliation British squadron bombards Algiers. Ship and crew released
1827	April: Ruler of Algiers strikes French consul. June: France imposes a naval blockade on the regency of Algiers. October: A British/French/Russian fleet destroys Ottoman/Egyptian fleet at battle of Navarino
1828	Neapolitan fleet bombards Tripoli
1828 –30	Naval conflict between Morocco and Austrian empire
1830	French naval and military expedition captures Algiers, beginning French conquest of Algeria. French impose new treaties on Tunis and Tripoli
1835	Ottoman expedition restores direct rule of Istanbul over Tripoli. French prevent Ottomans from imposing similar rule over Tunis
1845	Morocco agrees to end taking of tribute from foreign states in return for not carrying out corsair attacks
1848	French complete conquest of most of Algeria (rule until 1962)
1851	French warships bombard Salé after pirate attack on French ship
1881	French take control of Tunisia (rule until 1956)
1911	Italians seize Tripoli from Ottomans and begin conquest of Libya (rule until 1943)
1912	Morocco divided between Spain and France (rule until 1956)

REFERENCES

EI   *Encyclopedia of Islam* (2nd edn, Leiden, 1960–2002)
MM   *The Mariner's Mirror*
ODNB *Oxford Dictionary of National Biography* (Oxford, 2004)

INTRODUCTION: THE BARBARY LEGEND

1 M. N. Murphy, *Somalia: The New Barbary? Piracy and Islam in the Horn of Africa* (London, 2011), pp. 100–1.

2 The word 'kursan' (corsair) entered Arabic during the ninth century as a loan word from Italian because of the need to distinguish privateers from pirates (the Arabic term for the latter translated as 'sea robber'). See entry on 'kursan' in *EI*.

3 For books on the USA's two Barbary wars see chapter Four below.

4 See, for example, sections on Barbary corsairs in P. Earle, *The Pirate Wars* (London, 2003); T. Travers, *Pirates: A History* (Stroud, 2007) and A. Konstam, *Piracy: The Complete History* (Oxford, 2008).

5 For a recent survey of works on piracy, privateering etc. see D. J. Starkey, 'Voluntaries and Sea Robbers: A Review of the Academic Literature on Privateering, Corsairing, Buccaneering and Piracy', *MM*, 97 (2011), pp. 127–47.

6 M. Bonner (*Jihad in Islamic History: Doctrine and Practice* (Princeton, NJ, 2006), pp. 149–51) accepts the religious motivation of the Barbary corsairs, while W. G. Clarence-Smith (*Islam and the Abolition of Slavery* (London, 2006), pp. 28–30) is more sceptical. For corsair contributions to an Islamic religious foundation, see M. Hoexter, *Endowments, Rulers, and Community: Waqf al-Haramayn in Ottoman Algiers* (Leiden, 1998), pp. 12–15.

7 For a general history of Christian–Muslim conflict see A. G. Jamieson, *Faith and Sword: A Short History of Christian–Muslim Conflict* (London, 2006).

8 M. Greene, 'The Ottomans in the Mediterranean', in *The Early Modern Ottomans: Remapping the Empire*, ed. V. H. Aksan and G. Goffman (Cambridge, 2007), pp. 104–16; see also D. Abulafia, *The Great Sea: A Human History of the Mediterranean* (London, 2011), pp. 411–51.

9 See A. W. Fisher, *The Crimean Tatars* (Stanford, CA, 1978).

10   See S. O'Rourke, *The Cossacks* (Manchester, 2007).

11   See H.J.A. Sire, *The Knights of Malta* (New Haven, CT, and London, 1994).

12   J. Glete, *Warfare at Sea, 1500–1650: Maritime Conflicts and the Transforma-tion of Europe* (London, 2000), pp. 60–65, 93–111, 147–64.

13   J. M. Abun-Nasr, *A History of the Maghrib* (2nd edn, Cambridge, 1975), pp. 173–6.

14   See J. Waterson, *The Knights of Islam: The Wars of the Mamluks* (London, 2007).

15   S. Faroqhi, *The Ottoman Empire and the World Around It* (London, 2004), pp. 82–4.

16   C. R. Pennell, *Morocco: From Empire to Independence* (Oxford, 2003), pp. 93–6.

17   R. C. Davis, *Christian Slaves, Muslim Masters: White Slavery in the Mediter-ranean, the Barbary Coast, and Italy, 1500–1800* (Basingstoke, 2003), pp. 3–26.

18   A. W. Fisher, 'Muscovy and the Black Sea Slave Trade', *Canadian-American Slavic Studies*, 6 (1972), pp. 575–94. See also M. Ivanics, 'Enslavement, Slave Labour and Treatment of Captives in the Crimean Khanate', in *Ransom Slavery along the Ottoman Borders: Early Fifteenth–Early Eighteenth Centuries*, ed. G. David and P. Fodor (Leiden, 2007), pp. 193–220.

19   R. Segal, *The Black Diaspora: Five Centuries of Black Experience Outside Africa* (New York, 1995), p. 4.

20   D. Panzac, *Les corsaires barbaresques. La fin d'une épopée 1800–1820* (Paris, 1999). English translation, *The Barbary Corsairs: The End of a Legend 1800–1820* (Leiden, 2005).

21   See B. Vandervort, *Wars of Imperial Expansion in Africa, 1830–1914* (London, 1998).

22   Sir Godfrey Fisher produced a book entitled *Barbary Legend: War, Trade and Piracy in North Africa, 1415–1830* (Oxford, 1957). Conscious of the hostile attitude to the Barbary corsairs in most earlier books relating to them, Fisher went to the other extreme, shifting much of the blame for the maritime conflict onto the bad faith and aggressive actions of the Christian side.

I   VANGUARD OF THE SULTAN, 1492–1580

1   For Algiers 1541 see S. Lane-Poole, *The Story of the Barbary Corsairs* (London, 1890), pp. 112–23; A. C. Hess, *The Forgotten Frontier: A History of the Sixteenth Century Ibero-African Frontier* (Chicago, 1978), pp. 74–5; J. B. Wolf, *The Barbary Coast: Algeria under the Turks, 1500 to 1830* (New York, 1979), pp. 26–30; H.J.A. Sire, *The Knights of Malta* (New Haven, CT, and London, 1994), p. 65; H. Kamen, *Spain's Road to Empire: The Making of a World Power, 1492–1763* (London, 2002), pp. 75–6; J. D. Tracy, *Emperor Charles V, Impresario of War: Campaign Strategy, International Finance, and Domestic Politics* (Cambridge, 2002), pp. 170–76, 179–81; J. Heers, *The Bar-bary Corsairs: Warfare in the Mediterranean, 1480–1580* (English translation, London, 2003), p. 81; entry on Sir Thomas Chaloner the Elder in ODNB;

R. Crowley, *Empires of the Sea: The Final Battle for the Mediterranean, 1521–1580* (London, 2008), pp. 72–3; E. Garnier, *L'alliance impie. François Ier et Soliman le Magnifique contre Charles Quint (1529–1547)* (Paris, 2008), pp. 202–7; B. Rogerson, *The Last Crusaders: The Hundred-year Battle for the Centre of the World* (London, 2009), pp. 309–13.

2   C. Finkel, *Osman's Dream: The Story of the Ottoman Empire, 1300–1923* (London, 2005), pp. 48–114; M. Greene, 'The Ottomans and the Mediterranean', in *The Early Modern Ottomans: Remapping the Empire*, ed. V. H. Aksan and G. Goffman (Cambridge, 2007), pp. 104–16; J. J. Norwich, *A History of Venice* (New York, 1982), pp. 325–89.

3   J. N. Hillgarth, *The Spanish Kingdoms, 1250–1516*, 2 vols (Oxford, 1978), vol. II, pp. 366–93; J. Edwards, *The Spain of the Catholic Monarchs, 1474–1520* (Malden, MA, 2000), pp. 101–40; Rogerson, *Last Crusaders*, pp. 114–32.

4   Entry on Kemal Reis in *EI*; Hess, *Forgotten Frontier*, p. 60.

5   A. R. Disney, *A History of Portugal and the Portuguese Empire from the Beginnings to 1807*, 2 vols (Cambridge, 2009), vol. II, pp. 1–13; Hess, *Forgotten Frontier*, pp. 12–17, 26–34; Rogerson, *Last Crusaders*, pp. 13–62.

6   Hillgarth, *Spanish Kingdoms*, vol. II, pp. 570, 573; Hess, *Forgotten Frontier*, pp. 36–7.

7   M. Carr, *Blood and Faith: The Purging of Muslim Spain* (New York, 2009), pp. 52–69.

8   Kamen, *Spain's Road to Empire*, pp. 30–32; Hess, *Forgotten Frontier*, pp. 38–9; G. Sánchez Doncel, *Presencia de España en Orán (1509–1792)* (Toledo, 1991), pp. 125–64.

9   Hillgarth, *Spanish Kingdoms*, vol. II, pp. 574–5; Hess, *Forgotten Frontier*, 5pp. 39, 42.

10 Entries on Aruj and Barbarossa in *EI*; E. Bradford, *The Sultan's Admiral: Barbarossa – Pirate and Empire-builder* (repr London, 2009).

11 Sire, *Knights of Malta*, pp. 25–39; B. Galimard Flavigny, *Histoire de l'ordre de Malte* (Paris, 2006), pp. 127–44.

12 E. Jurien de la Gravière, *Doria et Barberousse* (Paris, 1886); S. A. Epstein, *Genoa and the Genoese, 958–1528* (Chapel Hill, NC, 1996), pp. 314–15; A.-M. Graziani, *Andrea Doria: un prince de la Renaissance* (Paris, 2008).

13 Wolf, *Barbary Coast*, pp. 8–14; W. Spencer, *Algiers in the Age of the Corsairs* (Norman, OK, 1976), pp. 16–22.

14 Rogerson, *Last Crusaders*, pp. 280–282.

15 For the janissaries see M. Uyar and E. J. Erickson, *A Military History of the Ottomans: From Osman to Atatürk* (Santa Barbara, CA, 2009), pp. 36–44.

16 Sire, *Knights of Malta*, pp. 57–9; Rogerson, *Last Crusaders*, pp. 157–8, 262–5; E. Brockman, *The Two Sieges of Rhodes, 1480–1522* (London, 1969).

17 Sire, *Knights of Malta*, pp. 59–61.

18 Wolf, *Barbary Coast*, p. 15; Crowley, *Empires of the Sea*, p. 46.

19 Crowley, *Empires of the Sea*, pp. 47–8.

20 Rogerson, *Last Crusaders*, p. 295.

21 Ibid., pp. 296–300, Tracy, *Emperor Charles V*, pp. 145–57.

22 Crowley, *Empires of the Sea*, pp. 62–3.

23 J. F. Guilmartin, *Gunpowder and Galleys: Changing Technology and Mediterranean Warfare at Sea in the 16th Century* (revd edn, London, 2003), pp. 57–71.

24 Rogerson, *Last Crusaders*, pp. 313–15; Crowley, *Empires of the Sea*, pp. 74–8.

25 Entry on Turgut Reis in *EI*.

26 Rogerson, *Last Crusaders*, p. 314.

27 F. Braudel, *The Mediterranean and the Mediterranean World in the Age of Philip II*, 2 vols (New York, 1973), vol. II, pp. 908–10; Rogerson, *Last Crusaders*, pp. 316–17.

28 Braudel, *Mediterranean*, vol. II, pp. 919–21; Rogerson, *Last Crusaders*, pp. 317–18; Sire, *Knights of Malta*, pp. 66–7.

29 Braudel, *Mediterranean*, vol. II, pp. 928–30. See also M. Vergé-Franceschi, *Sampiero Corso, 1498–1567: un mercenaire européen au XVIe siècle* (Ajaccio, 1999).

30 Braudel, *Mediterranean*, vol. II, pp. 933–4.

31 Ibid., pp. 944–5.

32 Ibid., p. 972; Hess, *Forgotten Frontier*, p. 78.

33 Guilmartin, *Gunpowder and Galleys*, pp. 137–48; Braudel, *Mediterranean*, vol. II, pp. 974–87.

34 Braudel, *Mediterranean*, vol. II, pp. 992–5.

35 Ibid., pp. 995–8.

36 Kamen, *Spain's Road to Empire*, pp. 156, 165; Hess, *Forgotten Frontier*, pp. 82, 84; Braudel, *Mediterranean*, vol. II, pp. 999–1001.

37 Galimard Flavigny, *Histoire de l'ordre de Malte*, pp. 192–3.

38 Hess, *Forgotten Frontier*, p. 84; Braudel, *Mediterranean*, vol. II, p. 1015.

39 For the siege of Malta 1565 see E. Bradford, *The Great Siege: Malta 1565* (repr Ware, Hertfordshire, 1999); S. C. Spiteri, *The Great Siege, Knights vs. Turks, MDLXV: Anatomy of a Hospitaller Victory* (Malta, 2005); S. O'Shea, *Sea of Faith: Islam and Christianity in the Medieval Mediterranean World* (Vancouver, 2006), pp. 286–309; Guilmartin, *Gunpowder and Galleys*, pp. 191–207; Braudel, *Mediterranean*, vol. II, pp. 1014–26; Sire, *Knights of Malta*, pp. 68–72; Crowley, *Empires of the Sea*, pp. 93–195; Rogerson, *Last Crusaders*, pp. 351–63.

40 Entry on Uluj Ali in *EI*; Rogerson, *Last Crusaders*, pp. 364–5; R. C. Davis, *Holy War and Human Bondage: Tales of Christian-Muslim Slavery in the Early Modern Mediterranean* (Santa Barbara, CA, 2009), pp. 93–5.

41 B. and L. Bennassar, *Les chrétiens d'Allah. L'histoire extraordinaire des renégats, XVIe et XVIIe siècles* (Paris, 1989), p. 174.

42 Carr, *Blood and Faith*, pp. 131–64; Braudel, *Mediterranean*, vol. II, pp. 1060–66, 1068–73.

43 Braudel, *Mediterranean*, vol. II, pp. 1066–68.

44 H. Bicheno, *Crescent and Cross: The Battle of Lepanto 1571* (London, 2003), p. 176; N. Capponi, *Victory of the West: The Great Christian–Muslim Clash*

at the Battle of Lepanto (Cambridge, MA, 2007), pp. 134–6.

45 Braudel, *Mediterranean*, vol. II, pp. 1073–87.

46 Ibid., pp. 1088–92.

47 M. Gemignani, 'The Navies of the Medici: The Florentine Navy and the Navy of the Sacred Military Order of St Stephen, 1547–1648', in *War at Sea in the Middle Ages and the Renaissance*, ed. J. B. Hattendorf and R. W. Unger (Woodbridge, 2003), pp. 169–86.

48 For the battle of Lepanto in 1571 see Bicheno, *Crescent and Cross*, pp. 227–56; Capponi, *Victory of the West*, pp. 253–86; Guilmartin, *Gunpowder and Galleys*, pp. 235–68; J. F. Guilmartin, *Galleons and Galleys* (London, 2002), pp. 138–49; Braudel, *Mediterranean*, vol. II, pp. 1100–105; Crowley, *Empires of the Sea*, pp. 251–86; Rogerson, *Last Crusaders*, pp. 390–94.

49 Capponi, *Victory of the West*, pp. 279–80.

50 Ibid., pp. 296–303.

51 D. Panzac, *La marine ottomane. De l'apogée à la chute de l'Empire (1572–1923)* (Paris, 2009), pp. 15–46.

52 Ibid., pp. 46–51.

53 Ibid., pp. 51–2; Braudel, *Mediterranean*, vol. II, pp. 1127–33.

54 Panzac, *La marine ottomane*, pp. 51–4; Braudel, *Mediterranean*, vol. II, pp. 1133–9.

55 C. R. Pennell, *Morocco: From Empire to Independence* (Oxford, 2003), pp. 83–5; E. W. Bovill, *The Battle of Alcazar: An Account of the Defeat of Don Sebastian of Portugal at El Ksar el Kebir* (London, 1952); P. Berthier, *La bataille de l'oued el-Makhasen, dite bataille des Trois-Rois (4 août 1578)* (Paris, 1985); Rogerson, *Last Crusaders*, pp. 399–422. See also W. F. Cook, *The Hundred Years War for Morocco: Gunpowder and the Military Revolution in the Early Modern Muslim World* (Boulder, CO, and Oxford, 1994).

56 Braudel, *Mediterranean*, vol. II, pp. 1160–65.

2 LORDS OF THE SEA, 1580–1660

1 B. Lewis, 'Corsairs in Iceland', in B. Lewis, *Islam in History: Ideas, People, and Events in the Middle East* (2nd edn, Chicago, 2001), pp. 239–46; G. Karlsson, *The History of Iceland* (Minneapolis, MN, 2000), pp. 143–5; B. Helgason, 'Historical Narrative as Collective Therapy: The Case of the Turkish Raid on Iceland', *Scandinavian Journal of History*, 22 (1997), pp. 275–89; R. C. Davis, *Holy War and Human Bondage: Tales of Christian–Muslim Slavery in the Early Modern Mediterranean* (Santa Barbara, CA, 2009), pp. 48, 92; A. Tinniswood, *Pirates of Barbary: Corsairs, Conquests and Captivity in the Seventeenth Century Mediterranean* (London, 2010), pp. 132, 134; C. Lloyd, *English Corsairs on the Barbary Coast* (London, 1981), pp. 98–9. For the raid on Baltimore see D. Ekin, *The Stolen Village: Baltimore and the Barbary Pirates* (Dublin, 2006); Tinniswood, *Pirates of Barbary*, pp. 126–42.

2 J. Glete, *Warfare at Sea, 1500–1650: Maritime Conflicts and the Transformation*

of Europe (London, 2000), pp. 108–9; J. Black, *Naval Power: A History of Warfare and the Sea from 1500* (Basingstoke, 2009), pp. 46–7.

3   R. C. Davis, *Christian Slaves, Muslim Masters: White Slavery in the Mediterranean, the Barbary Coast, and Italy, 1500–1800* (Basingstoke, 2003), pp. 28–9.

4   R. L. Playfair, *The Scourge of Christendom: Annals of British Relations with Algiers prior to the French Conquest* (London, 1884), pp. 26–8.

5   Entry on Edward Glemham (or Glenham) in *ODNB*.

6   D. Goodman, *Spanish Naval Power, 1589–1665: Reconstruction and Defeat* (Cambridge, 2003), pp. 1–10; N. Matar, *Britain and Barbary, 1589–1689* (Gainesville, FL, 2005), pp. 13–36; L. P. Harvey, *Muslims in Spain, 1500 to 1614* (Chicago, 2006), pp. 343–9.

7   F. Braudel, *The Mediterranean and the Mediterranean World in the Age of Philip II*, 2 vols (New York, 1973), vol. II, pp. 1232–4.

8   E. G. Friedman, *Spanish Captives in North Africa in the Early Modern Age* (Madison, WI, 1983), p. 11.

9   For expulsion of Moriscos 1609–14 see M. Carr, *Blood and Faith: The Purging of Muslim Spain* (New York, 2009), pp. 202–78.

10   Carr, *Blood and Faith*, p. 171; M. Garcia-Arenal and G. Wiegers, *A Man of Three Worlds: Samuel Pallache, a Moroccan Jew in Catholic and Protestant Europe* (Baltimore, MD, 2007), pp. 51–2.

11   Friedman, *Spanish Captives*, p. 24. Friedman views Morisco expulsion as important for the expansion of Barbary corsairing; for a more sceptical view see M. Jonsson, 'The Expulsion of the Moriscos from Spain in 1609–14: The Destruction of an Islamic Periphery', *Journal of Global History*, 2 (2007), pp. 202–11.

12   P. Earle, *The Pirate Wars* (London, 2003), pp. 26–33.

13   J. B. Wolf, *The Barbary Coast: Algeria under the Turks, 1500 to 1830* (New York, 1979), pp. 147, 181–2, 193, 197.

14   A. H. de Groot, *The Ottoman Empire and the Dutch Republic: A History of the Earliest Diplomatic Relations, 1610–1630* (Leiden and Istanbul, 1978), p. 36; J. Vermeulen, *Sultans, slaven en renegaten: de verborgen geschiedenis van de Ottomaanse rijk* (Leuven, 2001), pp. 321–5.

15   P. L. Wilson, *Pirate Utopias: Moorish Corsairs and European Renegadoes* (2nd edn, New York, 2003), pp. 96–100.

16   Entry on John Ward in *ODNB*; Wilson, *Pirate Utopias*, pp. 51–69; G. Bak, *Barbary Pirate: The Life and Crimes of John Ward, the Most Infamous Privateer of his Time* (Stroud, 2006). For William Lithgow see C. E. Bosworth, *An Intrepid Scot: William Lithgow of Lanark's Travels in the Ottoman Lands, North Africa, and Central Europe, 1609–21* (Aldershot, 2006).

17   Entry on Sir Henry Mainwaring in *ODNB*.

18   C. M. Senior, 'Robert Walsingham: A Jacobean Pirate', *MM*, 60 (1974); entry on Peter Easton in *Dictionary of Canadian Biography Online*. See also C. M. Senior, *A Nation of Pirates: English Piracy in its Heyday* (Newton Abbot, 1976).

19   D. Panzac, *La marine ottomane. De l'apogée à la chute de l'Empire (1572–1923)* (Paris, 2009), pp. 89–90.

20   Friedman, *Spanish Captives*, pp. 17–18.

21   Carr, *Blood and Faith*, p. 284.

22   Goodman, *Spanish Naval Power*, p. 16.

23   J. R. Bruijn, *The Dutch Navy in the Seventeenth and Eighteenth Centuries* (Columbia, SC, 1993), pp. 23–4; Vermeulen, *Sultans, slaven en renegaten*, pp. 191–2. Generally known as Admiral Lambert in English sources, his name was Lambrecht Hendrickszoon, nicknamed 'Moyen Lambert'.

24   O. Löwenheim, *Predators and Parasites: Persistent Agents of Transnational Harm and Great Power Authority* (Ann Arbor, MI, 2007), pp. 97–100.

25   Entry on Sir Robert Mansell in ODNB; Playfair, *Scourge of Christendom*, pp. 38–44; W. L. Clowes, *The Royal Navy: A History from the Earliest Times to the Present* (Annapolis, MD, 1996 reprint), vol. II, pp. 50–54; N.A.M. Rodger, *The Safeguard of the Sea: A Naval History of Britain, 660–1649* (London, 1997), pp. 352–3.

26   C. Finkel, *Osman's Dream: The Story of the Ottoman Empire, 1300–1923* (London, 2005), pp. 179–215.

27   Playfair, *Scourge of Christendom*, pp. 45–7. See M. Strachan, *Sir Thomas Roe, 1581–1644: A Life* (Salisbury, Wiltshire, 1989).

28   Entries on William Rainborow and Sir Thomas Roe in ODNB.

29   Bruijn, *Dutch Navy in Seventeenth and Eighteenth Centuries*, p. 51; J.J.A. Wijn, 'Maarten Harpertszoon Tromp', in *The Great Admirals: Command at Sea, 1587–1945*, ed. J. Sweetman (Annapolis, MD, 1997), pp. 38–9.

30   A. H. de Groot, 'Ottoman North Africa and the Dutch Republic in the Seventeenth and Eighteenth Centuries', *Revue de l'Occident musulman et de la Méditerranée*, 39 (1985), pp. 131–9.

31   For Dutch attempts to get a North African commercial outpost in 1625 see M.-C. Engels, *Merchants, Interlopers, Seamen, and Corsairs: The 'Flemish' Community in Livorno and Genoa (1615–1635)* (Hilversum, 1997), pp. 58–9.

32   A. James, *The Navy and Government in Early Modern France, 1572–1661* (Woodbridge, 2004), pp. 94–5; see also G. L. Weiss, *Captives and Corsairs: France and Slavery in the Early Modern Mediterranean* (Stanford, CA, 2011), pp. 27–51.

33   V. L. Tapié, *France in the Age of Louis XIII and Richelieu* (2nd edn, Cambridge, 1984), p. 258. For Bastion of France see P. Masson, *Histoire des établissements et du commerce français dans l'Afrique barbaresque (1560–1793): Algérie, Tunisie, Tripolitaine, Maroc* (Paris, 1903).

34   Wolf, *Barbary Coast*, pp. 202–9.

35   Tinniswood, *Pirates of Barbary*, pp. 186–7.

36   See A. Tenenti, *Piracy and the Decline of Venice, 1580–1615* (London, 1967).

37   K. M. Setton, *Venice, Austria, and the Turks in the Seventeenth Century* (Philadelphia, 1991), pp. 108–9.

38   For Knight see Tinniswood, *Pirates of Barbary*, pp. 143–5.

39 For Lazarists and consuls see Wolf, *Barbary Coast*, pp. 212–14.

40 Playfair, *Scourge of Christendom*, pp. 63–5, 68–70; Tinniswood, *Pirates of Barbary*, pp. 195–202.

41 B. Rogerson, *The Last Crusaders: The Hundred-year Battle for the Centre of the World* (London, 2009), pp. 158–9.

42 Carr, *Blood and Faith*, pp. 203, 250, 285, 291–2.

43 The best survey of the Salé corsairs remains R. Coindreau, *Les corsaires de Salé* (Paris, 1948). Although dealing primarily with corsair activities after 1660, there is material relating to Salé in the first half of the seventeenth century in L. Maziane, *Salé et ses corsaires (1666–1727). Un port de course marocain au XVIIe siècle* (Caen, 2007). See also J. B. Bookin-Weiner, 'The "Sallee Rovers": Morocco and its Corsairs in the Seventeenth Century', in *The Middle East and North Africa: Essays in Honor of J. C. Hurewitz*, ed. R. S. Simon (New York, 1990), pp. 307–31; C. R. Pennell, *Morocco: Empire to Independence* (Oxford, 2003), pp. 93–6; and Earle, *Pirate Wars*, pp. 44–6.

44 Wilson, *Pirate Utopias*, pp. 96–141.

45 For a romanticized view of the 'pirate republic' of Salé see Wilson, *Pirate Utopias*, pp. 71–92.

46 Pennell, *Morocco*, pp. 89, 94.

47 Earle, *Pirate Wars*, p. 45.

48 K. R. Andrews, *Ships, Money, and Politics: Seafaring and Naval Enterprise in the Reign of Charles I* (Cambridge, 1991), pp. 161–2. See also D. D. Hebb, *Piracy and the English Government, 1616–1642* (Aldershot, 1994).

49 Entry on John Harrison in ODNB.

50 Tapié, *France in Age of Louis XIII and Richelieu*, pp. 180–181, 259. Razilly was also told to establish a French colony in Morocco at Mogador, but this did not prove possible. He played a more important colonizing role in New France. See entry on Isaac de Razilly in *Dictionary of Canadian Biography Online*.

51 For Rainborow's expedition see Andrews, *Ships, Money, and Politics*, pp. 171–8; Rodger, *Safeguard of the Sea*, pp. 384–5; entry on William Rainborow in ODNB.

52 For Pallache see M. Garcia-Arenal and G. Wiegers, *A Man of Three Worlds: Samuel Pallache, a Moroccan Jew in Catholic and Protestant Europe* (Baltimore, MD, 2007).

53 J. M. Abun-Nasr, *A History of the Maghrib* (2nd edn, Cambridge, 1975), pp. 221–3.

54 Quoted in Andrews, *Ships, Money, and Politics*, p. 181.

55 For the captivity of Cervantes see M. A. Garcés, *Cervantes in Algiers: A Captive's Tale* (Nashville, TN, 2002) and Friedman, *Spanish Captives*, pp. 57–8, 71, 73, 120, 149.

56 Wolf, *Barbary Coast*, pp. 151–2; Davis, *Christian Slaves, Muslim Masters*, pp. 3–26.

57 Panzac, *La marine ottomane*, pp. 137–8.

58 Ibid., pp. 130–31.

59 Ibid., pp. 133–4. Between 1615 and 1629 some 20 Lübeck ships were captured by the Barbary corsairs; see P. Dollinger, *The German Hansa* (Stanford, CA, 1970), p. 346.

60 R. C. Davis, 'Rural Slavery in the Early Modern Mediterranean. The Significance of Algiers', in *Human Bondage in the Cultural Contact Zone: Transdisciplinary Perspectives on Slavery and its Discourses*, ed. R. Hörmann and G. Mackenthun (Münster, 2010), pp. 81–94.

61 S. Clissold, *The Barbary Slaves* (London, 1977) remains a useful summary of the experiences of Christian captives.

62 Clissold, *Barbary Slaves*, p. 55.

63 See J. I. Israel, 'The Jews of Spanish Oran and their Expulsion in 1669', in J. I. Israel, *Conflicts of Empires: Spain, the Low Countries, and the Struggle for World Supremacy, 1585-1713* (London, 1997), pp. 219–39.

64 Friedman, *Spanish Captives*, pp. 105–6, 110–28, 145. For Italian organizations set up to ransom captives see Davis, *Christian Slaves, Muslim Masters*, pp. 150–74.

65 Friedman, *Spanish Captives*, pp. 146–7.

66 Ibid., pp. 147–8.

67 Ibid., pp. 136–8.

68 B. and L. Bennassar, *Les chrétiens d'Allah. L'histoire extraordinaire des rénégats, XVIe et XVIIe siècles* (Paris, 1989), pp. 27–42.

69 Ibid., pp. 260, 446–7.

70 N. Matar, *Europe Through Arab Eyes, 1578–1727* (New York, 2008), pp. 48–50.

71 P. Fodor, 'Maltese Pirates, Ottoman Captives, and French Traders in the Early Seventeenth Century Mediterranean', in *Ransom Slavery along the Ottoman Borders: Early Fifteenth–Early Eighteenth Centuries*, ed. G. David and P. Fodor (Leiden, 2007), pp. 221–38.

72 Entry on Laurence Aldersey in *ODNB*; A. H. de Groot, 'Ottoman North Africa and the Dutch Republic', p. 131.

73 Davis, *Holy War and Human Bondage*, pp. 39–40, 60–61, 63.

74 Panzac, *La marine ottomane*, p. 125.

75 Ibid., pp. 112–15.

76 Ibid., pp. 118, 122.

77 Ibid., pp. 127–8.

78 T. Astarita, *Between Salt Water and Holy Water: A History of Southern Italy* (New York, 2005), p. 98; H. Kamen, *Early Modern European Society* (New York, 2000), p. 204; Davis, 'Rural Slavery . . . Significance of Algiers', *Human Bondage in the Cultural Contact Zone*, p. 82.

79 Friedman, *Spanish Captives*, pp. 67–8; see also R. Pike, *Penal Servitude in Early Modern Spain* (Madison, WI, 1983), pp. 27–40.

80 Panzac, *La marine ottomane*, p. 126.

81 For more on the composition of galley crews, see S. Bono, 'D'esclaves à marins dans la Méditerranée de l'époque moderne', in *D'esclaves à soldats:*

miliciens et soldats d'origine servile, XIIIe–XXIe siècles, ed. C. Bernard and A. Stella (Paris, 2006), pp. 68–9.

82 B. Galimard Flavigny, *Histoire de l'ordre de Malte* (Paris, 2006), pp. 212–13. See also T. Freller and D. Campoy, *Padre Ottomano and Malta* (Malta, 2006).

83 Davis, *Holy War and Human Bondage*, pp. 18–19.

84 Matar, *Europe Through Arab Eyes*, pp. 47–8.

3 FACING THE SEA POWERS, 1660–1720

1 P. W. Bamford, *Fighting Ships and Prisons: The Mediterranean Galleys of France in the Age of Louis XIV* (Minneapolis, MN, 1973), p. 138.

2 J. Boudriot and H. Berti, *The Bomb Ketch Salamandre* (Robertsbridge, 1991), pp. 8–9; C. Ware, *The Bomb Vessel: Shore Bombardment Ships of the Age of Sail* (London, 1994), pp. 9–10.

3 For Abraham Duquesne see E. Taillemite, *Histoire ignorée de la marine française* (Paris, 2003), pp. 157–61, and M. Vergé-Franceschi, *Abraham Duquesne, huguenot et marin de Roi Soleil* (Paris, 1992). For bombardments of Algiers in the 1680s see also G. L. Weiss, *Captives and Corsairs: France and Slavery in the Early Modern Mediterranean* (Stanford, CA, 2011), pp. 72–91.

4 The 'consular cannon' that killed Le Vacher and others in 1683 was captured when the French took Algiers in 1830. It was moved to Brest in France in 1833 and still exists as a monument.

5 R. L. Playfair, *The Scourge of Christendom: Annals of British Relations with Algiers prior to the French Conquest* (London, 1884), pp. 141–3, 146.

6 D. Panzac, *La marine ottomane. De l'apogée à la chute de l'Empire (1572–1923)* (Paris, 2009), p. 148.

7 A. Tinniswood, *Pirates of Barbary: Corsairs, Conquests and Captivity in the Seventeenth- century Mediterranean* (London, 2010), p. 195.

8 N.A.M. Rodger, *The Command of the Oceans: A Naval History of Britain, 1649–1815* (London, 2004), pp. 21–2; Tinniswood, *Pirates of Barbary*, pp. 220–27. See also J. D. Davies, *Pepys's Navy: Ships, Men and Warfare, 1649–1689* (London, 2008).

9 Panzac, *La marine ottomane*, p. 148.

10 Entries on Murrough O'Brien and William O'Brien, 1st and 2nd earls of Inchiquin, in ODNB; Playfair, *Scourge of Christendom*, p. 79; Tinniswood, *Pirates of Barbary*, p. 227.

11 See section on Tangier in L. Colley, *Captives: Britain, Empire and the World, 1600–1850* (London, 2002), pp. 23–41, and chapter 12 in Tinniswood, *Pirates of Barbary*.

12 B. Galimard Flavigny, *Histoire de l'ordre de Malte* (Paris, 2006), pp. 220–28.

13 J. B. Wolf, *The Barbary Coast: Algeria under the Turks, 1500 to 1830* (New York, 1979), pp. 226–8; E. H. Jenkins, *A History of the French Navy: From Its Beginnings to the Present Day* (London, 1973), p. 45. See also P. McClusky, 'Commerce Before Crusade? France, the Ottoman Empire, and the

Barbary Pirates, 1661–1669', *French History*, 23 (2009), pp. 1–21.

14 Entries on Wenceslaus Hollar and John Kempthorne in ODNB; G. A. Kempthorne, 'Sir John Kempthorne and his Sons', *MM*, 12 (1926), pp. 289–31.

15 A. H. de Groot, 'Ottoman North Africa and the Dutch Republic in the Seventeenth and Eighteenth Centuries', *Revue de l'Occident musulman et de la Méditerranée*, 39 (1985), pp. 139–42.

16 For campaigns of Narbrough and Herbert against the Algerines see S. R. Hornstein, *The Restoration Navy and English Foreign Trade, 1674–1688: A Study of the Peacetime Use of Sea Power* (Aldershot, 1991), pp. 109–47. See also P. Le Fevre, 'Arthur Herbert, Earl of Torrington, 1648–1716', in *Precursors of Nelson: British Admirals of the Eighteenth Century*, ed. P. Le Fevre and R. Harding (London, 2000), pp. 19–41.

17 S. Willis, *The Admiral Benbow* (London, 2010), p. 56.

18 Ibid., pp. 40–41.

19 W. L. Clowes, *The Royal Navy: A History from the Earliest Times to the Present* (repr Annapolis, MD, 1996), vol. II, pp. 455–7; Willis, *The Admiral Benbow*, pp. 65–6; Kempthorne, 'Sir John Kempthorne and his Sons', *MM*, 12 (1926), pp. 289–317.

20 P. M. Holt, A. K. S. Lambton and B. Lewis, eds, *Cambridge History of Islam*, 2 vols (repr. Cambridge, 1977), vol. II, p. 264.

21 For Jean d'Estrées see Taillemite, *Histoire ignorée de la marine française*, pp. 153–7.

22 See C. R. Pennell, ed., *Piracy and Diplomacy in Seventeenth-Century North Africa: The Journal of Thomas Baker, English Consul in Tripoli, 1677–1685* (London, 1989).

23 Ibid., p. 188.

24 Playfair, *Scourge of Christendom*, p. 158.

25 D. Panzac, 'The Manning of the Ottoman Navy in the Heyday of Sail (1660–1850)', in *Arming the State: Military Conscription in the Middle East and Central Asia, 1775–1925*, ed. E. J. Zürcher (London, 1999), pp. 41–4.

26 Entry on Hadji Husayn Pasha (Mezzomorto) in *EI*.

27 Playfair, *Scourge of Christendom*, p. 166.

28 P. Earle, *Sailors: English Merchant Seamen, 1650–1775* (London, 1998), pp. 115–18, 120, 123–4. The English sent out privateers as well and in the Mediterranean these corsairs clashed with Ottoman authority; see C. Heywood, 'Ottoman Territoriality Versus Maritime Usage: The Ottoman Islands and English Privateering in the Wars with France, 1689–1714', in *Insularités ottomanes*, ed. N. Vatin and G. Veinstein (Paris, 2004), pp. 145–73.

29 Wolf, *The Barbary Coast*, pp. 282–4; G. Sánchez Doncel, *Presencia de España en Orán (1509–1792)* (Toledo, 1991), pp. 211–13.

30 C. R. Pennell, *Morocco: From Empire to Independence* (Oxford, 2003), pp. 101–2.

31 Colley, *Captives*, p. 30; Tinniswood, *Pirates of Barbary*, pp. 242–53.

32 L. Maziane, *Salé et ses corsaires (1666–1727). Un port de course marocain au XVIIe siècle* (Caen, 2007), p. 172.

33 Ibid., p. 179; R. Coindreau, *Les corsaires de Salé* (Paris, 1948), pp. 78–84.

34 Entry on Thomas Phelps in *ODNB*.

35 Colley, *Captives*, p. 55.

36 Ibid.; Pennell, *Morocco*, p. 103.

37 See G. Milton, *White Gold: The Extraordinary Story of Thomas Pellow and North Africa's One Million European Slaves* (London, 2004).

38 Milton, *White Gold*, pp. 172–202; Colley, *Captives*, p. 68.

4 DECLINE, REVIVAL AND EXTINCTION, 1720–1830

1 For the war of 1815 see F. C. Leiner, *The End of Barbary Terror: America's 1815 War against the Pirates of North Africa* (New York, 2006). For Stephen Decatur see J. T. de Kay, *A Rage for Glory: The Life of Commodore Stephen Decatur USN* (New York, 2004); R. J. Allison, *Stephen Decatur: American Naval Hero, 1779–1820* (Amherst, MA, 2005); S. Tucker, *Stephen Decatur: A Life Most Bold and Daring* (Annapolis, MD, 2005); and L. F. Guttridge, *Our Country, Right or Wrong: The Life of Stephen Decatur, the US Navy's Most Illustrious Commander* (New York, 2006). For Hamidou Reis see A. Devoulx, *Le raïs Hamidou* (Algiers, 1859); P. Earle, *Corsairs of Malta and Barbary* (London, 1970), pp. 195–262; J. de Courcy Ireland, 'Rais Hamidou', *MM*, 60 (1974), pp. 187–96; and D. Panzac, *Les corsaires barbaresques. La fin d'une épopée, 1800–1820* (Paris, 1999), pp. 54–5, 226, and in English translation, *The Barbary Corsairs: The End of a Legend, 1800–1820* (Leiden, 2005).

2 See G. Hills, *Rock of Contention: A History of Gibraltar* (London, 1974), and D. Gregory, *Minorca, the Illusory Prize: A History of the British Occupations of Minorca between 1708 and 1802* (London, 1990). See also L. Colley, *Captives: Britain, Empire and the World, 1600–1850* (London, 2002), pp. 69–72.

3 J. Lynch, *Bourbon Spain, 1700–1808* (Oxford, 1989), p. 129; W. N. Hargreaves-Mawdsley, *Eighteenth-century Spain, 1700–1788* (Totowa, NJ, 1979), pp. 67–8; H. Kamen, *Spain's Road to Empire: The Making of a World Power, 1492–1763* (London, 2002), pp. 455–6.

4 H.J.A. Sire, *The Knights of Malta* (New Haven, CT, and London, 1994), pp. 95, 97–8; R. Cavaliero, *The Last of the Crusaders: The Knights of St John and Malta in the Eighteenth Century* [1960] (London, 2009), pp. 44–51.

5 E. G. Friedman, *Spanish Captives in North Africa in the Early Modern Age* (Madison, WI, 1983), pp. 157–8.

6 Ibid., pp. 158–61.

7 R. Rezette, *The Spanish Enclaves in Morocco* (Paris, 1976), p. 42.

8 Entry on Alexander (Alejandro) O'Reilly in *ODNB*; Lynch, *Bourbon Spain*, pp. 294–5, 311–12; Hargreaves-Mawdsley, *Eighteenth-century Spain*, pp. 124–5.

9 Lynch, *Bourbon Spain*, pp. 321–2; Hargreaves-Mawdsley, *Eighteenth-*

century Spain, pp. 139–40.

10 J. B. Wolf, *The Barbary Coast: Algeria under the Turks, 1500 to 1830* (New York, 1979), pp. 305–7; Lynch, *Bourbon Spain*, p. 322; G. Sánchez Doncel, *Presencia de España en Orán (1509–1792)* (Toledo, 1991), pp. 309–20.

11 S. Dearden, *A Nest of Corsairs: The Fighting Karamanlis of the Barbary Coast* (London, 1976), pp. 46–55.

12 E. H. Jenkins, *A History of the French Navy: From its Beginnings to the Present Day* (London, 1973), p. 145. See also J. Pianelli, *Corsi e Turchi: les barbaresques et la Corse* (Ajaccio, 2003).

13 J. R. Bruijn, *The Dutch Navy in the Seventeenth and Eighteenth Centuries* (Columbia, SC, 1993), pp. 150–51, 155, 159; A. H. de Groot, 'Ottoman North Africa and the Dutch Republic in the Seventeenth and Eighteenth Centuries', *Revue de l'Occident musulman et de la Méditerranée*, 39 (1985), pp. 143–5.

14 L. Müller, *Consuls, Corsairs, and Commerce: The Swedish Consular Service and Long-Distance Shipping, 1720–1815* (Uppsala, 2004), pp. 54–69, 124–31; D. H. Andersen and H.-J. Voth, 'Neutrality and Mediterranean Shipping under the Danish Flag, 1747–1807', *Scandinavian Economic History Review*, 48 (2000), pp. 5–23.

15 J. J. Norwich, *A History of Venice* (New York, 1982), pp. 598–9.

16 Cavaliero, *Last of the Crusaders*, pp. 81–5.

17 Colley, *Captives*, pp. 85–7.

18 Ibid., pp. 126–7, 131–2. See also L. Colley, *The Ordeal of Elizabeth Marsh: A Woman in World History* (New York, 2007), pp. 50–86.

19 C. L. Lewis, *Admiral de Grasse and American Independence* (Annapolis, MD, 1945), pp. 41–3.

20 L. J. Hall, *The United States and Morocco, 1776–1956* (Metuchen, NJ, 1971), p. 44; C. R. Pennell, *Morocco: From Empire to Independence* (Oxford, 2003), pp. 108–9.

21 Hall, *United States and Morocco*, pp. 43–57.

22 Quote from entry on James Irving in ODNB. See also S. Schwarz, *Slave Captain: The Career of James Irving in the Liverpool Slave Trade* (revd edn, Liverpool, 2008).

23 Panzac, *Les corsaires barbaresques*, p. 23.

24 Hall, *United States and Morocco*, pp. 62–3; M. El Mansur, 'The Anachronism of Maritime Jihad: The US–Morocco Conflict of 1802–3', in *The Atlantic Connection: 200 Years of Moroccan-American Relations, 1786–1986*, ed. J. B. Bookin-Weiner and M. El Mansur (Rabat, 1990); I. W. Toll, *Six Frigates: The Epic History of the Foundation of the US Navy* (New York, 2006), pp. 181–4.

25 L. Sondhaus, *The Habsburg Empire and the Sea: Austrian Naval Policy, 1797–1866* (West Lafayette, IN, 1989), pp. 14, 74–5.

26 Hall, *United States and Morocco*, p. 64; Jenkins, *History of French Navy*, p. 293.

27 Cavaliero, *Last of the Crusaders*, pp. 223–35, 243.

28 Panzac, *Les corsaires barbaresques*, p. 64.

29 Ibid., pp. 82–3, 94–5; Sondhaus, *Habsburg Empire and the Sea*, pp. 7–8.

30 Statistics about corsair fleets, cruises, prizes and so on between 1793 and 1815 given here and below are from Panzac, *Les corsaires barbaresques*, especially chapters 2, 3 and 4.

31 For Lyle see Dearden, *A Nest of Corsairs*, pp. 133–4, 136, 142–3, 148, 155, 158, 219–20.

32 Panzac, *Les corsaires barbaresques*, pp. 72–3. See also D. Gregory, *Malta, Britain, and the European Powers, 1793–1815* (London, 1996).

33 Quoted in T. Pocock, *Breaking the Chains: The Royal Navy's War on White Slavery* (Annapolis, MD, 2006), p. 8.

34 See Panzac, *Les corsaires barbaresques*, chapters 6, 7 and 8.

35 For the US/Tripoli war of 1801–5 see J. Wheelan, *Jefferson's War: America's First War on Terror, 1801–1805* (New York, 2003); J. London, *Victory in Tripoli: How America's War with the Barbary Pirates Established the US Navy and Built a Nation* (Hoboken, NJ, 2005); F. Lambert, *The Barbary Wars: American Independence in the Atlantic World* (New York, 2005); R. Zacks, *The Pirate Coast: Thomas Jefferson, the First Marines, and the Secret Mission of 1805* (New York, 2005) and D. Smethurst, *Tripoli: The United States' First War on Terror* (New York, 2006). See also G. W. Allen, *Our Navy and the Barbary Corsairs* [1905] (Cranbury, NJ, 2005) and M.L.S. Kitzen, *Tripoli and the United States at War: A History of American Relations with the Barbary States, 1785–1805* (Jefferson, NC, 1993).

36 Entry on Sir John Acton in *ODNB*. See also H. Acton, *The Bourbons of Naples* (London, 1957).

37 Pocock, *Breaking the Chains*, pp. 5–23. See also T. Pocock, *A Thirst for Glory: The Life of Admiral Sir Sydney Smith* (London, 1996).

38 Pocock, *Breaking the Chains*, pp. 32–41; N. B. Harding. 'North African Piracy, the Hanoverian Carrying Trade, and the British State, 1728–1828', *The Historical Journal*, 43 (2000), pp. 25–47. See also C. N. Parkinson, *Edward Pellew, Viscount Exmouth, Admiral of the Red* (London, 1934).

39 In contemporary writings the consul's name is given as Hugh McDonell. His son British diplomat Sir Hugh Guion MacDonell preferred a different spelling (see his entry in *ODNB*).

40 Quoted in Pocock, *Breaking the Chains*, p. 43.

41 For bombardment of Algiers 1816 see William Shaler, *Sketches of Algiers, Political, Historical, and Civil, etc.* (Boston, 1826), pp. 135–8, 279–94; R. L. Playfair, *The Scourge of Christendom: Annals of British Relations with Algiers prior to the French Conquest* (London, 1884), pp. 259–73; Pocock, *Breaking the Chains*, pp. 54–67; R. Perkins and K. J. Douglas-Morris, *Gunfire in Barbary* (Havant, Hampshire, 1982).

42 Panzac, *Les corsaires barbaresques*, p. 45; Shaler, *Sketches of Algiers*, p. 37.

43 Shaler, *Sketches of Algiers*, p. 164.

44 Ibid., pp. 184–5; Playfair, *Scourge of Christendom*, p. 290.

45 Pocock, *Breaking the Chains*, pp. 92–103.

46 D. Panzac, *La marine ottomane. De l'apogée à la chute de l'Empire (1572–1923)* (Paris, 2009), p. 274.

47 Ibid., pp. 280–83; Pocock, *Breaking the Chains*, pp. 141–65.

48 Playfair, *Scourge of Christendom*, pp. 311, 313; G. Fleury, *Comment l'Algérie devint française (1830–1848)* (Paris, 2004), pp. 57–9, 63–6.

49 Playfair, *Scourge of Christendom*, p. 314; Fleury, *Comment l'Algérie devint française*, pp. 89–94.

50 Fleury, *Comment l'Algérie devint française*, pp. 14, 43–5. See also J. Marchioni, *Boutin: le Lawrence de Napoléon, espion à Alger et en Orient, pionnier de l'Algérie française* (Paris, 2007).

51 Shaler, *Sketches of Algiers*, pp. 51–2.

52 For conquest of Algiers 1830 see Playfair, *Scourge of Christendom*, pp. 315–22; W. E. Watson, *Tricolor and Crescent: France and the Islamic World* (Westport, CT, 2003), pp. 18–21; Fleury, *Comment l'Algérie devint française* (Paris, 2004), pp. 101–126.

53 Quoted in Fleury, *Comment l'Algérie devint française*, p. 132. (Author's translation.)

54 Entry on Hanmer George Warrington in ODNB; Dearden, *A Nest of Corsairs*, pp. 223–314.

55 Dearden, *A Nest of Corsairs*, pp. 297–311; J. M. Abun-Nasr, *A History of the Maghrib* (2nd edn, Cambridge, 1975), pp. 188–9, 200–1.

56 Shaler, *Sketches of Algiers*, p. 38.

CONCLUSION: A NEW BARBARY?

1 For the *Maersk Alabama* incident see M. N. Murphy, *Somalia: The New Barbary? Piracy and Islam in the Horn of Africa* (London, 2011), pp. 104–6, and R. Phillips and S. Talty, *A Captain's Duty: Somali Pirates, Navy SEALs, and Dangerous Days at Sea* (New York, 2010). See also I. Lewis, *Understanding Somalia and Somaliland* (London, 2008); P. Eichstaedt, *Pirate State: Inside Somalia's Terrorism at Sea* (Chicago, 2010); M. N. Murphy, *Small Boats, Weak States, Dirty Money: Piracy and Maritime Terrorism in the Modern World* (New York and London, 2009); N. Cawthorne, *Pirates of the 21st Century* (London, 2009); J. C. Payne, *Piracy Today: Fighting Villainy on the High Seas* (Dobbs Ferry, NY, 2010); D. Marley, *Modern Piracy: A Reference Handbook* (Santa Barbara, CA, 2011); J. Bahadur, *The Pirates of Somalia: Inside their Hidden World* (London, 2011).

Abulafia, D., ed., *The Mediterranean in History* (London, 2003)

—, *The Great Sea: A Human History of the Mediterranean* (London, 2011)

Abun-Nasr, J. M., *A History of the Maghrib* (2nd edn, Cambridge, 1975)

Acton, H., *The Bourbons of Naples* (London, 1957)

Aksan, V. H., and G. Goffman, eds, *The Early Modern Ottomans: Remapping the Empire* (Cambridge, 2007)

Allen, G. W., *Our Navy and the Barbary Corsairs* [1905] (Cranbury, NJ, 2005)

Allison, R. J., *The Crescent Obscured: The United States and the Muslim World, 1776–1815* (New York and Oxford, 1995)

—, *Stephen Decatur: American Naval Hero, 1779–1820* (Amherst, MA, 2005)

Andersen, D. H., and H.-J. Voth, 'Neutrality and Mediterranean Shipping under the Danish Flag, 1747–1807', *Scandinavian Economic History Review*, 48 (2000), pp. 5–23

Anderson, M. S., 'Great Britain and the Barbary States in the Eighteenth Century', *Bulletin of the Institute of Historical Research*, 29 (1956), pp. 87–107

Anderson, R. C., *Naval Wars in the Levant, 1559–1853* (Liverpool, 1952)

Andrews, K. R., *Ships, Money, and Politics: Seafaring and Naval Enterprise in the Reign of Charles I* (Cambridge, 1991)

Astarita, T., *Between Salt Water and Holy Water: A History of Southern Italy* (New York, 2005)

Atauz, A. D., *Eight Thousand Years of Maltese Maritime History: Trade, Piracy, and Naval Warfare in the Central Mediterranean* (Gainsville, FL, 2008)

Attard, J., *The Knights of Malta* (Malta, 1992)

Aylmer, G. E., 'Slavery under Charles II: The Mediterranean and Tangier', *English Historical Review*, 114 (1999), pp. 378–88

Baepler, P., ed., *White Slaves, African Masters: An Anthology of American Barbary Captivity Narratives* (Chicago, 1999)

Bahadur, J., *The Pirates of Somalia: Inside their Hidden World* (London, 2011)

Bak, G., *Barbary Pirate: The Life and Crimes of John Ward, the Most Infamous*

Privateer of his Time (Stroud, 2006)

Bakker, J. de, *Slaves, Arms and Holy War: Moroccan Policy vis-à-vis the Dutch Republic during the Establishment of the Alawi Dynasty (1660–1727)* (Amsterdam, 1991)

Bamford, P. W., *Fighting Ships and Prisons: The Mediterranean Galleys of France in the Age of Louis XIV* (Minneapolis, MN, 1973)

Barnby, H. G., *The Prisoners of Algiers: An Account of the Forgotten American-Algerian War, 1785–1797* (London, 1966)

Belhamissi, M., *Histoire de la marine algérienne* (Algiers, 1983)

—, *Les captifs algériens et l'Europe chrétienne* (Algiers, 1988)

—, *Marine et marins d'Alger, 1518–1830*, 3 vols (Algiers, 1996)

Bennassar, B. and L., *Les chrétiens d'Allah. L'histoire extraordinaire des renégats, XVIe et XVIIe siècles* (Paris, 1989)

Bernard, C., and A. Stella, eds, *D'esclaves à soldats: miliciens et soldats d'origine servile, XIIe–XXIe siècles* (Paris, 2006)

Berthier, P., *La bataille de l'oued el-Makhasen, dite bataille des Trois-Rois (4 août 1578)* (Paris, 1985)

Bicheno, H., *Crescent and Cross: The Battle of Lepanto 1571* (London, 2003)

Black, J., *The British Seaborne Empire* (New Haven, CT, and London, 2004)

—, *Naval Power: A History of Warfare and the Sea from 1500* (Basingstoke, 2009)

—, ed., *European Warfare, 1453–1815* (New York, 1999)

Bonaffini, G., *La Sicilia e i Barbareschi: Incursioni corsare e riscatto degli schiavi (1570–1606)* (Palermo, 1983)

—, *Sicilia e Maghreb tra Sette e Ottocento* (Caltanissetta, 1991)

Bonner, M., *Jihad in Islamic History: Doctrine and Practice* (Princeton, NJ, 2006)

Bono, S., *I Corsari barbareschi* (Turin, 1964)

—, *Corsari nel Mediterraneo* (Milan, 1993); French trans., *Les corsaires en Méditerranée* (Rabat, 1998)

—, *Schiavi musulmani nell'Italia moderna* (Naples, 1999)

—, *Lumi e corsari: Europa e Maghreb nel Settecento* (Perugia, 2005)

—, 'D'esclaves à marins dans la Méditerranée de l'époque moderne', in *D'esclaves à soldats: miliciens et soldats d'origine servile, xiie–xxie siècles*, ed. C. Bernard and A. Stella (Paris, 2006), pp. 67–74

Bookin-Weiner, J. B., '"The Sallee Rovers": Morocco and its Corsairs in the Seventeenth Century', in *The Middle East and North Africa: Essays in Honor of J. C. Hurewitz*, ed. R. S. Simon (New York, 1990), pp. 307–31

—, 'The Origins of Moroccan-American Relations', in J. B. Bookin-Weiner and M. El Mansur, eds, *The Atlantic Connection: 200 Years of Moroccan-American Relations, 1786–1986* (Rabat, 1990)

—, 'Corsairing in the Economy and Politics of North Africa', in *North Africa: Nation, State, and Region*, ed. E.G.H. Joffé (London, 1993), pp. 3–33

—, and M. El Mansur, eds, *The Atlantic Connection: 200 Years of Moroccan–American Relations, 1786–1986* (Rabat, 1990)

Boot, M., *The Savage Wars of Peace: Small Wars and the Rise of American Power* (New York, 2002)

Bosworth, C. E., *An Intrepid Scot: William Lithgow of Lanark's Travels in the Ottoman Lands, North Africa, and Central Europe, 1609–21* (Aldershot, 2006)

—, ed., *Historic Cities of the Islamic World* (Leiden, 2007)

Boudriot, J., and H. Berti, *The Bomb Ketch Salamandre* (Robertsbridge, 1991)

Bovill, E. W., *The Battle of Alcazar: An Account of the Defeat of Don Sebastian of Portugal at El Ksar el Kebir* (London, 1952)

Bradford, E., *The Great Siege: Malta 1565* [1961] (Ware, Hertfordshire, 1999)

—, *The Sultan's Admiral: Barbarossa – Pirate and Empire-builder* [1969] (London, 2009)

Brandi, K., *The Emperor Charles V* (London, 1939)

Braudel, F., *The Mediterranean and the Mediterranean World in the Age of Philip II*, 2 vols (New York, 1973)

Brockman, E., *The Two Sieges of Rhodes, 1480–1522* (London, 1969)

Brogini, A., *Malte, frontière de chrétienté (1530–1670)* (Rome, 2006)

Bromley, J. S., *Corsairs and Navies* (London, 1987)

Bruijn, J. R., *The Dutch Navy in the Seventeenth and Eighteenth Centuries* (Columbus, SC, 1993)

Brummett, P. J., *Ottoman Seapower and Levantine Diplomacy in the Age of Discovery* (Albany, NY, 1994)

Bulut, M., *Ottoman–Dutch Economic Relations in the Early Modern Period, 1571–1699* (Hilversum, 2001)

Capponi, N., *Victory of the West: The Great Christian–Muslim Clash at the Battle of Lepanto* (Cambridge, MA, 2007)

Carr, M., *Blood and Faith: The Purging of Muslim Spain* (New York, 2009)

Castillo, D., *The Maltese Cross: A Strategic History of Malta* (Westport, CT, 2006)

Cavaliero, R., *The Last of the Crusaders: The Knights of St John and Malta in the Eighteenth Century* [1960] (London, 2009)

—, *Admiral Satan: The Life and Campaigns of Suffren* (London, 1994)

Cawthorne, N., *Pirates of the 21st Century* (London, 2009)

Chelebi, K., *History of the Maritime Wars of the Turks* (London, 1831)

Cheyne, A. G., *Islam and the West: The Moriscos* (Albany, NY, 1983)

Clarence-Smith, W. G., *Islam and the Abolition of Slavery* (London, 2006)

Clark, G. N., 'The Barbary Corsairs in the Seventeenth Century', *Cambridge Historical Journal*, 8 (1944), pp. 22–35

Clissold, S., *The Barbary Slaves* (London, 1977)

Clot, A., *Suleiman the Magnificent* (London, 1992)

Clowes, W. L., *The Royal Navy: A History from the Earliest Times to the Present*, 7 vols (repr Annapolis, MD, 1996), vol. II

Coindreau, R., *Les corsaires de Salé* (Paris, 1948)

Colley, L., *Captives: Britain, Empire and the World, 1600–1850* (London, 2002)

—, *The Ordeal of Elizabeth Marsh: A Woman in World History* (New York, 2007)

Cook, M. A., ed., *A History of the Ottoman Empire to 1730* (Cambridge, 1976)

Cook, W. F., *The Hundred Years War for Morocco: Gunpowder and the Military Revolution in the Early Modern Muslim World* (Boulder, CO, and Oxford, 1994)

Corbett, J. S., *England in the Mediterranean, 1603–1713*, 2 vols (London, 1904)

Courtinat, R., *La piraterie barbaresque en Méditerranée, XVIe–XIXe siècle* (Coulommiers, 2008)

Crowley, R., *Empires of the Sea: The Final Battle for the Mediterranean, 1521–1580* (London, 2008)

Currey, E. H., *Sea-Wolves of the Mediterranean* (London, 1910)

Dan, P., *Histoire de Barbarie et des corsaires* (Paris, 1637)

David, G., and P. Fodor, eds, *Ransom Slavery along the Ottoman Borders: Early Fifteenth–Early Eighteenth Centuries* (Leiden, 2007)

Davies, J. D., *Pepys's Navy: Ships, Men and Warfare, 1649–1689* (London, 2008)

Davis, R., *The Rise of the English Shipping Industry in the 17th and 18th Centuries* (London, 1962)

Davis, R. C., *Christian Slaves, Muslim Masters: White Slavery in the Mediterranean, the Barbary Coast, and Italy, 1500–1800* (Basingstoke, 2003)

—, *Holy War and Human Bondage: Tales of Christian-Muslim Slavery in the Early Modern Mediterranean* (Santa Barbara, CA, 2009)

—, 'Rural Slavery in the Early Modern Mediterranean. The Significance of Algiers', in *Human Bondage in the Cultural Contact Zone: Transdisciplinary Perspectives on Slavery and its Discourses*, ed. R. Hörmann and G. Mackenthun (Münster, 2010), pp. 81–94

De Kay, J. T., *A Rage for Glory: The Life of Commodore Stephen Decatur USN* (New York, 2004)

Dearden, S., *A Nest of Corsairs: The Fighting Karamanlis of the Barbary Coast* (London, 1976)

Desportes, C., *Le siege de Malte. La grande défaite de Soliman le Magnifique* (Paris, 1998)

Dessert, D., *La Royale: vaisseaux et marins du Roi Soleil* (Paris, 1996)

—, *Tourville* (Paris, 2002)

Devoulx, A., *Le raïs Hamidou* (Algiers, 1859)

Disney, A. R., *A History of Portugal and the Portuguese Empire from the Beginnings to 1807*, 2 vols (Cambridge, 2009)

Dollinger, P., *The German Hansa* (Stanford, CA, 1970)

Earle, P., *Corsairs of Malta and Barbary* (London, 1970)

—, *Sailors: English Merchant Seamen, 1650–1775* (London, 1998)

—, *The Pirate Wars* (London, 2003)

Edwards, J., *The Spain of the Catholic Monarchs, 1474–1520* (Malden, MA, 2000)

Eichstaedt, P., *Pirate State: Inside Somalia's Terrorism at Sea* (Chicago, 2010)

Ekin, D., *The Stolen Village: Baltimore and the Barbary Pirates* (Dublin, 2006)

El Mansur, M., 'The Anachronism of Maritime Jihad: The US–Morocco Conflict of 1802–3', in *The Atlantic Connection: 200 Years of Moroccan-American Relations, 1786–1986*, ed. J. B. Bookin-Weiner and M. El Mansur (Rabat, 1990)

Elliot, J. H., *Imperial Spain, 1469–1716* (London, 1963)

Engels, M.-C., *Merchants, Interlopers, Seamen and Corsairs: The 'Flemish' Community in Livorno and Genoa (1615–1635)* (Hilversum, 1997)

Epstein, S. A., *Genoa and the Genoese, 958–1528* (Chapel Hill, NC, 1996)

—, *Speaking of Slavery: Color, Ethnicity, and Human Bondage in Italy* (Ithaca, NY, 2001)

Faroqhi, S., *The Ottoman Empire and the World Around It* (London, 2004)

—, ed., *The Cambridge History of Turkey: The Later Ottoman Empire, 1603–1839* (Cambridge, 2006)

Fernández Armesto, F., *Ferdinand and Isabella* (London, 1975)

Fernández Duro, C., *Armada española desde la union de los reinos de Castilla y Aragón*, 9 vols (Madrid, 1896)

Field, J. A., *America and the Mediterranean World, 1776–1882* (Princeton, NJ, 1969)

Finkel, C., *Osman's Dream: The Story of the Ottoman Empire, 1300–1923* (London, 2005)

Fisher, A. W., 'Muscovy and the Black Sea Slave Trade', *Canadian-American Slavic Studies*, 6 (1972), pp. 575–94.

—, *The Crimean Tatars* (Stanford, CA, 1978)

Fisher, G., *Barbary Legend: War, Trade and Piracy in North Africa, 1415–1830* (Oxford, 1957)

Fleury, G., *Comment l'Algérie devint française (1830–1848)* (Paris, 2004)

Fodor, P., 'Maltese Pirates, Ottoman Captives and French Traders in the Early Seventeenth Century Mediterranean', in *Ransom Slavery Along the Ottoman Borders: Early Fifteenth–Early Eighteenth Centuries*, ed. G. David and P. Fodor (Leiden, 2007), pp. 221–38

Folayan, K., *Tripoli during the Reign of Yusuf Pasha Qaramanli* (Ife, Nigeria, 1979)

Fontenay, M., 'Les missions des galères de Malte (1530–1798)', in *Guerre et commerce en Méditerranée, IXe–XXe siècles*, ed. M. Vergé-Franceschi (Paris, 1991), pp. 103–22

—, 'Le Maghreb barbaresque et l'esclavage méditerranéen aux XVIe–XVIIe siècles', *Les Cahiers de Tunisie*, 43 (1991), pp. 7–43

—, *La Méditerranée entre la Croix et le Croissant: navigation, commerce, course et piraterie (XVIe–XIXe siècles)* (Paris, 2010)

—, and A. Tenenti, 'Course et piraterie méditerranéennes de la fin du moyen âge au début du xixème siècle', in *Course et piraterie*, ed. M. Mollat, 2 vols (Paris, 1975), pp. 78–136

Freller, T., and D. Campoy, *Padre Ottomano and Malta* (Malta, 2006)

Friedman, E. G., *Spanish Captives in North Africa in the Early Modern Age* (Madison, WI, 1983)

Galimard Flavigny, B., *Histoire de l'ordre de Malte* (Paris, 2006)

Garcés, M. A., *Cervantes in Algiers: A Captive's Tale* (Nashville, TN, 2002)

García-Arenal, M., and M.-A. de Bunes Ibarra, *Los españoles en el Norte de África, siglos XV–XVIII* (Madrid, 1992)

García-Arenal, M., and G. Wiegers, *A Man of Three Worlds: Samuel Pallache, a Moroccan Jew in Catholic and Protestant Europe* (Baltimore, MD, 2007)

García Hernán, E., *La Armada española en la monarquía de Felipe ii y la defensa del Mediterráneo* (Madrid, 1995)

Garnier, E., *L'âge d'or des galères de France: le champ de bataille Méditerranéen à la Renaissance* (Paris, 2005)

—, *L'alliance impie. François Ier et Soliman le Magnifique contre Charles Quint (1529–1547)* (Paris, 2008)

Gemignani, M., 'The Navies of the Medici: The Florentine Navy and the Navy of the Sacred Military Order of St Stephen, 1547–1648', in *War at Sea in the Middle Ages and the Renaissance*, ed. J. B. Hattendorf and R. W. Unger (Woodbridge, 2003), pp. 169–86

Glete, J., *Navies and Nations: Warships, Navies and State Building in Europe and America, 1500–1860*, 2 vols (Stockholm, 1993)

—, *Warfare at Sea, 1500–1650: Maritime Conflicts and the Transformation of Europe* (London, 2000)

Goffman, D., *The Ottoman Empire and Early Modern Europe* (Cambridge, 2002)

Goodman, D., *Spanish Naval Power, 1589–1665: Reconstruction and Defeat* (Cambridge, 2003)

Grammont, H. D. de, *Histoire d'Alger sous la domination turque (1515–1830)* (Paris, 1887)

Graziani, A.-M., *Andrea Doria: un prince de la Renaissance* (Paris, 2008)

Greene, M., 'Beyond the Northern Invasion: The Mediterranean in the Seventeenth Century', *Past and Present*, 174 (2002), pp. 42–71

—, 'The Ottomans in the Mediterranean', in *The Early Modern Ottomans: Remapping the Empire*, ed. V. H. Aksan and G. Goffman (Cambridge, 2007), pp. 104–16

—, *Catholic Pirates and Greek Merchants: A Maritime History of the Mediter-*

ranean (Princeton, NJ, 2010)

Gregory, D., *Sicily, the Insecure Base: A History of the British Occupation of Sicily, 1806–1815* (London, 1988)

—, *Minorca, the Illusory Prize: A History of the British Occupations of Minorca between 1708 and 1802* (London, 1990)

—, *Malta, Britain, and the European Powers, 1793–1815* (London, 1996)

Groot, A. H. de, *The Ottoman Empire and the Dutch Republic: A History of the Earliest Diplomatic Relations, 1610–1630* (Leiden and Istanbul, 1978)

—, 'Ottoman North Africa and the Dutch Republic in the Seventeenth and Eighteenth Centuries', *Revue de l'Occident musulman et de la Méditerranée*, 39 (1985), pp. 131–47

Guilmartin, J. F., *Gunpowder and Galleys: Changing Technology and Mediterranean Warfare at Sea in the 16th Century* (revd edn, London, 2003)

—, *Galleons and Galleys* (London, 2002)

Guttridge, L. F., *Our Country, Right or Wrong: The Life of Stephen Decatur, the US Navy's Most Illustrious Commander* (New York, 2006)

Haedo, D. de, *Topografía e historia general de Argel* (Valladolid, 1612)

Hall, L. J., *The United States and Morocco, 1776–1956* (Metuchen, NJ, 1971)

Hanlon, G., *The Twilight of a Military Tradition: Italian Aristocrats and European Conflicts, 1560–1800* (London, 1998)

—, *Early Modern Italy, 1550–1800: Three Seasons in European History* (New York, 2000)

Harding, N. B., 'North African Piracy, the Hanoverian Carrying Trade, and the British State, 1728–1828', *The Historical Journal*, 43 (2000), pp. 25–47

Harding, R., *Seapower and Naval Warfare, 1650–1830* (London, 1999)

—, 'Naval Warfare, 1453–1826', in *European Warfare, 1453–1815*, ed. J. Black (New York, 1999), pp. 96–117

Hargreaves-Mawdsley, W. N., *Eighteenth Century Spain, 1700–1788* (Totowa, NJ, 1979)

Harper, G., ed., *Colonial and Post-Colonial Incarceration* (New York, 2001)

Harvey, L. P., *Muslims in Spain, 1500 to 1614* (Chicago, 2006)

Hattendorf, J. B., ed., *Naval Policy and Strategy in the Mediterranean: Past, Present and Future* (London, 2000)

—, and R. W. Unger, eds, *War at Sea in the Middle Ages and the Renaissance* (Woodbridge, Suffolk, 2003)

Hebb, D. D., *Piracy and the English Government, 1616–1642* (Aldershot, 1994)

Heers, J., *The Barbary Corsairs: Warfare in the Mediterranean, 1480–1580* (London, 2003)

Helgason, B., 'Historical Narrative as Collective Therapy: The Case of the Turkish Raid on Iceland', *Scandinavian Journal of History*, 22 (1997), pp. 275–89

Hess, A. C., *The Forgotten Frontier: A History of the Sixteenth Century Ibero-*

African Frontier (Chicago, 1978)

—, 'The Forgotten Frontier: The Ottoman North African Provinces during the Eighteenth Century', in *Studies in Eighteenth Century Islamic History*, ed. A. T. Naff and R. Owen (Carbondale, IL, 1977), pp. 74–87

Heywood, C., 'Ottoman Territoriality Versus Maritime Usage: The Ottoman Islands and English Privateering in the Wars with France, 1689–1714', in *Insularités ottomanes*, ed. N. Vatin and G. Veinstein (Paris, 2004), pp. 145–73

Hillgarth, J. N., *The Spanish Kingdoms, 1250–1516*, 2 vols (Oxford, 1978)

Hills, G., *Rock of Contention: A History of Gibraltar* (London, 1974)

Hoexter, M., *Endowments, Rulers, and Community: Waqf al-Haramayn in Ottoman Algiers* (Leiden, 1998)

Holt, P. M., A. K. S. Lambton and B. Lewis, eds, *Cambridge History of Islam*, 2 vols (repr. Cambridge, 1977)

Hopkins, J. F. P., *Letters From Barbary, 1576–1774* (Oxford, 1982)

Hordern, P., and N. Purcell, *The Corrupting Sea: A Study of Mediterranean History* (Oxford, 2000)

Hörmann, R., and G. Mackenthun, eds, *Human Bondage in the Cultural Contact Zone: Transdisciplinary Perspectives on Slavery and Its Discourses* (Münster, 2010)

Hornstein, S. R., *The Restoration Navy and English Foreign Trade, 1674–1688: A Study of the Peacetime Use of Sea Power* (Aldershot, 1991)

Horodowich, E., *A Brief History of Venice* (London, 2009)

Housley, N. J., *The Later Crusades, 1274–1580: From Lyons to Alcazar* (Oxford, 1992)

Imber, C., *The Ottoman Empire, 1300–1650: The Structure of Power* (2nd edn, Basingstoke, 2009)

Inalcik, H., *The Ottoman Empire: The Classical Age, 1300–1600* (London, 1973)

Ireland, J. de Courcy, 'Rais Hamidou', *The Mariner's Mirror*, 60 (1974), pp. 187–96

—, 'The Corsairs of North Africa', *The Mariner's Mirror*, 62 (1976), pp. 271–83

Israel, J. I., 'The Jews of Spanish Oran and their Expulsion in 1669', in J. I. Israel, *Conflicts of Empires: Spain, the Low Countries, and the Struggle for World Supremacy, 1585–1713* (London, 1997), pp. 219–39

Ivanics, M., 'Enslavement, Slave Labour and Treatment of Captives in the Crimean Khanate', in *Ransom Slavery along the Ottoman Borders: Early Fifteenth-Early Eighteenth Centuries*, ed. G. David and P. Fodor (Leiden, 2007), pp. 193–220

James, A., *The Navy and Government in Early Modern France, 1572–1661* (Woodbridge, 2004)

Jamieson, A., 'The Tangier Galleys and the Wars against the Mediterranean

Corsairs', *The American Neptune*, 23 (1963), pp. 95–112

Jamieson, A. G., *Faith and Sword: A Short History of Christian–Muslim Conflict* (London, 2006)

Jenkins, E. H., *A History of the French Navy: From its Beginnings to the Present Day* (London, 1973)

Joffé, E.G.H., ed., *North Africa: Nation, State, and Region* (London, 1993)

Jonsson, M., 'The Expulsion of the Moriscos from Spain in 1609–14: The Destruction of an Islamic Periphery', *Journal of Global History*, 2 (2007), pp. 195–212

Julien, C.-A., *History of North Africa* (London, 1970)

Jurien de la Gravière, E., *Doria et Barberousse* (Paris, 1886)

—, *Les Corsaires barbaresques et la marine de Soliman le Grand* (Paris, 1887)

Kamen, H., *Philip of Spain* (New Haven, CT, and London, 1997)

—, *Early Modern European Society* (New York, 2000)

—, *Spain's Road to Empire: The Making of a World Power, 1492–1763* (London, 2002)

Karlsson, G., *The History of Iceland* (Minneapolis, MN, 2000)

Kempthorne, G. A., 'Sir John Kempthorne and his Sons', *The Mariner's Mirror*, 12 (1926), pp. 289–317.

Khiari, F., *Vivre et mourir en Alger: l'Algérie ottomane aux XVIe–XVIIe siècles: un destin confisqué* (Paris, 2002)

Kirk, T. A., *Genoa and the Sea: Policy and Power in an Early Modern Maritime Republic, 1559–1684* (Baltimore, MD, 2005)

Kitzen, M.L.S., *Tripoli and the United States at War: A History of American Relations with the Barbary States, 1785–1805* (Jefferson, NC, 1993)

Kleinschmidt, H., *Charles V: The World Emperor* (Stroud, 2004)

Konstam, A., *Piracy: The Complete History* (Oxford, 2008)

Krieken, G. van, *Corsaires et marchands: les relations entre Alger et le Pays-Bas, 1604–1830* (Paris, 2002)

Lambert, A., *The Last Sailing Battlefleet: Maintaining Naval Mastery, 1815–1850* (London, 1991)

—, *Warfare at Sea in the Age of Sail, 1650–1850* (London, 2000)

Lambert, F., *The Barbary Wars: American Independence in the Atlantic World* (New York, 2005)

Lane, F. C., *Venice: A Maritime Republic* (Baltimore, 1973)

Lane-Poole, S., *The Story of the Barbary Corsairs* (London, 1890)

Le Fevre, P., 'Arthur Herbert, Earl of Torrington, 1648–1716', in *Precursors of Nelson: British Admirals of the Eighteenth Century*, ed. P. Le Fevre and R. Harding (London, 2000), pp. 19–41

Le Fevre, P., and R. Harding, eds, *Precursors of Nelson: British Admirals of the Eighteenth Century* (London, 2000)

Leiner, F. C., *The End of Barbary Terror: America's 1815 War against the Pirates of North Africa* (New York, 2006)

Lewis, B., *Race and Slavery in the Middle East: An Historical Enquiry* (New York, 1992)

—, 'Corsairs in Iceland', in B. Lewis, *Islam in History: Ideas, People, and Events in the Middle East* (2nd edn, Chicago, 2001), pp. 239–46

Lewis, C. L., *Admiral de Grasse and American Independence* (Annapolis, MD, 1945)

Lewis, I., *Understanding Somalia and Somaliland* (London, 2008)

Lloyd, C., *English Corsairs on the Barbary Coast* (London, 1981)

Loades, D., *England's Maritime Empire: Seapower, Commerce and Piracy, 1490–1690* (London, 2000)

London, J., *Victory in Tripoli: How America's War with the Barbary Pirates Established the US Navy and Built a Nation* (Hoboken, NJ, 2005)

Lopez Nadal, G., 'Corsairing as a Commercial System: The Edges of Legitimate Trade', in *Bandits at Sea: A Pirates Reader*, ed. C. R. Pennell (New York, 2001), pp. 125–36

Löwenheim, O., *Predators and Parasites: Persistent Agents of Transnational Harm and Great Power Authority* (Ann Arbor, MI, 2007)

Lynch, J., *Spain under the Habsburgs*, 2 vols (New York, 1984)

—, *Bourbon Spain, 1700–1808* (Oxford, 1989)

Mackesy, P., *The War in the Mediterranean, 1803–1810* (London, 1957)

McClusky, P., 'Commerce before Crusade? France, the Ottoman Empire, and the Barbary Pirates, 1661–1669', *French History*, 23 (2009), pp. 1–21

McNeill, W. H., *Venice: The Hinge of Europe, 1081–1797* (Chicago, 1974)

Marchioni, J., *Boutin: le Lawrence de Napoléon, espion à Alger et en Orient, pionnier de l'Algérie française* (Paris, 2007)

Marley, D., *Modern Piracy: A Reference Handbook* (Santa Barbara, CA, 2011)

Masson, P., *Histoire des établissements et du commerce français dans l'Afrique barbaresque (1560–1793): Algérie, Tunisie, Tripolitaine, Maroc* (Paris, 1903)

Matar, N., *Turks, Moors and Englishmen in the Age of Discovery* (New York, 1999)

—, *In the Lands of the Christians: Arabic Travel Writing in the Seventeenth Century* (London, 2003)

—, *Britain and Barbary, 1589–1689* (Gainesville, FL, 2005)

—, *Europe Through Arab Eyes, 1578–1727* (New York, 2008)

Maziane, L., *Salé et ses corsaires (1666–1727) Un port de course marocain au XVIIe siècle* (Caen, 2007)

Merino Navarro, J. P., *La Armada española en el siglo XVIII* (Madrid, 1981)

Milton, G., *White Gold: The Extraordinary Story of Thomas Pellow and North Africa's One Million European Slaves* (London, 2004)

Moalla, A., *The Regency of Tunis and the Ottoman Porte, 1777–1814* (London, 2004)

Mollat, M., ed., *Course et piraterie*, 2 vols (Paris, 1975)

Moreau, F., ed., *Captifs en Méditerranée (XVI–XVIIIe siècles): histories, récits et legendes* (Paris, 2008)

Morrison, J., and R. Gardiner, eds, *The Age of the Galley: Mediterranean Oared Vessels since Pre-Classical Times* (London, 1995)

Müller, L., *Consuls, Corsairs, and Commerce: The Swedish Consular Service and Long-Distance Shipping, 1720–1815* (Uppsala, 2004)

Murphy, M. N., *Small Boats, Weak States, Dirty Money: Piracy and Maritime Terrorism in the Modern World* (New York and London, 2009)

—, *Somalia: The New Barbary? Piracy and Islam in the Horn of Africa* (London, 2011)

Naff, A. T., and R. Owen, eds , *Studies in Eighteenth Century Islamic History* (Carbondale, IL, 1977)

Naphy, W. G., and P. Roberts, eds., *Fear in Early Modern Society* (Manchester, 1997)

Naylor, P. C., *North Africa: A History from Antiquity to the Present* (Austin, TX, 2009)

Nicholson, H. J., *The Knights Hospitaller* (Woodbridge, Suffolk, 2001)

Norwich, J. J., *A History of Venice* (New York, 1982)

—, *The Middle Sea: A History of the Mediterranean* (London, 2006)

O'Rourke, S., *The Cossacks* (Manchester, 2007)

O'Shea, S., *Sea of Faith: Islam and Christianity in the Medieval Mediterranean World* (Vancouver, 2006)

Panzac, D., 'La guerre de course à Tripoli de Barbarie dans la seconde moitié du XVIIIe siècle', in *Guerre et commerce en Méditerranée, IXe–XXe siècles*, ed. M. Vergé-Franceschi (Paris, 1991), pp. 255–78

—, 'The Manning of the Ottoman Navy in the Heyday of Sail (1660–1850)', in *Arming the State: Military Conscription in the Middle East and Central Asia, 1775–1925*, ed. E. J. Zürcher (London, 1999), pp. 41–58

—, *Les corsaires barbaresques. La fin d'une épopée, 1800–1820* (Paris, 1999); trans. into English, *The Barbary Corsairs: The End of a Legend, 1800–1820* (Leiden, 2005)

—, *La marine ottomane. De l'apogée à la chute de l'Empire (1572–1923)* (Paris, 2009)

Paolitti, C., *A Military History of Italy* (Westport, CT, 2008)

Parker, G., *The Dutch Revolt* (London, 1977)

—, *The Grand Strategy of Philip II* (New Haven, CT, and London, 1998)

Parkinson, C. N., *Edward Pellew, Viscount Exmouth, Admiral of the Red* (London, 1934)

Payne, J. C., *Piracy Today: Fighting Villainy on the High Seas* (Dobbs Ferry, NY, 2010)

Pennell, C. R., *Morocco: From Empire to Independence* (Oxford, 2003)

—, ed., *Piracy and Diplomacy in Seventeenth-century North Africa: The Journal of Thomas Baker, English Consul in Tripoli, 1677–1685* (London, 1989)

—, ed., *Bandits at Sea: A Pirates Reader* (New York, 2001)

Perkins, R., and K. J. Douglas-Morris, *Gunfire in Barbary* (Havant, Hampshire, 1982)

Peskin, L. A., *Captives and Countrymen: Barbary Slaves and the American Public, 1785–1816* (Baltimore, MD, 2009)

Peter, J., *Les barbaresques sous Louis XIV. Le duel entre Alger et la Marine du roi (1681–1698)* (Paris, 1997)

Petrie, C., *Don John of Austria* (London, 1967)

Phillips, R., and S. Talty, *A Captain's Duty: Somali Pirates, Navy Seals, and Dangerous Days at Sea* (New York, 2010)

Pianelli, J., *Corsi e Turchi: les barbaresques et la Corse* (Ajaccio, 2003)

Pike, R., *Penal Servitude in Early Modern Spain* (Madison, WI, 1983)

Planhol, X. de, *L'Islam et la mer. La mosque et le matelot, VIIe–XXe siècles* (Paris, 2000)

Playfair, R. L., *The Scourge of Christendom: Annals of British Relations with Algiers prior to the French Conquest* (London, 1884)

Pocock, T., *A Thirst for Glory: The Life of Admiral Sir Sydney Smith* (London, 1996)

—, *Breaking the Chains: The Royal Navy's War on White Slavery* (Annapolis, MD, 2006)

Pryor, J. H., *Geography, Technology and War: Studies in the Maritime History of the Mediterranean, 649–1571* (Cambridge, 1988)

Rahn Phillips, C., 'Navies and the Mediterranean in the Early Modern Period', in *Naval Policy and Strategy in the Mediterranean: Past, Present and Future*, ed. J. B. Hattendorf (London, 2000), pp. 3–16

Reston, J., *Dogs of God: Columbus, the Inquisition, and the Defeat of the Moors* (New York, 2005)

—, *Defenders of the Faith: Charles v, Suleyman the Magnificent, and the Battle for Europe, 1520–1536* (New York, 2009)

Rezette, R., *The Spanish Enclaves in Morocco* (Paris, 1976)

Rodger, N.A.M., *The Safeguard of the Sea: A Naval History of Britain, 660–1649* (London, 1997)

—, *The Command of the Oceans: A Naval History of Britain, 1649–1815* (London, 2004)

Rogers, P. G., *A History of Anglo–Moroccan Relations to 1900* (London, c. 1970)

Rogers, W. L., *Naval Warfare under Oars, 4th to 16th Centuries: A Study of Strategy, Tactics and Ship Design* (Annapolis, MD, 1967)

Rogerson, B., *The Last Crusaders: The Hundred-year Battle for the Centre of the*

World (London, 2009)

Rogoziński, J., *Pirates! An A–Z Encyclopedia* (New York, 1995)

Routh, E.M.G., *Tangier: England's Lost Atlantic Outpost, 1661–1684* (London, 1912)

Ruedy, J. D., *Modern Algeria: The Origins and Development of a Nation* (2nd edn, Bloomington, IN, 2005)

Sánchez Doncel, G., *Presencia de España en Orán (1509–1792)* (Toledo, 1991)

Scammell, G. V., *The World Encompassed: The First European Maritime Empires, c. 800–1650* (London, 1981)

Schwarz, S., *Slave Captain: The Career of James Irving in the Liverpool Slave Trade* (revd edn, Liverpool, 2008)

Sebag, P., *Tunis au XVIIe siècle. Une cité barbaresque au temps de la course* (Paris, 1989)

Segal, R., *The Black Diaspora: Five Centuries of Black Experience Outside Africa* (New York, 1995)

Senior, C. M., 'Robert Walsingham: A Jacobean Pirate', *The Mariner's Mirror*, 60 (1974)

—, *A Nation of Pirates: English Piracy in its Heyday* (Newton Abbot, 1976)

Setton, K. M., *The Papacy and the Levant, 1204–1571*, 4 vols (Philadelphia, 1984)

—, *Venice, Austria, and the Turks in the Seventeenth Century* (Philadelphia, 1991)

Seward, D., *The Monks of War: The Military Religious Orders* (London, 1972)

Shaler, W., *Sketches of Algiers, Political, Historical, and Civil* (Boston, 1826)

Simon, R. S., ed., *The Middle East and North Africa: Essays in Honor of J. C. Hurewitz* (New York, 1990)

Sire, H.J.A., *The Knights of Malta* (New Haven, CT, and London, 1994)

Smethurst, D., *Tripoli: The United States' First War on Terror* (New York, 2006)

Smithers, A. J., *The Tangier Campaign: The Birth of the British Army* (Stroud, 2003)

Sola, E., *Un Mediterráneo de piratas: corsarios, renegados y cautivos* (Madrid, 1988)

Sondhaus, L., *The Habsburg Empire and the Sea: Austrian Naval Policy, 1797–1866* (West Lafayette, IN, 1989)

—, *Naval Warfare, 1815–1914* (London, 2001)

Spencer, W., *Algiers in the Age of the Corsairs* (Norman, OK, 1976)

Spiteri, S. C., *The Great Siege, Knights vs. Turks, mdlxv: Anatomy of a Hospitaller Victory* (Malta, 2005)

Starkey, D. J., 'Voluntaries and Sea Robbers: A Review of the Academic Literature on Privateering, Corsairing, Buccaneering and Piracy', *The Mariner's Mirror*, 97 (2011), pp. 127–47

Strachan, M., 'Sampson's Fight with the Maltese Galleys, 1628', *The Mariner's Mirror*, 55 (1969), pp. 281–9

—, *Sir Thomas Roe, 1581–1644: A Life* (Salisbury, Wiltshire, 1989)

Stella, A., *Histoire d'esclaves dans la peninsule ibérique* (Paris, 2000)

Sumner, C., *White Slavery in the Barbary States* (Boston, 1853)

Sweetman, J., ed., *The Great Admirals: Command at Sea, 1587–1945* (Annapolis, MD, 1997)

Taillemite, E., *Histoire ignorée de la marine française* (Paris, 2003)

Tapié, V. L., *France in the Age of Louis XIII and Richelieu* (2nd edn, Cambridge, 1984)

Taylor, B., 'The Enemy Within and Without: An Anatomy of Fear in the Spanish Mediterranean Littoral', in *Fear in Early Modern Society*, ed. W. G. Naphy and P. Roberts (Manchester, 1997), pp. 78–99

Tenenti, A., *Piracy and the Decline of Venice, 1580–1615* (London, 1967)

Thomson, A., *Barbary and Enlightenment: European Attitudes towards the Maghreb in the 18th Century* (Leiden, 1987)

Thomson, J. E., *Mercenaries, Pirates, and Sovereigns: State-Building and Extra-territorial Violence in Early Modern Europe* (Princeton, NJ, 1994)

Tinniswood, A., *Pirates of Barbary: Corsairs, Conquests and Captivity in the Seventeenth-century Mediterranean* (London, 2010)

Toll, I. W., *Six Frigates: The Epic History of the Foundation of the US Navy* (New York, 2006)

Tracy, J. D., *Emperor Charles V, Impresario of War: Campaign Strategy, International Finance, and Domestic Politics* (Cambridge, 2002)

Travers, T., *Pirates: A History* (Stroud, 2007)

Tueller, J. B., *Good and Faithful Christians: Moriscos and Catholicism in Early Modern Spain* (New Orleans, LA, 2002)

Tucker, S., *Stephen Decatur: A Life Most Bold and Daring* (Annapolis, MD, 2005)

Ungerer, G., *The Mediterranean Apprenticeship of British Slavery* (Madrid, 2008)

Uyar, M., and E. J. Erickson, *A Military History of the Ottomans: From Osman to Atatürk* (Santa Barbara, CA, 2009)

Valensi, L., *On the Eve of Colonialism: North Africa before the French Conquest (1790–1830)* (New York, 1977)

Vandervort, B., *Wars of Imperial Expansion in Africa, 1830–1914* (London, 1998)

Vatin, N., and G. Veinstein, eds, *Insularités ottomanes* (Paris, 2004)

Vergé-Franceschi, M., ed., *Guerre et commerce en Méditerranée, IXe–XXe siècles* (Paris, 1991)

—, *Abraham Duquesne, huguenot et marin de Roi Soleil* (Paris, 1992)

—, *Sampiero Corso, 1498–1567: un mercenaire européen au XVIe siècle* (Ajaccio, Corsica, 1999)

Vermeulen, J., *Sultans, slaven en renegaten: de verborgen geschiedenis van de Ottomaanse rijk* (Leuven, 2001)

Vilar, J. B., and R. Lourido, *Relaciones entre España y el Magreb, siglos XVII y XVIII* (Madrid, 1994)

Vitkus, D. J., 'The Circulation of Bodies: Slavery, Maritime Commerce and English Captivity Narratives in the Early Modern Period', in *Colonial and Post-Colonial Incarceration*, ed. G. Harper (New York, 2001), pp. 23–37

—, and N. Matar, *Piracy, Slavery and Redemption: Barbary Captivity Narratives from Early Modern England* (New York, 2001)

Ware, C., *The Bomb Vessel: Shore Bombardment Ships of the Age of Sail* (London, 1994)

Waterson, J., *The Knights of Islam: The Wars of the Mamluks* (London, 2007)

Watson, W. E., *Tricolor and Crescent: France and the Islamic World* (Westport, CT, 2003)

Weiss, G. L., *Captives and Corsairs: France and Slavery in the Early Modern Mediterranean* (Stanford, CA, 2011)

Wettinger, G., *Slavery in the Islands of Malta and Gozo, c. 1000–1812* (Malta, 2002)

Wheelan, J., *Jefferson's War: America's First War on Terror, 1801–1805* (New York, 2003)

Wijn, J.J.A., 'Maarten Harpertszoon Tromp', in *The Great Admirals: Command at Sea, 1587–1945*, ed. J. Sweetman (Annapolis, MD, 1997), pp. 36–57

Willis, S., *The Admiral Benbow* (London, 2010)

Wilson, P. L., *Pirate Utopias: Moorish Corsairs and European Renegadoes* (2nd edn, New York, 2003)

Wolf, J. B., *The Barbary Coast: Algeria under the Turks, 1500 to 1830* (New York, 1979)

Wood, A. C., *A History of the Levant Company* (London, 1964)

Zachariadou, E., ed., *The Kapudan Pasha: His Office and his Domain* (Rethymnon, Crete, 2002)

Zacks, R., *The Pirate Coast: Thomas Jefferson, the First Marines, and the Secret Mission of 1805* (New York, 2005)

Zürcher, E. J., ed., *Arming the State: Military Conscription in the Middle East and Central Asia, 1775–1925* (London, 1999)

Zysberg, A., *Les Galériens. Vies et destins de 60 000 forçats sur les galères de France, 1680–1748* (Paris, 1987)

—, 'Les galères de France entre 1661 et 1748. Restauration, apogée et survivance d'une flotte de guerre en Méditerranée', in *Guerre et commerce en Méditerranée, IXe–XXe siècles*, ed. M. Vergé-Franceschi (Paris, 1991), pp. 123–60

PHOTO ACKNOWLEDGEMENTS

Photo courtesy of the Amsterdam Historical Museum, Amsterdam: p. 130; from Georg Braun and Franz Hogenberg, *Civitates Orbis Terrarum*, vol. II (Cologne, 1575): p. 22; from Pierre Dan, *Histoire de Barbarie et de ses Corsaires* (Paris, 1637): p. 74; maps courtesy of Mapping Specialists Ltd., Fitchburg, Wisconsin: pp. 6–7, pp. 8–9; U.S. Navy photograph by Mass Communication Specialist 2nd Class Vincent J. Street: p. 217; photo courtesy of the National Maritime Museum, London: p. 10; photo courtesy the U.S. Naval History and Heritage Command, Washington DC: p. 164; photo courtesy the Rijksmuseum, Amsterdam: p. 205; courtesy of Wesleyan University, Middletown, Connecticut: p. 147.

INDEX